FOUNDATIONS OF AN AFRICAN ETHIC

Foundations of an African Ethic

Beyond the Universal Claims of Western Morality

Bénézet Bujo

Translated by Brian McNeil

A Herder and Herder Book
The Crossroad Publishing Company
New York

The Crossroad Publishing Company
481 Eighth Avenue, New York, NY 10001

Originally published in German under the title *Wider den Universalanspruch westlicher Moral* © 2000 by Verlag Herder, Freiburg im Breisgau

Printed in the United States of America

Library of Congress Cataloging-in-Publication Data

Bujo, Benezet.
[Wider den Universalanspruch westlicher Moral. English]
Foundations of an African ethic : beyond the universal claims of western morality / Benezet Bujo ; translated by Brian McNeil.
p. cm.
"A Herder and Herder book."
Includes bibliographical references and index.
ISBN 0-8245-1905-1 (alk. paper)
1. Ethics—Africa. 2. Christian ethics. 3. Ethics, Comparative. I. Title.
BJ980.B8513 2001
170'.96—dc21

2001000504

1 2 3 4 5 6 7 8 9 10 05 04 03 02 01

For
Narcisse Pilo Kamaragi
and
Jean-Benoît Kiza Katanga

Contents

PART 2
Identity and the Understanding of Freedom

Foreword to the English Edition

COLONIALISM HAS DIVIDED AFRICA IN MANY COUNTRIES AND languages reflecting the dominant colonial powers. However, the most important of these are English and French.

This book was originally written in German, the language in which I teach, and is a result of experiences I have gathered from my regular pastoral and academic work in Africa. However, the experiences I brought to Europe can offer a real challenge to Europeans and Americans only if Africans are deeply involved in the process. To this aim it is necessary to return to the African "palaver," and here the language is one of the capital elements that cannot be neglected. For all these reasons I am grateful for an English edition of this book. First of all I wish to thank the Crossroad Publishing Company for having accepted to edit this work. In a very special way I thank Michael G. Parker, the academic editor, who has warmly encouraged and initiated the translation of the book. My thanks go as well to Brian McNeil, the translator, and to my assistant, Mrs. Anita Zocchi Fischer, who made sure that the English translation was in accordance with the original text and who selected the bibliography for the present edition.

My hope is that this modest book may contribute to a truly African Christianity.

Fribourg, February 2001
Bénézet Bujo

Preface

TODAY'S WORLD IS MORE THAN EVER CONFRONTED WITH NEW AND complex problems, which pose equally new challenges that are utterly decisive for the future of humanity; it suffices here to recall the breakneck speed with which modern technology conquers and transforms the world.

Modern technology certainly inspires hope in the improvement of the quality of life. For example, modern information technologies enable such high-quality communication that we will be able to resolve international conflicts, or to denounce injustices and offenses against human rights—in short, to make peace—more quickly than ever before. Genetic technology makes it possible today to fight against world famine by improving agriculture and foodstuffs. Many illnesses can be more easily brought under control, and others we may justifiably hope will be overcome before too long. However, these positive aspects should not blind us to the ambivalence of modern technology, which can also lead to fear. Philipp Schmitz is correct to insist that technology is no less unsettling than life itself: "Nothing is so frightening as a life that misses its goal or is lost. Value systems can be destroyed by technology; it can go so far as to call into question the autonomy of the human person, dissolving the cohesion of societies and frustrating the state's claim to power."[1] We have become acutely aware that technology is capable of destroying nature and producing catastrophe on a global scale.

Here, however, we must draw attention to the fact that modern technology creates a *monoculture.* This applies especially to the cultures of the non-Western world, which can scarcely assert themselves technologically and make their voices heard in the process of globalization. Remarkably few people appear troubled by this threat of a monoculture. Everywhere, we hear protests against the mass destruction of species of plants and animals, but globalization and a kind of "cloning" on the level of the "human cultures" are taken for granted—it seems to be forgotten that the progress and future of humanity can be realized only in the plural. Thus, without overlooking the clear advantages implied here, it is absolutely essential to point out the danger of modern mass media; often, while disseminating information, they also spread ideologies that destroy the good in the non-Western cultures. The mass media, protégés of the West, are not concerned about the ideas of the human person held by their audience in the Third World. Their presupposition is often that what is good for Europe or North America must be equally good everywhere and for all cultures.

The example of Western democracy allows us to observe with especial clarity the negative consequences of such a global culture on Black Africa. Democracy is transposed to the black continent without question, and promoted vis-à-vis a largely illiterate populace by means of modern media such as television and radio. This new culture, even when it claims to be democratic, destroys the world in which Africans have traditionally lived. Political life was organized in an extremely *communitarian* manner by means of the palaver. Today, however—and precisely thanks to the mass media—a few individuals hold the monopoly of the word. Admittedly, globalization is no new phenomenon in Africa; one could say that it began with the slave trade, since the black male and female slaves were persons without culture, who could be bought and sold; their duty was to submit to their owner. Since, however, their status as slaves was the reason for this disparagement of their culture, this negative judgment was extended de facto to Black Africa as a whole.[2]

It must however be understood that globalization is much more radical and total today than in the past, when it was simply impossible to bring the whole world so swiftly to accept uniformity in thought and action. This is why it is not by chance that some groups have called for a world ethos that would work against the negative effects of globalization. Accordingly, in the course of our investigation we shall have to discuss how far the project for a world ethos can be an appropriate response to a multicultural world.

This also brings us to the problem of inculturation, which must be very significant for the Christian ethos. To put it briefly: Christians cannot avoid paying close attention to the process of globalization precisely because it tends to a *monoculture,* with clear consequences for evangelization. If the good news of Jesus is to *make its home* among every people, it cannot identify itself with one specific culture, not even a global or monoculture. The Congregation of Propaganda Fide warned against this as long ago as 1659, under Pope Alexander VII. The Apostolic Vicars who were appointed for China and Korea and other regions were urged *not* to compel the peoples whom they sought to evangelize, even merely by the arguments they used, to abandon their rites, practices, and customs, "unless these are *obviously* in contradiction of religion and morality. What could be more absurd than to transport France, Spain, Italy or some other European country to China? Do not introduce our countries among them, but the faith . . . ."[3] These wise words were not completely forgotten in the following centuries; they were, for example, repeated with regard to the work of evangelization in Congo, where the same Congregation held that the "Catholic Church is neither Belgian, nor French, nor English, nor Italian or American; it is Catholic. This is why it is Belgian in Belgium, French in France, English in England, etc. In Congo, it must be Congolese."[4] Despite this—and although many other documents of the magisterium[5] spoke of the necessity of respecting cultures in the process of evangelization—this problem ultimately received insufficient attention in practice. A new impetus came here only with the Second Vatican Council, which meant a new spring for the movement of inculturation. The Decree on Missions encourages the young churches to take seriously and not abandon the "customs and tradition of their peoples," their wisdom, knowledge, and art, etc., in view of the proclamation of the Gospel (*Ad Gentes* 22; *Gaudium et Spes* 44). This teaching of the council not only had a refreshing effect but also was liberating, since the young churches had undergone profound Western influence, as Suso Brechter remarks: "It is a depressing historical fact that, apart from in the West and in the new world, the church was no longer able to incorporate any new foreign culture into herself and transform it. It never again became truly at home anywhere, but remained Western wherever she was."[6] This observation is particularly applicable to Black Africa, since Westerners did not believe that they had discovered any genuine "culture" or great religion there, with the result that a genuine dialogue between Christianity and African religion was long seen as irrelevant. This topic was explicitly mentioned only many years after Vatican II, and even then only in a hesitant manner.[7] The dialogue that must be initiated concerns not only the sphere of faith but also that of morals, in the sense of an orthodoxy that must lead into orthopraxis.

This is the context in which the present book must be understood. It takes up earlier reflections which one might call "fragments of an African ethic."[8] In his review of my previous book, my colleague and friend Franz Furger, who died all too young, wrote that one "might wish that the . . . author would one day go beyond studies of individual questions to produce a systematic synthesis from the African perspective."[9] As I indicated in the preface to my earlier book, I had proposed such a work even before Furger expressed this wish.[10] Nevertheless, what is presented here cannot be a synthesis of African ethics, since this itself has not yet been elaborated in a totally systematic matter. In what follows, I aim at the development of only one aspect of earlier reflections on the foundations of African ethics. When I present a comparison with Western systems here, this does not in the least mean that the African ethic is constructed on the basis of those systems; on the contrary, this comparison intends to demonstrate clearly the autonomy of the world of African thought, which cannot simply be subsumed under other modes of thought, but demands to be taken seriously as a dialogue partner. In other words, African ethics seeks no self-legitimation. It accepts the confrontation with other ethical systems because it hopes for a reciprocal give and take that can enrich both sides. Nor do Christian orthodoxy and orthopraxis need to fear any kind of loss; for if they honestly enter the debate about that which is good, true, and right in other, non-Western cultures, they will harvest a rich yield and have available a wider and deeper reflection on the treasure of the faith.

As the council notes, what is involved here is a "contribution to praising the glory of the Creator, exalting the grace of the Redeemer, and shaping the Christian life aright" (*Ad Gentes*). In the period after the council, this theme has been studied in greater depth, so that it is not a mere question of adaptation.[11] Rather, African theology has accepted the term "inculturation" into its own vocabulary, and its goal is the incarnation of the message of Christ in every sphere. The present attempt at interpreting African ethics does indeed discuss Western systems of thought in great detail, but I never forget that the ultimate goal of the whole endeavor must be the better understanding and living, in a genuinely Black African context, of the realities connected to the Christian faith.

This study has two parts. The first asks about the foundations of African ethics and provides an introduction to the anthropology of this ethics. Here we see that the community and anamnetic thinking play such an important role that African ethical norms do not derive from natural law; nor can they be discovered and justified according to communitarianism or discourse ethics. This will be made clear by a comparison with these three philosophical systems.

The second part of this book discusses the question whether an ethic (such as the African) that emphasizes the community does not deprive the individual of his or her identity. This debate involves above all the problem of autonomy and freedom, especially as regards the individual conscience and the understanding of sin. After this, the negative and positive elements of the African worldview are presented; both of these pose a challenge to the Christian message and the church. The following reflections assume the necessity of an African ethics, which must be articulated in such a manner that Africans do not lose their own identity: they are to make their own contribution, through their cultural specificity, to the enrichment of humanity as a whole and to the deepening of the Christian faith.

Many persons, sometimes without knowing it, have played a role in the genesis of this investigation. While I was doing the preliminary work for this book, the convent of the Little Sisters of the Presentation in Bunyuka in the diocese of Butembo-Beni (eastern Congo) gave me hospitality as a brother. Despite their great poverty, they went without many things in order to support me in my work. I should like to express my deepest thanks to all the members of this generous convent. I also thank the many parishes, priests, and religious communities—especially the "Wamama Watumishi wa Yezu"—of my home diocese of Bunia, who often gave me the opportunity to encounter African realities through retreats, sermons, and sharing in parish work; I wish to mention Mudzi-Maria and Nyakasanza in particular.

But above all I wish to thank my two closest collaborators, Mrs. Anita Zocchi Fischer and Mrs. Marie-Thérèse Soler. The former, my assistant, selflessly took on the task of proposing corrections in style and content and also saw to the photocopying of texts needed; the latter, my secretary, did not hesitate to accept the job of typing the entire manuscript without a pause, even though it includes difficult expressions in African languages. Finally, I should like to thank my colleague Peter Hünermann, the editor who accepted this book for the series Quaestiones disputatae, as well as Dr. Peter Suchla of Herder Verlag, who saw the work through the press. I remain deeply indebted to all those who supported me in whatever way.

This book is dedicated to two dear friends, Narcisse Pilo Kamaragi and Jean-Benoît Kiza Katanga, whose consistent helpfulness and fidelity are a sign to me of that continuing African solidarity which belongs to the precious elements of the ancestral tradition of the black continent.

FRIBOURG
DECEMBER

Abbreviations

AAS	*Acta Apostolicae Sedis*
CCC	*Catechism of the Catholic Church*
CIC	Codex iuris canonici
CSEL	Corpus scriptorum ecclesiasticorum latinorum
DH	*Dignitatis humanae*
DThA	*Deutsche Thomas-Ausgabe*
DV	*Donum veritatis*
FR	*Fides et ratio*
GE	*Gravissimum educationis*
HK	*Handbuch der Kirchengeschichte*
LThK	*Lexikon fürTheologie und Kirche*
LThK-E	*Lexikon fürTheologie und Kirche–Atlas*
MThZ	*Münchener theologische Zeitschrift*
OT	*Optatam totius*
PhJ	*Philosophisches Jahrbuch*
PL	Patrologia Latina
RThom	*Revue Thomiste*
StdZ	*Stimmen der Zeit*
ThG	*Theologie und Glaube*
Thomas Aquinas	
CTh	*Compendium theologiae*
In Eth. Nic.	*Commentary on Nicomachean Ethics*
SCG	*Summa contra gentiles*
Sent.	*Scriptum super libros Sententiarum*
STh	*Summa theologiae*
ThPh	*Theologie und Philosophie*
ThQ	*Theologische Quartalschrift*
TWNT	*Theologische Wörterbuch zum Alten Testament*
VS	*Veritatis splendor*

PART 1

Fundamental Questions of African Ethics

WE BEGIN THIS STUDY WITH ONE OF THE FOUNDATIONS OF African ethics, viz., the question of its anthropology, since it is possible to understand many norms and modes of ethical conduct aright only when one is aware of how Africans understand the human person.

It is especially important here to understand the decisive role of the community. Many scholars, above all Western thinkers, have long asserted that African ethics is exclusively anthropocentric, without any connection to God as *Person* (whatever they have understood this term to mean).[1] This is not the place to examine the question about God, but two points must be made. First, the definition of "person" in Africa is certainly not coterminous with the Western definition; second, those who still insist that African morality is concerned exclusively with human persons and that its perspective excludes a monotheistic God, have failed to comprehend African thought. It must be emphasized (a point to which we shall return above all in part 2) that Africans do not think in "either/or," but rather in "both/and" categories. While it is unambiguously true that the idea of community is the starting point for African ethics, this is not limited only to the visible community: the invisible community, which is equally important for Africans, embraces not only one's deceased ancestors but also those not yet born and even God. Africans tend in practice to speak about human beings rather than about God; this is due to the view that one who pays heed to the dignity of the human person also pleases God, and that one who acts against the human person offends precisely this God.[2] African ethics treats the dignity of the human person as including the dignity of the entire creation, so that the cosmic dimension is one of its basic components.

It follows—if one looks at the entire panorama—that ethical conduct not only is based on the individual, but is realized primarily by means of a relational network that is equally anthropocentric, cosmic, and theocentric. Thus, norms come into being through a reciprocal relationship that is expressed in a symmetrical or asymmetrical palaver. In this whole process, one must not lose sight of the decisive role of *anamnesis,* for it is impossible to overlook the "remembering" dimension of the word, which is of preeminent importance in the palaver.

This, however, means that the presuppositions of African ethics are not the same as those involved in natural-law approaches. The main goal of African ethics is fundamentally life itself. The community must guarantee the promotion and protection of life by specifying or ordaining ethics and morality. In the next two chapters we compare this communitarian character of African ethics both with discourse ethics and with communitarianism.

CHAPTER 1

Starting Point and Anthropology

AS I HAVE SAID, THE COMMUNITY HAS A CENTRAL PLACE IN African ethics. It must be emphasized that this ethics is not the product of the Western rationality with which we are familiar (as in Descartes or Kant), where discursive reason is central. The present chapter seeks to show that African ethics, unlike Western models of thought, sees relatedness as the decisive issue; it is, however, impossible to categorize this as biological, since relatedness signifies merely an openness that goes beyond what is present and visible in a given situation. In the ethical sphere, attention is paid to that which is good and correct. As has been said above, this can be discerned and realized in a procedure that is both anamnetic and oriented to the future.

THE PROBLEM OF THE *COGNATUS SUM*

Many investigations, covering other fields besides ethical questions, have shown the differences between African and European-American modes of thought.[1] Place Tempels, for example, laid especial emphasis on the principle of the vital force as the central dimension in African thinking. In ethics, it is of primary importance to underline the significance of the community. While the idea of the vital force is not insignificant in ethics, the key to understanding this idea is supplied by one's membership in the community; and this means that the vital force is a consequence and goal of ethical conduct rather than its basis—individuals live only thanks to the community. At the same time, life is the highest principle of ethical conduct.

African ethics is like North American communitarianism in its emphasis on community, although (as we shall see later) there are important differences between the two in the process by which norms are established. The concern that motivates communitarianism in its critique of the "unfettered self" or of "atomism" against liberalism[2] is entirely in keeping with African ethics, which rejects the idea that being a human person and acting responsibly is merely the result of having assented to rational principles, or arguing and thinking rationally. For Black Africa, it is not the Cartesian *cogito ergo sum* ("I think, therefore I am") but an existential *cognatus sum, ergo sumus* ("I am known, therefore we are") that is decisive.[3] It is interesting to note that Joseph Ratzinger arrives at a similar conclusion by means of his christological reflections: "Christian faith does not find its starting-point in the atomized individual, but comes from the knowledge that the merely individual person does not exist. Rather, the human person is himself only in an orientation to the totality of humanity, of history, and of the cosmos. This is an appropriate and essential dimension of the human person as 'spirit in a body.'"[4]

In my opinion, Ratzinger shows very convincingly that an isolated individual or human monad cannot exist, since no human person is a *tabula rasa* whose life is an entirely new project.[5] To be human always means sharing life with others in such a way that, as Ratzinger puts it, "the past and the future of humanity are also present in every human being."[6] The very fact of language allows us to observe this reality, since it links us to the past, determines our present, and allows us to project the future.[7] The dependence of human beings on one another which we note in the case of language naturally holds even more true in the case of our bodiliness: human beings are descended from one another. And something similar must then be said of the human spirit too, as Ratzinger affirms: "We initially affirm this descendance in physical terms, . . . but it means that for the human being, who is spirit only in the body and as a body, that the spirit too—in simple terms, the single and entire human being—is marked most profoundly by the fact that one belongs to the totality of humanity, of the one 'Adam.'"[8] This approach allows Ratzinger to distance himself from the Cartesian *cogito, ergo sum,* since the real human person cannot exist as a solitary "I"—even in the act of knowing, one exists only in *the fact of being known.*[9] Ratzinger quotes with approval Franz von Baader's criticism of Descartes, when von Baader calls for a turn from the *cogito ergo sum* to a *cogitor ergo sum,* that is, "I am thought, therefore I am." Ratzinger comments: "it is only on the basis of his being known that the knowledge of the human person and this person himself can be understood."[10]

This approach, which explicitly emphasizes the "relational dimension,"[11] is very close to the approach of Black African anthropology. One must, however, point out that the latter does not limit itself to the "relational dimension" between individuals, as in personalistic philosophy, but is concerned rather with the relationship of the individual to the *community* and vice versa. This is why I believe that the transformation of the Cartesian formulation into a *cogitor* achieves too little, as long as it remains within the metaphor of "knowledge." For in the last analysis, a whole community could go so far as to refuse to let an individual "be known," as happens all too often, especially in Western society with its emphasis on individual achievements[12]; by contrast the principle *cognatus sum* does not depend on society's assent. It is not only a given; it is existential to such a degree that refusal to accept it must lead to the death, not only of the individual but even of the community itself. This kind of relational dimension does not primarily or exclusively involve a historical dependence on bodiliness and spirit such as Ratzinger emphasizes; from the Black African perspective, the concrete and unbroken interaction among all the members of the community seems to be much more decisive.[13]

How does this approach compare with communitarianism? African ethics too is concerned with the significance of the community for the discernment and laying down of norms and for ethical conduct as a whole, but, unlike communitarianism, Black African ethics goes beyond the concrete, visible community to embrace the dead as well; indeed, even those not yet born constitute an important dimension. This inalienable fundamental principle of African ethics has been repeated so often, in an almost proverbial formula, that people virtually know it by heart: "I am because we are, and because we are, I am too."[14] This principle articulates the conviction that each one becomes a human being only in a fellowship of life with others. This does not refer exclusively to an ethnic group, although such groups are the initial basis for all further "relations." Behind this lies the view that the human person acts more effectively to the extent that he holds fast to solidarity with those like himself; for thus he raises the quality of the vital force not only for himself, but rather for the entire community, indeed for the whole of humanity. This shows us a universalist perspective, since hospitality, daily friendship, and dialogue with the members of other ethnic groups are vital laws from which no one is excepted. One who is not a member of my own group is ultimately also the "property of the other," just as I myself am, and this means that I owe him respect and esteem. Thus one is ultimately related to all human beings.[15]

This principle of solidarity does not in the least mean that the individual loses his identity in and because of the group. As we shall discuss in greater detail, the individual is indispensable, since each person must express his ethical conviction in such a way that he includes the entire community. For example, individuality in Africa is emphasized by the fact that each one has his own name, which is different from that of his parents.[16] Besides this, African ethics attaches great importance to *intentionality* in the ethical conduct of the individual. In the past, some scholars have asserted that the human person in Africa is ethically subsumed under the ethnic group to such an extent that he scarcely merits to be considered as an autonomous ethical subject;[17] but recent research has proven conclusively that the group does not at all dissolve the ethical identity of the individual. This is confirmed in a number of proverbs. For ethical reflection, the heart of each individual is an important locus of ethical conduct and of the integration of ethical norms.[18]

Alexis Kagame has correctly drawn attention to another decisive organ for individual responsibility in the ethical realm, viz., the liver, which, among the Baluba, for example, is regarded as the locus of a number of feelings such as love, desires, and suffering, but is also decisively significant for the will, since intentional actions likewise proceed from the liver.[19]

Ethical insight involves, however, more than just the individual, who depends on others if he is to understand and discern moral norms aright. There is a great deal of evidence for the decisive importance of community in regard to morally correct action; one obvious example is sexuality. It has been rightly noted that homosexuality is rare in traditional Black Africa, and the reason for this is precisely the communal dimension: south of the Sahara, the fundamental anthropological conception in Africa is both bipolar and tripolar. One is a human being only in the duality of man and woman, and this bipolarity generates the triad man-woman-child, which leads to full community. Against this background, a man-man or woman-woman relationship would not only be looked on as an egotistic isolationism which dares not take the step to full human existence; it also leads to a sexist discrimination against part of the human race and shows an unwillingness to accept the enrichment that comes from heterogeneity. This argumentation, which is not based on natural law, can be maintained even where there is no progeny (so that the triad man-woman-child is lacking), since where the bipolarity exists, it is possible for the tripolarity to be supplied in another way, for example, by means of polygamy, thus integrating a childless bipolarity into the triad. Naturally, this does not mean the model is above question. As we shall see later, the community can certainly arrive at a different ethical model—a process that nevertheless must be carried out by the community itself, not by reflection on metaphysics and natural law.

Something similar must be said about the question of incest. The prohibition of incest has deep roots in the concept of community and is thus not to be legitimated (as in the West) on the grounds that incest is contrary to nature. Rather, the *homo incurvatus in se* is the one who is unwilling to share with other human persons. One who has sexual intercourse with his own relatives not only offends against a "natural" feeling. The gravity of his action consists in the fact that both partners are unwilling to approach others outside their own familial or ethnic group in order to exchange or share their *blood* with them.[20]

Africans argue against lifelong celibacy along precisely these lines: one who remains unmarried for life withdraws from solidarity with other human persons, offending against the law of life. He is like a magician who ruthlessly destroys life, since a celibate is unwilling to take a share in the growth of life on the biological level and refuses to take his place in the duality of man and woman, which alone constitutes full humanity.[21]

Precisely because the community is an inalienable dimension of sexuality, prostitution in the modern sense is scarcely possible in traditional Africa. Sexuality is not for sale. It finds expression only in the fellowship of the living and the dead.

Let us mention one other example, that of private property, which also does not exist in Africa in the Western sense. The individual indeed possesses a right of administration, but this is not devoid of the sense of community, since this right must always take into account the members of the family fellowship as a whole. The social doctrine of the Catholic Church, which justifies the right to private property in Aristotelian-scholastic terms by appealing to natural law, has nothing in common with the African attitude. Nor is the patristic justification in terms of a universal right to the use of material goods[22] the same thing as the fundamental conception held by Africans south of the Sahara.

Let us once again emphasize that none of the arguments presented here claims absolute validity for what it says; they are certainly open to further dialogue with other models that argue along different lines. But it is decisive for them that the starting point should lie not in abstract principles but in concrete communities, whether inside or outside one's own group. In this sense, we may borrow Michael Walzer's expression and call African ethics *radically anti-Platonic,* since it remains in the "cave," "in the city, on the ground."[23] Nevertheless, here too we can follow the line of thought that Walzer calls "rights of reiteration" and speak of "reiterative universalism." The fundamental principle of reiterative universalism consists "in the reciprocal acknowledgment of the other as 'architect of morality,' as a being who determines himself in and with a fellowship."[24] "Reiterative universalism" allows universal principles to take on validity in particular instances, unlike the "covering-law universalism" in which the principles of justice and the standards for the good individual and political life are established in general terms, without any real possibility of self-articulation. This is why one can speak here only of images or incipient forms of true justice.[25] This means that the African community ethic involves a "contextualistic" or "context-sensitive" universalism that is not reduced to a "covering-law" universalism; both the cultural group and individuals within the community have the possibility of self-articulation. However, this context-sensitive self-articulation remains open to dialogue and receptive to other contexts. To sum up: both the specific cultural communities and the individuals within these must always speak in a locally defined manner, out of the "cultural cave," but at the same time their intention is to express something obligatory for members outside their own contexts. Similarly, their acknowledgment of the right of other specific communities to formulate obligatory norms impels them to dialogue with these communities.

This is certainly what happened on the black continent south of the Sahara in the confrontation with Western culture, as we see in the example of the pre- and postnatal sexual taboos which understood the sexual acts as an attack on the life of the child. Thanks to improved information in the area of modern medicine, many African women and men have at least to some extent called these traditional prohibitions into question. In concrete terms, this means that a husband can no longer appeal to these taboos to legitimate polygamy or occasional infidelities. However, the basic idea of the tradition is preserved, viz., respect for a woman because of the child she is carrying or has just borne: this life lays a heavier burden than normal on the mother, and the husband must show consideration for this fact.

Another example that can be observed within this area of marital life concerns the problem of the individual's freedom to contract a marriage.

In many regions, especially in the large cities, the individual freedom of the couple is expressed more clearly than in the past, where sometimes the family could exert a strong pressure to override any objections on the part of the young people. Better education (including religious education) and living alongside the Western way of life have shown the limitations of some traditional practices. Young people no longer accept uncritically the fact that they are "predestined" from childhood for marriage with particular persons and that this may not be changed. Nevertheless, it remains true that the community plays a significant role in the correct praxis of individual freedom in the incipient marriage. This community must find an expression different from that of the ancestral tradition: its essence must be the effective transmission of the established tradition, integrating both past and present.

Another problem concerns health and suffering, which were almost always seen as the outcome of magic. Education in school and improved contact with Western thought through radio, television, and so on, as well as Western medicine have given people in Black Africa better knowledge of the causes of illness, so that there has been a decline in exaggerated mutual suspicions when illness and accidents occur. But this ancestral tradition of magic contains one component that has proved capable of survival, viz., the idea of the community, confirmed rather than weakened by modern medicine and the dialogue with Western culture. Good neighbors or a good, healthy, peaceful community can play a decisive role in the health of the individual members, and this is the contribution of African thinking, as far as magic is concerned—for a community that is devoid of love "consumes" the vital force of its members and leads to their death. In this wider sense, African thinking about magic can provide food for thought to the individualistic perspective of the West.

In view of what has just been said, it is inappropriate to call the African community ethic an ethnocentric error, which leads to a fundamentalistic ghetto mentality. African ethics recognizes a *minimum moral code* which, "formally" speaking, deserves recognition in every human group, even if it is expressed variously in keeping with specific cultures and communities. Rainer Forst is correct when he says: "It is the *human* experiences in all cultures which demand the elaboration of a *human morality,* although this is never found in a pure form. We share the feelings of others who suffer under oppression and experience pain, and we have feelings like theirs. As a result of this shared feeling, we emphasize the same moral claims which are born of negative experiences."[26] Nevertheless, there is no "moral Esperanto," but only a "plurality of languages" inspired by the common experiences of different persons.[27] This minimum must certainly be preserved in all cases. But the minimum moral code also includes the right of each particular community to translate its laws into practice in a substantially different manner, provided that this praxis does not "morally" injure the minimum itself.

The example of monogamy and polygamy in the African tradition can make clear what is meant here. Traditional society never looked on polygamy as institutionalized prostitution; in general, the ideal demanded the same respect for women in polygamy as in monogamy. At this stage of the tradition, it was believed that women's dignity could be maintained only by means of a marital bond that was *monogamous* and/or *polygamous.* Thus, the heart of this praxis was not in the least immoral: it certainly amounted to a high ethical ideal. But as soon as society accepts the insight that there are other and better ways of defending woman's dignity than polygamy, or that one can no longer defend this practice, a new language must be learned or developed in order to do justice to the value the tradition sought to maintain. Seen from this perspective, a cultural community is no ghetto community, but rather what Michael Walzer calls a "justifying community."[28] We shall return to this in the chapter about the palaver.

Finally, we must take up an important question, that of rationality. While the problem of the *cognatus sum* that we have discussed here certainly diverges from the Western standard of rationality, this does not necessarily imply irrationality but merely a non-Western form of rationality. Many scholars have called the African mode of thought "pre-logical,"[29] identifying this as one of the main reasons for the underdevelopment of the black continent. The question is whether rationality is primarily defined as goal-oriented, formal-logical, and mathematical. But even when rationality is no longer teleologically defined, rather than in terms of communicative behavior, it is distinct from African rationality to the extent that it emphasizes the rational, argumentative power of reason.[30] Black African rationality is much more inclusive. In the process of establishing norms for ethical-moral conduct, it admits the contribution of that which cannot be justified in terms of reason. This is because it wishes to consider the human being holistically—and the mystery that surrounds the human person cannot be grasped by reason alone.

This incomprehensibility does not necessarily or primarily entail that we are confronted by meaninglessness or irrationality. The value of some things may be experienced and observed as a fact; yet it can take years or centuries before later generations are convinced of their truth. The clearest example here is traditional African medicine. Many people found the assumption of the fellowship of the living and the dead absurd—for how can one regain one's health by bringing food to a deceased member of the family? The fundamental underlying attitude, that is, that reconciliation with the community leads to regaining health, was not recognized by those who thought and acted differently. Today one can observe that modern Western society attempts, above all in psychotherapy, to rehabilitate relevant practices in African medicine that used to be condemned out of hand. This is a good example of the mistake made when one particular rationality is absolutized, as if it alone could encompass every aspect of the truth. In our pluralistic thinking, there are also truths that are forgotten. Walzer is correct when he affirms that a justifying interpretation that explains absolutely everything is an ideology: "It is false, because neither we ourselves in our daily conduct, nor a society, ever truly lives up to the criteria which apply to ourselves, or to it. Criticism is always necessary, in order to remind us."[31]

In the book *Zweifel und Einmischung: Gesellschaftsethik im 20. Jahrhundert* (Frankfurt a.M., 1991), Walzer demonstrates the errors and mistakes of eleven of the most important social critics of the twentieth century and concludes they are unable to reach a consensus about moral judgments: all they can attain is a "temporary and preliminary final point." This is why it sometimes happens that persons are declared guilty, and this judgment later proves to have been false.[32] If one takes this line of argument further and bears in mind that Black Africans prefer this way of thinking, one will more readily understand why they have immense difficulties with natural-law ethics. Those who consider the *status quaestionis* in moral judgments as something always preliminary, since it is related to and determined by the community, will need to maintain a critical distance vis-à-vis an ethic that speaks of the *intrinsece malum.* The *Catechism of the Catholic Church* and papal documents such as *Humanae vitae* and *Veritatis splendor* fall on deaf ears, since they do not accept this concern of Black African ethics. This is why it is appropriate here to make a comparison between natural-law moral theology and African ethics.

Questioning Natural-Law Thinking

In view of the discussion of relativism in ethical theories,[33] it is important to affirm that African ethics does not call into question the possibility of universal validity in ethics; all that is at stake is the problem of its justification. For does there not exist a legitimate pluralism in argumentation and the way in which norms are established, a pluralism that can ultimately lead to divergent (though not contradictory) forms of praxis?

This question is perhaps not quite so naive as it may at first sight appear. It is, for example, not unfair to say that the absolutization of natural law means that the Catholic Church is not very open to an intercultural dialogue *in rebus moralibus.* This prescinds from the question whether this natural-law tradition argues correctly or incorrectly; it asks only whether the truth may be grasped by one kind of methodology, via a "one-way street." There is no doubt that natural-law moral theologians have developed an ingenious methodology that is impressive and can even be convincing.[34] However, those not trained in this way of thinking, especially those from other cultural milieux, will not find it particularly fruitful. This is why the attempt is made here to examine other ethical models in relation to the African way of thinking; nevertheless, natural-law theology remains an important dialogue partner. However, the natural-law model, which is based on one particular philosophy, is one among many models of ethical reflection. The ethos of the Old Testament takes a different path, and natural-law ethics begins with the attempt to understand and systematize this biblical concept, a procedure already adopted by Thomas Aquinas.[35] Thomas does not always argue strictly in terms of natural law. An example here is his argument about masturbation. It is considered wrong not primarily because it is contrary to nature, but in view of the function of male sperm within the community: "Even if the sperm is superfluous in view of the maintenance of the individual, it is nevertheless necessary for the propagation of the species."[36] And he continues: "This makes it obvious that every emission of semen which cannot result in procreation is contrary to the good of the human person. And if one were to behave in this way with deliberate intent, this must be a sin."[37] Thomas's explanation is interesting. He does not understand nature in the strictly Stoic sense; thus his aim is not a servile respect for the natural ends. Accordingly, he can write: "Nor should one consider it a light sin if one procures the emission of semen apart from the duty of procreation and education—arguing that a minor sin, or none at all, is involved if one employs some part of the body for a use other than that to which it is ordained in accordance with nature, for example if one were to walk on one's hands or do something with the feet that ought to be done by the hands. Such disordered uses do not thwart the good of the human person to any great extent, but the disordered emission of semen is contrary to the good of nature, which is the conservation of the species."[38]

L. Oening-Hanhoff correctly notes that the significant point in this text is not "that this argument of Thomas is obsolete, but that Thomas requires one to evaluate an ethical norm, not on the basis of the goals of nature, but of the *bonum humanum*."[39] A different kind of argumentation, alongside the *lex naturalis,* can also be discerned in the case of polygamy in *4 Sent.* d. 33 q. 1 a. 2c; q. 2a a. 2 sol. 2, where marriage to several wives is permissible under certain circumstances. Thomas, like Augustine in the patristic period,[40] legitimates the Old Testament praxis from a wholly communitarian perspective, in terms of the necessary growth of the people of God in preparation for the fulfillment to come in the new covenant.[41]

Not only does Thomas argue in some places along lines other than the natural law; he also clearly recognizes the boundaries of reason—first because reason needs a long time until it can clearly recognize some truths, and also because, even where the truth can be known, it is sometimes an object of dispute among specialists; in some cases, only a minority of persons can recognize the truth. This leads Thomas to postulate the necessity of divine revelation, which allows the human being to know in a manner genuinely free of error. He writes:

> Even those truths about God which per se can be reached by the human reason had to be revealed to the human person, since only a few persons would have the possibility of investigating these truths; this would involve a great amount of time and would even then be linked to error. Yet it is on the knowledge of these truths that the entire salvation of the human person (a salvation which is in God) depends.[42]

We should note that these words of Thomas are not restricted only to those truths most directly linked to revelation. He also emphasizes the general limitation of reason in relation to the knowledge of truth.

The clinching proof of this is the position of women in Thomas's doctrine. It was not possible for him to establish the equality of men and women on the basis of rational arguments, since according to such arguments women can have only an inferior position vis-à-vis men. This limitation on reason is, however, transcended by the statement of faith that man and woman were equally created as the image of God.[43] Today we are able to use rational arguments to establish the equal dignity of men and women, but Thomas Aquinas was prevented by the dominant anthropology and the science and philosophy of his period from discerning something that today is taken for granted, for example, in the area of human rights. What we can observe in Thomas recalls the "forgotten truths" mentioned above, which are discovered by later generations only later on and then are universally taken for granted. Pagan scientists and philosophers ignorant of the Jewish-Christian faith and who accepted that period overlooked the inalienable dignity of women. In this sense, the biblical message was a forgotten truth; this truth, which had in fact been revealed so long before, was discovered and established at a very late date by our "rational" or "natural-law" thinking. Similar observations can be made not only about that which can be discerned by faith but also in the case of cultural convictions. Initially, these may seem unimportant to a rationalist way of thinking, as in the case of African art. People in the West dismissed it as worthless, since it did not accord with Western criteria for art, until it was rehabilitated by Pablo Picasso. The same thing can happen in ethics; for the difficulty indicated by a Thomas Aquinas with regard to knowing and attaining the truth involves not only theoretical but also practical reason.

In view of all this, it sometimes seems too trivial and hasty when scholars refer to Lawrence Kohlberg's theory of moral development, which attempts to point out that there are stages of moral development in cultures too, and notes that many cultures are still at the lowest stage.[44] In my view, studies such as those by Gertrud Nummer-Winkler relativize this view when she makes it clear that even small children are already capable of understanding and internalizing moral concepts. For example, they know that one may not torture another person without doing him an injustice.[45] The child would not be able to provide a rational justification of the underlying moral value, yet (to use Kohlberg's language) it is at a very high stage of development. The same may also be said of the so-called primitive cultures.

After these general reflections on the rational, natural-law argumentation, we can now speak of the genuinely African problems. Some examples will help to make the issue clear. If we ask (as we have done above) when one may speak of a prohibition of incest, we note a clear difference between many African cultures and those of the West: in some African peoples, the boundary against incest is reached much more quickly than in central Europe. In Western culture, at least in central Europe, sexual intercourse between cousins does not count as incest, but this is strictly prohibited by many African peoples. This sometimes covers all degrees of relationships, reaching even the smallest branches of the family tree. The Bathema in the eastern area of the Democratic Republic of the Congo are an example of this: they practice an extremely strict sexual morality as far as incest is concerned.

The difference between the Western and the African prohibition of incest is ultimately due to different understandings of life, which are transmitted by the very languages employed. Many African languages have no word to express what is meant by the German, French, or English term "cousin." In these African languages, "cousins" (in European languages) are "brother" and "sister," in the case of children of one's father's brother or one's mother's sister. Even the children of what Europeans would call two cousins can be brother and sister. Further, the brother of one's father is equally "father," just as the sister of one's mother is equally "mother." They are not "uncle" and "aunt"—"aunt" is only the sister of one's father, and "uncle" only the brother of one's mother. Consequently, the children of this uncle are just as much "uncle" as their father, or "mothers" in the case of daughters.

The intention of this lengthy and somewhat complicated explanation is to show that language exercises a decisive influence on ethical conduct in the sexual sphere. It goes without saying that one does not marry one's own brother or sister, any more than one would marry an uncle or aunt from one's own family. It is even less possible to imagine a marriage between a mother and her son or a father and his daughter. This, however, makes it obvious that church praxis, which determines the degrees of relationship in keeping with the Western pattern, does not fully take account of the African situation. Thus Christianity can appear to permit and encourage behavior that is ethically abominable. It is unnecessary to emphasize that African and Western ethics differ not in the condemnation of incest as such but rather in the question of who determines what is to count as incest. Only then can one agree about the so-called *intrinsece malum.*

The problem of polygamy, mentioned above, is similar. E. Schockenhoff is right to point out that even when "the crime involved in specific fields of action such as theft, adultery or murder" can be defined in various ways, in keeping with particular cultures or epochs, the value judgment that is the basis of the "behavioral type" remains constant: "Thus, although the modes of conduct which count as adultery in a polygamous or in a monogamous ordering of society may diverge widely, this does not alter the ethical disapproval of adultery."[46] This may be true, but in view of the official ecclesiastical moral attitude, and that of Western society, it does not seem very helpful to those concerned, since polygamy is held above all by the Christian church to be adultery, even where people consider this institution to be legitimate, and condemn an act of adultery just as much as those who live in a monogamous marriage do. The decisive existential question for those in this situation is no longer how they themselves establish and understand morality, but how the church establishes and justifies its norms. Another factor, especially in the case of incest, is that some African traditions go even further than the church's demands, since they hold that marriage lasts not only until death separates the partners, but even after the death of one's spouse. It is not helpful here to appeal to Jesus' logion in Matthew 22:30, which affirms that there is no more marriage after the resurrection, since these ethnic groups hold that marriage lasts for eternity: thus, it is possible to incur guilt in relation to the deceased partner, by marrying again.[47] Marriage to an in-law does not offend against this idea, since the widow remains faithful to her husband by maintaining fidelity to his family or to society. This makes her a living "sacrament" which recalls the dead man. Thus there is ultimately a community dimension in marriage with the widow, and this in turn has a social function. A woman who is widowed continues to belong to the family of her husband. She may not abandon this family; her task is to integrate it into the community by means of a new, visible bond and to look after this family in purely societal terms. This means that even when the church admits the possibility of a dispensation, canon 1092 of the Code of Canon Law is speaking a fundamentally different language from African reality, which justifies ethical conduct in "communitarian" terms, that is, on the basis of the community.[48]

This kind of justification applies to virtually all spheres of African ethics. For example, if we take the problem of insemination or of *in vitro* fertilization with anonymous donors of sperm, the decisive and convincing argument will not be an abstract one, drawn from natural law: it is only the community dimension that supplies lasting justification for the prohibition. African society, where *cognatus sum, ergo sumus* is significant, does not admit any anonymity. This is ultimately linked to the anamnetic thinking of African anthropology; we shall return to this in greater detail below. Here it is essential that each child knows its father and mother by name and remains in a living contact with them after their death; and it is equally essential that parents know their children by name and remain in the warmest contact with them, for it is only this mutual bond that constitutes them as persons. It is extraordinarily important to insist on this precisely in Africa, where the desire for children and yearning for community can have disastrous consequences on some persons—for modern technology and medicine could pervert a good tradition into its opposite, for example, when the mother or the married couple desire children to satisfy their own ideals or egoistic desires, to bring about the community that they picture to themselves in egotistic terms, but to the disadvantage of the child, without concern for his true identity in the community.

An abstract argument, proceeding in an unequivocally rational or natural-law manner, cannot convince people not to use the possibilities offered through modern technology and medicine. The Instruction *Donum vitae* of the Roman Congregation for the Doctrine of the Faith (1987) points in this direction (II/2),[49] but despite its attempts to keep up with the advance of science, this document does not move beyond the framework of the traditional doctrine of the natural law. If it is read from a non-Western perspective, it inevitably creates the impression of having been written for Westerners, although it ultimately makes the claim of universal validity. One place where this impression arises is the justification of natural rights, or where the document speaks of "the natural prerequisites of the human person" (*Donum vitae* III). And the encyclical *Humanae vitae* (1968) would have found a readier hearing among people in Black Africa if it had addressed their ethical attitude, oriented toward the community, instead of giving the central position to *natura.*[50]

Regrettably, similar passages can be found in the recent *Catechism of the Catholic Church.* If we take once again the example of homosexuality, we find that the *Catechism* begins by rejecting homosexual practices *inter alia* on the basis of a natural-law argument: its moral justification is that homosexuality contradicts what is given by nature. At the same time, however, this very *Catechism* acknowledges the results of modern scientific research, which affirm that many people have a primarily homosexual orientation. The *Catechism* recommends that one take these scientific results into consideration; but these people cannot be allowed to engage in any homosexual genital encounter.[51] In my view, this mode of argument involves the *Catechism* in a contradiction. For homosexuals could turn things around and state that they cannot understand why heterosexuals should be allowed to engage in sexual fellowship, *inter alia* on the basis of their natural disposition, while they are strictly prohibited from doing so.

From the perspective of African ethics, homosexual persons can be encountered within the African communitarian-anamnetic framework. The idea of a community embracing the living and the dead could help those persons who are attracted to the same gender to overcome this natural disposition, without, however, requiring them to abandon their own identity. The survival of the community depends on their committed action in favor of those not yet born, who constitute an essential dimension of the community. Additionally, we must also recall here the bipolarity between man and woman, mentioned above which constitutes the entire person in an all-embracing sense, even where there are no offspring. The argument of the *Catechism* recalls the problem of the *inclinationes naturales* in Thomas Aquinas. Unlike Thomas, however, the *Catechism* seems not to pay sufficient attention to the function of reason in structuring the natural inclinations. He does indeed take the natural endeavor and disposition of the human person so seriously that he goes so far as to speak of the "vice against nature";[52] but one must analyze more precisely what he means by "against nature," "according to nature," and "beyond nature."[53] He employs a very nuanced language here, although the *inclinationes naturales* provide him with the framework for the formulation of his definition of the *lex naturalis.* At any rate, in keeping with the spirit of Thomas (who did not discuss this problem in detail), there can be no doubt that the decisive role is played by reason. This is not simply an organ that merely registers and accommodates itself to the natural inclination; it must integrate its own given nature in such a way that the human person can act responsibly. This is why everything that is against reason is sin, and whatever contradicts reason is equally contradictory of nature itself.[54] This question should be seen in connection with the so-called natural desire to see God. Thomas repeatedly asserts: "A natural desire cannot be in vain"; "nature does nothing in vain"; and so on.[55] This natural striving, as an instinct, is in turn subject to a higher instinct, viz., reason, and is structured in such a way that it may reach its goal.[56] This can also be seen on the level of *amor* as a quasi-erotic element, which, however, passes over into *caritas* or *amor amicitiae,* where reason assumes a leading role.[57] On the other hand, however, the *ratio* must take the natural dispositions seriously, since they provide it with guidelines for its orientation, so that it starts aright and remains on course and can proceed efficiently with its work of investigation.[58]

Everything indicates that it is natural-law thinking that casts suspicion on many African forms of marriage, especially the so-called marriage by stages. To begin with, ecclesiastical marriage takes place at one point in time (as does civil marriage, which bears a Western imprint), whereas African marriage is a process, even where the future married couple are not permitted to live together before marriage; the intention is that they shall get to know each other thoroughly, not least with the help of the community. This brings up the communitarian character of African marriage. While Western marriage is primarily something brought about by a contract between two persons, African marriage is understood as a covenant between two families, each embracing a community of several generations. A contractual marriage has traits belonging unambiguously to the sphere of the natural law, and it can cease to exist at one point in time, just as it began at one point in time. Communitarian thinking forbids this in the case of African marriage, which (as we have seen) remains indissoluble even after death in the view of some ethnic groups. Here too the *Catechism of the Catholic Church* remains external to African reality, though its argumentation is equivocal, since it takes both covenant and contract as the basis of marriage.[59]

In my view, the examples presented here make it clear that the dialogue between ecclesiastical moral theology, based on natural law, and African moral theology, based on the community, would be made easier if the church paid more heed to the Thomistic distinction between *ius naturale* and *ius gentium.* Although this distinction does not do full justice to African ethics, it can nevertheless facilitate dialogue, since the concept of *ius gentium* includes a historical-communitarian element. The *ius naturale* speaks of the existing state of affairs as something that has assumed a fixed, stable form; but the *ius gentium* points to the elaboration of the *ius naturale* in terms of the goal at which a specific context and society consciously aim.[60] It is surely the doctrine of *ius gentium* that supplied Aquinas with the framework for a nuanced treatment in his evaluation of polygamy and polyandry[61] and of the right to property and slavery.[62] Together with the *ius gentium,* the doctrine of *desiderium naturale* creates sufficient points of contact for dialogue with African ethics, especially where Thomas says that "nature does nothing in vain." If we take the ecological question as our example, it could be possible to motivate and compel reason to discover the function of various elements in the entire governance of the world and the cosmos as a whole, and to provide a posteriori justification of this and elaborate it in a new manner. This procedure corresponds exactly to the idea of African anthropology, which does not simply attempt naively (as many people suppose) to establish the causalities in the cosmos. An assertion such as "there exist interaction and mutual influence in nature" indicates a deeper reality and makes it clear that the human person recognizes that he is inextricably embedded in the cosmos as a whole. It is only this recognition that makes the human person capable of assuming the stewardship and protection of the environment in a comprehensive fashion.[63]

In view of these observations, one may not accuse African ethics of cutting itself off from the rest of the world, or of the ethnocentric fallacy: it intends to raise its voice in the universal dimension—but it does so in the plural. It may be true to say that the claim made by natural law refers "only to the minimum presuppositions" that all human persons, irrespective of the culture to which they belong, ought to acknowledge, since they are included in the ethical phenomenon.[64] One must, however, ask whether the acknowledgment of the *universale* suffices to identify the boundary beyond which no more questions can be posed; as long as there exists a moral authority that defines ecclesiastically or internationally binding norms—or even only the ethical minimum—without consulting those concerned, the acknowledgment of a purely formal "universal" is of little help. This has at least been indicated above, in the example of the prohibition of incest. We should also mention the rules of hospitality in the ethnic groups in Rwanda, where a husband hands over his wife to the friend who is visiting him, and she spends the night with him. This is not looked on as adultery, since adultery is disparaged just as much here as elsewhere. A similar, though not exactly comparable example, is found among the Gikuyu in Kenya. A woman who is not able to satisfy her husband fully looks for another woman and brings her to the husband as herself—a second "I"—but this does not count as adultery.[65]

No one will dispute that these peoples recognize the same formal principle as the Christian churches, namely, the prohibition of adultery; the real question begins when one demands to know what counts as adultery, and when one can say adultery has taken place. It is clear that the churches, as well as civil society at least in the West, define not only *formally,* but also *substantially,* what constitutes adultery, and this is why the above-mentioned African practices are very severely condemned by the Catholic Church. Moral theoreticians will surely agree with Schockenhoff's conclusion: "To speak of the natural rights of each human person presupposes a modest anthropology which makes no ultimately definitive statements beyond the general goals of life that allow human existence to succeed as a whole, and stake out the circumstances within which human existence is possible. The statements of natural law are thus made within a 'preliminary area' which points beyond itself to that 'fullness of the basis of life' to which the biblical revelation bears witness."[66] Schockenhoff clearly has in mind here the so-called world religions (Buddhism, Hinduism, Islam, etc.) and "lofty ethical traditions of humanity."[67] If we consider the examples from the Black African experience, this thesis does not seem quite accurate. In praxis, no attention is paid to Schockenhoff's warning that one should not extend "the sphere of validity of the natural law" as if this were an integral ethos "covering all areas of life."[68] As our examples show, it often happens that the justification of the formalistic principles is immediately filled out with substance, so that the substantial element itself also lays claim to universal validity. It is then very questionable whether in this case the common basis of natural law "defines a culturally neutral lowest common denominator of what it is to be human," even though it does not aim to give an exhaustive answer to "the question of what positively constitutes an existence worthy of the human person,"[69] in accordance with E. Troeltsch, who pointed out the impossibility of elaborating a cultural ethics of substance.[70]

It is precisely such reservations that make it difficult to give a clear answer to the problem of the *intrinsece malum.*[71] As has already been emphasized several times, people in Black Africa agree with the doctrine of natural law that adultery must always be condemned, without any exceptions; but the question is, to what form of marriage this rule applies. Schockenhoff replies as follows:

> The recognition that marital love obligates both partners in their personal selves and in their reciprocal subjectivity implies the recognition of the monogamous structure of marriage and the obligation of marital fidelity. Fidelity to one's partner cannot be considered an external, preethical value in such a sense that the prohibition against infringing this fidelity would be the consequence only of other goods external to marriage itself.[72]

This thesis is certainly correct and irrefutable in terms of Western anthropology and understanding of marriage, but the definition of marriage is only partial from the traditional African perspective if it remains limited to monogamy—as if the second and third and any subsequent wives in a polygamous marriage were "non-spouses," and the husband were not their husband. In African eyes, the husband's infidelity to his second and third and subsequent wives (and their infidelity to him) is just as much adultery as is his infidelity to his first wife. Now, if one wishes to assert the *intrinsece malum,* it is only logical to apply it also to infidelity in a polygamous marriage; likewise, the *intrinsece malum* in the case of the prohibition of incest must apply not only in the Western, limited sense, but must include (without any exceptions) the African cases of incest too.

It is, however, well known that the contextual argument here proceeds along the lines of natural law.[73] When, for example, the encyclical *Veritatis splendor* says that *praecepta negativa* are valid *semper et pro semper,*[74] it will be necessary, in view of the cases discussed above, to find a contextual solution to some questions that ought to be investigated. Let me repeat that the question is not whether one *theoretically* acknowledges the absolute claim to validity of the *intrinsece malum,* but how, by whom, and according to what rationality this is established or asserted. One can then go on to question whether a distinction between *bonum* and *bona,* suggested by some proponents of the doctrine of natural law, ought not to receive more attention and recognition.[75] Franz Böckle is one of those who hold that we live in a contingent world, where contingent goods so compete with one another that we are able to recognize the absolute *bonum* only in the contingent *bona.* This differentiation might perhaps be better suited to carry on the dialogue between African ethics and the doctrine of natural law. Although such examples as torture, rape, the killing of innocent persons, and adultery are impressive and convincing as *intrinsece mala,* it is difficult in many other substantial questions of ethics to specify when prohibitions are valid *semper et pro semper* as clearly as the theoretical justification attempts to do. Thus, it seems rather like an *a posteriori* attempt to exculpate Old Testament ethics, when the killing of Isaac, Abraham's lie, Hosea's whoring or adultery, and the like are justified in terms of natural law (e.g., on the basis of God's ordering of things). Here Thomas too is a child of his own time.[76] On *STh* I-II q. 100 a. 8 ad 3, P. Grelot remarks that people of the thirteenth century had difficulties with a literal understanding of scripture; in many cases, it was necessary to find or invent excuses for characters in the Old Testament and even for God himself.[77] It is, however, primarily those ethical norms filled with substance that are relevant and existential: it is here that the theory must demonstrate its worth.

Let us note here that this debate does not concern the validity of natural law or African ethics. Rather, it involves two different procedures for justifying and positing moral norms. Whereas the natural-law argumentation proceeds in a rational and abstract manner, African ethical justification also includes a narrative dimension, which allows one to question an excessively idealistic theory and to put it to the test by means of an example. The natural-law argumentation gives the impression of looking for the absolute "ultimate justification," whereas African ethics is content with a less ambitious goal —not an absolute "ultimate justification" but only an "ultimate justification" until a better argument turns up. Thus African ethics also arrives at a point where questioning has to cease, but this involves a certain reservation (though not an arbitrariness). The claim its argumentation makes to absoluteness is a claim made in a specific context, and this makes Jürgen Habermas, although he argues differently, an interesting dialogue partner for African ethics. Unlike Karl-Otto Apel, he too renounces the goal of an "ultimate justification," although his discourse ethics emphasizes the absolute boundary to questioning in his argument and the transcendental-pragmatic presuppositions of the argumentation which the speaker "must have acknowledged *a priori,* if the argumentation is to maintain a *meaning.*"[78] Habermas's real concern is a "recursive-reflexive and formal-pragmatic reconstruction of the principle of a justifying reason," where the practical reason has no recourse to ultimate reasons or substantial "external" values in order to deduce norms, since norms must be able to justify their claims to reciprocal and universal obligatory validity "reciprocally" and "universally."[79] Rainer Forst comments: "This reconstruction cannot however itself be more than a self-reconstruction of a reason (employing the best means). As such, it cannot lay claim to absolute authority (what Apel calls 'ultimately justified' authority), but only to an authority justified 'recursively' as well as possible in relation to its object, viz. the 'rational' validity of norms."[80] The emphasis here on the norms' claim to validity and on the reciprocal and universal justification of these norms does not in the least mean that one abandons content; but practical reason both transcends context and is immanent to context. This means that while moral problems arise contingently, we may not be content with contingent answers. Unlike ethical values or legal norms, moral norms are not "rational" when they are "particularistic" (i.e., valid only for "me" or for "us"); this means that one cannot reasonably demand that others observe them, nor uphold these norms in relation to others.[81] The fact that practical reason both transcends context and is immanent to context indicates, however, that various contexts correct and supplement one another. "Persons are always members of various contexts, which offer a plurality of possibilities for conflict and critique."[82] In other words, ethics and morality (in Habermas's sense) are mutually determinative.

With regard to the discussion between the natural-law theory of the justification of norms and African ethics, this means that the theories with universal claims must be brought down to earth by particular practices which concretize the universal; more than this, they must also expose themselves to questioning and demonstrate their worth. On the other hand, the particular must allow itself to be questioned by a principle that has been justified in formal universal terms. African ethics does this in its own fashion, in that the community plays an active role in shaping a meaningful moral life. This involves effective and active participation not only in the establishing of norms but also in the positing and the *application* of these norms. This very significant participation in the ethical community is realized by means of the palaver, which—though not without similarities to the discourse ethics of a Habermas or an Apel—has its own characteristics, which provide interesting pointers to a fruitful dialog not only with procedural ethics but also with the natural-law model and communitarianism.

We will discuss this in greater detail later, although we cannot present every relevant detail and nuance. However, before we can study this theme, we must take up the problem of virtue, since it allows us most clearly to see a moral theology filled with substance.

Virtue and Morality

A consideration of virtue is an essential element in our reflections on African anthropology. It can readily be imagined that a moral theology of virtue in this context will not look the same as in the Aristotelian-Thomistic context.

Fairy Tales, Proverbs, Riddles, and Initiation

We must begin by noting that African communities believe that their future depends on the ethical conduct of their members. Education in ethical conduct that promotes the good of the community plays a decisive role here. The methods used to teach virtues vary in accordance with the age of the children and young people; for example, the fairy tales and legends that are told to children again and again, with especial emphasis on the vices and virtues of the protagonists. The children are to internalize these as lessons for daily dealings with their fellow human beings. Proverbs are equally important. These play a decisive role in communicating ethical goods and correct behavior, and they often supplement and correct one another by means of contradictory assertions. For example, the Bahema in eastern Congo say: "If a tree is not set in an upright position very early on, it remains crooked for ever."[83] This means that if a child is not corrected, it will be too late for it to learn correct behavior when it is an adult. We are also told: "You can bend a tree only when it is young."[84] The meaning is similar: if you do not take care of a child when it is young, it will be too late. There is no contradiction between these two proverbs, which are complementary; however, other proverbs virtually contradict each other, and their antithetical character allows the totality of life to come into view. I give only a few examples here. A Swahili proverb says: "The tortoise does not bite the leg of the leopard."[85]

This means that inferiors should not do anything against their superiors. But this affirmation must be corrected and balanced by another proverb: "The boat shows respect for the water, just as the water shows respect for the boat,"[86] which demands that superiors and inferiors display mutual respect. Other proverbs emphasize and relativize the authority of the chief, for example, "The ears are not higher than the head,"[87] which means that everyone should have his fixed station. This might mean that the chief is inviolable, but then a second proverb says: "When the river roars, rocks and stones are hidden in it."[88] This means that the chief can be angry only because he has inferiors—without these, he would have no kind of rank and dignity. He in turn must show respect in his dealings with the inferiors who are entrusted to his care; and in fact he can be deposed by them.

We have looked at only a few examples, but it must be emphasized that fairy tales and proverbs embrace every sphere of life. The morality that is transmitted in this way has a primarily sapiential character. To put it more precisely, it is the word that is eaten and digested and becomes wisdom for all the situations in life.[89] So that the proverbs can be easily learned, the formulations are intentionally brief, and sometimes even poetic.[90] The context in which young people learn them is fellowship with older, wise persons. In a society in which the spoken word is more important than the written, fellowship with old, experienced persons is an essential task in life, since the young person who is growing up must not only learn how to master life, but must also acquire the art of speaking. Here the proverbs, which express the synthesis of past experiences, play a great role for the future and for the coming generations. Since, however, this morality is sapiential, the virtues communicated and acquired by means of fairy tales and proverbs are not intended to be applied in a static manner to the various situations in life. Rather, they must be continually expounded and actualized anew. In this process, present-day life is enriched by new proverbs drawn from recent history and experience.

"Guessing games" must also be mentioned here. Not only children but also adults take part. One member of the group (it may even be a child) poses a puzzling question, and each one attempts to answer it. The answer presupposes that one interprets correctly the realities observed in daily life or in nature. This game encourages quick and creative thinking, as well as the invention of new questions and answers. The guessing games prepare the child to behave reflectively and creatively in all existential situations, including the ethical sphere. The child must always take care to interpret and describe events and contexts correctly and appropriately.

Initiation plays an even more decisive function in the education of the young. This term covers the period of life in which young people are integrated into the community of their ethnic groups, the time in which they must learn with particular intensity the entire history of their ancestors and of their ethnic group as a whole. In other words, the goal here is to recall and internalize the mighty deeds and the specific virtues of one's ancestors. The aim in the period of initiation is to attain to a new birth and become a new person, in order thereby to contribute a new dynamism to the community and to pass on to the coming generations the virtues acquired through the new birth. Anselme Titianma Sanon's observations about the Bobo of Burkina Faso are fundamental principles applicable to the morality of initiation in general: "The hare says: 'Prudence is not a right of the first-born. For if it were linked to that status, then I, the hare, would have entered the world with great prudence on the day of my birth. But since it is not like the rights of the first-born, each one who looks on the light of the world should listen to those who were born before him.'"[91] Sanon interprets this text to mean that prudence does not come with age; rather, one must listen to the tradition, or to one's ancestors.[92] Understanding or reason alone cannot suffice to make a person capable of living and of giving life—for this, each one needs to be integrated *actively* into the community, seeking contact with its other members, and in particular taking into consideration the experience of past generations. It is only thus that the young person can become wise and prudent. *Active* integration into the community means more than just a conscious act of incorporation; the accent lies on a holistic acquisition of virtues and experiences.

In order to grasp this point, one must recall that no dichotomy exists in Black Africa between body and soul, or between theory and praxis—or, in the present instance, between the body and knowledge. The initiation presupposes that virtue and experience are not only acquired by means of reason but also "conquered" by means of the whole body. Sanon notes that the Bobo distinguish between initiates and non-initiates by saying that one acquires knowledge only through initiation; this, however, concerns first of all the body, which must register the knowledge. Indeed, it is the body that links one to the community and to the spirits.[93] Sanon writes pointedly: "It is also the communitarian 'body' of learners which receives the tradition, and each individual assumes this into his own body, which is the field in which the seed of the word of initiation is sown deeply, supported by gestures, attitudes, rhythms and (if necessary) even by punishments."[94] Endurance and perseverance are also particular characteristics of initiation. One who has accepted and endured all the strenuous initiatory practices has internalized the virtues in an excellent manner and is prepared to meet all situations in life. Not only will he encounter difficulties in his private life (e.g., in his marriage) head-on; he will be able to support the community in every way. He will be a "stronghold" for the community. All this is possible because recourse is made to the past, in order to hand it on (not without criticism) and to narrate it so that the present and the future may be capable of life.

The Narrative Dimension of Virtue

In his much-discussed book *After Virtue,* Alasdair MacIntyre explicitly emphasizes the narration of stories, fables, and parables as characteristic dimensions of virtue above all in so-called heroic societies.[95] The narrative element here is not restricted to stories as such or to fables and parables, nor does it apply exclusively to heroic societies. MacIntyre holds that this dimension has an inalienable significance for the correct interpretation of our life even today. "Story" here refers simply to our past, which is handed on in narration. "We are, whether we acknowledge it or not, what the past has made us and we cannot eradicate from ourselves . . . those parts of ourselves which are formed by our relationship to each formative stage in our history."[96]

We must point out two complementary aspects of the narrative dimension. First, we have the literal narration of stories, events of the past, fairy tales, and so on. We have contexts that supply outlines and "body" to that which is narrated, molds without which the narration loses some of its significance. The first aspect is essential, if ethics is to come alive; one can observe this, for example, in the case of initiation in Africa. Although the initiation phase in puberty is more important, it nevertheless presupposes the narrative phase; and even later on, this narrative phase is continually reactivated and recalled. Indeed, in the case of many ethnic groups in Black Africa, one might speak of a "cantatory-narrative" ethic, which concerns the transmission not only of virtues but also vices, which are to be avoided. For example, the Bahema in Congo-Kinshasa had a celebrated song in the 1950s sung into the 1960s about a young woman who murdered a child. It criticized both the deed and the manner in which it was done: "Germana, can one kill a child at the breast? Germana, you used a razor blade to kill a child at the breast!" This song—which became popular in the whole area, not least because of its fine melody— had an important function in the education of people's consciences. It summoned everyone to get involved in the protection of children (including the unborn).

Another song from the same period, and just as famous, told of a young woman whose feet were attacked by sand fleas and totally deformed. "Irena, you have (thousands of) sand fleas on your foot! You notice these sand fleas at night above all (because they itch)!" By telling the story of Irena, the composers wanted to draw attention to the young woman's responsibility: she herself is to blame for her present state, which exposes her to laughter. At the same time, this song aimed at educating everyone, especially young people, since it is a disgrace when an adult behaves negligently and irresponsibly. The song also points out the responsibility of parents for small children; parents are disgraced when a child suffers this kind of bodily disfigurement, since it means that they have failed to carry out their duty of education and care.

It is purely by chance that these examples refer to women. There are songs with narratives that publicly criticize young men, and men in general, in exactly the same way. They are all intended to promote the good of the community. But, as these examples show, education in virtue and the promotion of ethical living are tasks incumbent upon the entire community, and this implies that the community gives expression to itself through each individual action. The action of the individual narrates the history of the community; at the same time, the individual narrates his own self.[97] This dimension is expressed already when a name is bestowed: in many ethnic groups, the name does not pass from the parents to their children, and this makes it clear that the self is narrative. Circumstances before or during the birth may be narrated, but the name can also relate the history of the family and of one's ancestors. This makes it perfectly obvious that the individual cannot be an unbound self. And the individual should make this known in everything he does.

It is impossible to overlook the similarities and points of contact between this presentation of the African understanding and communitarianism. Nevertheless, one important difference is the way in which African ethics and communitarianism understand concretely how ethical behavior is put into practice. As far as I can see, communitarianism emphasizes the community—the moral context, history, and the narrative dimension. Yet in concrete ethical behavior, the individual ultimately acts in the knowledge that his conduct is explained by the past, which is handed on here in narration. In African ethics, on the other hand, context is not all-important—one could not speak of a predetermined framework within which ethical behavior is realized. History and the experience of one's ancestors and of the elders are indeed taken seriously, but they are not merely repristinated or copied; rather, ethical conduct means that the individual does not consider himself to be the only one involved in his actions. As we shall see in greater detail later, there is a "circumincessory" relationship between the individual and the community in its three dimensions (the unborn, the living, and the dead) so that without the community, correct ethical decisions and acts of virtue are impossible.

We shall discuss later what this implies for such themes as the decisions of conscience. Here we note only that the communitarianism that is put forward by important representatives of modern philosophy deserves this name from the African viewpoint only in a *limited* sense, especially since it does not understand the dead as agents and pays no attention at all to the significance of the unborn. Despite all its criticism of liberalism, communitarianism ultimately cannot detach itself from its Western origin. Even when it speaks of the agent as one who remains in the "cave" of daily living, one who appears on the scene in the name of the "context," the agent nevertheless appears as an individual whose action can be fully deciphered only by means of context and history. The common denominator linking discourse ethics and communitarianism can be clearly seen here too, since both underline the position of the community in the establishing or justifying of ethical norms. But whereas discourse ethics demands that all concerned participate in an unlimited communicative community, communitarianism emphasizes the significance of tradition and community for the understanding of ethical norms. To a large extent, African ethics constructs a bridge between these two. Nevertheless, the fundamental difference remains which is not connected with their underlying philosophies, but is culturally determined.

Various Understandings of Virtue

MacIntyre points out that different societies can have different views and rules about virtues. He cites the example of the Lutheran pietists, who educate their children to tell the truth always, without respect to circumstances and consequences, as was the case with Immanuel Kant.[98] Bantu parents provide another example. MacIntyre writes: "Traditional Bantu parents brought up their children not to tell the truth to unknown strangers, since they believed that this could render the family vulnerable to witchcraft."[99] The reason he adduces is not entirely correct, for magic is not necessarily the point here. Rather, the basic rule is education in care and prudence. Ultimately, the parents want to communicate to their children wisdom and the right way to handle *words.* At the same time, one must agree with MacIntyre's fundamental thesis that there is a universal intention to secure the acknowledgment of the virtue of love of truth, which is non-negotiable. This observation points however to the context which alone makes it possible to understand virtue and ethical actions.[100] This is why it is important to emphasize that sensitivity to particular virtues can vary in accordance with culture historical epoch.

We can make this clear by taking the example of truthtelling. If one looks with African eyes at the attitude of Western people to the truth, one has the impression that Europeans and North Americans are much more sensitive to falsehood than is the case in Black Africa, while stealing seems of much more importance in Black Africa than in the West. If someone in the West is accused of lying, we assume that he will feel deeply offended, since in the last analysis, everything (perhaps even theft) comes down to a question of truth and truthfulness. A comparison with African sensibilities shows that one of the worst insults appears to be the accusation of theft; indeed, one who is reported to have incurred suspicion of stealing (even in very small matters) is unable to contract a marriage—or at the very least, such a person will find it difficult to find a marriage partner.[101] It is interesting here to note that Western ethics links such matters as adultery with falsehood: one who is unfaithful has deceived his or her partner, whereas in Africa adultery is associated with theft. This, however, does not mean that a human being is degraded to the level of "property" in the Western sense. Nor should one be too quick to quote Exodus 20:17, where the wife's relationship to her husband is that of property to its proprietor. Adultery here applies to both partners, husband and wife.[102] The point here will be grasped if we recall what was said above: wife and husband form a unity, since it is only the two genders *together* that constitute a whole human person. Adultery separates the human person in his or her totality, so that one loses one of one's essential parts. This is why it is included under the category of theft. It is important to emphasize here that these examples are not intended to assert that Africans approve of lying, while the West treats theft as a peccadillo. My aim is only to bring out the significance of contextuality and ethical sensibilities in the area of virtue. One who is at home in the Black African culture and worldview may perhaps find the Western view of truth too intellectualistic. Words, expressions, and so on are dissected with conceptual precision; they possess a priori a precisely established and defined meaning, which also has important legal implications. In Black Africa, however, truth is seen more in a dynamic manner. We shall see later that the word must always be considered not only in its communitarian dimension, but also in its function of creating community, since its aim is to give the community life in fullness. Whether one particular word can be called a lie does not depend on a stable meaning defined with conceptual precision. The word must be interpreted in connection with gestures, looks, proverbs—in short, contextually. Besides this, if the word is to create community, one must pay heed to the direction intended by its communication. A word that results in the destruction of the community loses its communicative significance. Understood in this way, truth must be uttered not for its own sake but for the sake of the human person, who is a communal being. Truth per se, independent of context, does not exist; it must mean something for the common life.

These remarks about truth and falsehood are meant only for clarification. One could present similar reflections on all the virtues, with the same result: virtues cannot be prescribed *ab extra,* but depend concretely on a specific context. It is precisely here that the proclamation of Christian morality must submit to inculturation. The most sensitive area for Christianity is in fact that of ethical problems, which must find corresponding solutions with a plurality of cultures; and this is not a question for the non-European world alone, since voices urging a new understanding of virtue can be heard in the West itself. Otto Friedrich Bollnow is correct to note:

> Old virtues, which set their stamp on an earlier period, get forgotten, so that even their name is scarcely understood today, as for example with "humility." Even where the names of other virtues are retained, the understanding—and hence also the evaluation—of these virtues changes. This was true with the word "virtue" itself. In each instance, the individual virtue takes on substance in the framework of a particular understanding of the human person. This substance changes, when the virtue is taken into a different framework.[103]

This altered appearance of a "virtue" is certainly not to be equated with moral degeneration, since it could also mean the chance for a new dynamism which in turn would perhaps even recall forgotten values to people's consciousness.[104]

Our world seems to react with greater sensitivity today to questions of social justice. We see more demonstrations, more posters, greater solidarity with the Third World, and so on. The option for the poor, promoted by liberation theology, is a fundamental attitude of many Christians today. Likewise, even the world of politics pays attention to the ecological questions which awaken a new awareness of the cosmos. There can be no doubt that this ecological challenge is beginning to change people's behavior; it is surely not false to say that ecology has become one of the new virtues of the modern world. Modern Westerners have developed a sensitivity to new values, and it is necessary to pay attention to this. The section of the official German catechism dealing with ethics notes that, in addition to the classical cardinal virtues, modern people find other fundamental attitudes such as "openness, reliability, respect, tolerance, love of peace, and solidarity" important.[105] This is because many believe that these virtues help to make "true humanity" possible for people today.

It is regrettable that the *Catechism of the Catholic Church* does not take up the question of this new sensitivity to virtues, and a fortiori ignores the question of multiculturalism. On the contrary, the *Catechism* levels down the differences which can be decisive for the identity of the various local churches. It really seems as if the *Catechism* proclaims a world ethos! It has, however, already been pointed out that there cannot be an "Esperanto" in moral theology. I believe that Josef Fuchs is correct when he maintains that no world ethos exists that can give concrete guidance for humanity as a whole. Indeed, Fuchs holds that such a moral theology cannot exist. Even when one appeals to faith, there exists no moral theology "handed down" to humanity "from on high." From the perspective of the natural law, we are also always confronted with a plural moral theology. Fuchs takes the example of human sexuality, which can be interpreted variously; thus we find Catholic moral theologians who see the goal of human sexuality in biological procreation, or in the human "founding of a marriage and family," or in "relaxation for body and spirit."[106] Josef Fuchs goes on to ask whether the idea of one single world ethos or a world ethic "thought out and proclaimed by Christian moralists and theologians" (including popes) with exclusive validity in questions of what is good and evil, is a utopia. His answer is clear: "No sufficiently similar interpretation, still less an equal evaluation, within the various spheres of life exists in the various groups, societies, populations, nations, etc., which have inherited such a variety of intellectual attitudes, traditions, experiences of life and environments. This is why it is not possible for agreement everywhere about ethical insights into good and evil, into behavior that is worthy of the human person and behavior that is sinful."[107] This affirmation is supremely important precisely in the question of the inculturation of moral theology within the framework of the Christian faith. In the proclamation of morality, one must stop imposing from on high one particular ideal of virtue on other peoples, if this is a contextually and culturally determined ideal. This is why one may regret that the *Catechism of the Catholic Church,* while addressing a multicultural world, fails to open up new perspectives, limiting itself to one particular ethical model. Some critics accuse the *Catechism* of adhering too closely to Thomism in its sections on morals, including the passages about the virtues.[108] Such a moral theology must sound even stranger outside Europe, although one should not ignore other ethical models—the narrative dimension in African ethics should not lead to the ethnocentric fallacy. African ethics is open to other experiences outside its own tradition, so that a sustainable future can be constructed. The experiences and testimonies of one's ancestors and of the community elders do indeed provide points of orientation, but they demand a critical confrontation with posterity,[109] since only such a confrontation can show what is substantially correct for today's generation. Philipp Schmitz is correct to say: "Virtue prepares one to take a decision in favor of what is right and gives insight into what morality demands, by activating the experience of the human person, his readiness to pay heed to others, and his alertness."[110] However, the individual's *ratio* does not suffice to establish whether a traditional virtue is right and truly serves today's context. Nor is it sufficient to share in a discussion of one particular virtue or norm and then leave the decision to each individual.[111] Rather—and here we see the difference between African ethics and the communitarian model—the community *qua* community must reach a consensus. The discourse ethics of Jürgen Habermas and Karl-Otto Apel are very close to African ethics on this point, even though the latter shares many similarities with communitarianism.

CHAPTER 2

Ethics and Anamnesis

IT IS ONLY IN THE CONTEXT OF A "MORALITY OF *MEMORIA*" that we can fully grasp the problem of African ethics as presented in the previous chapter. As I indicated there this *memoria* is realized within an all-embracing fellowship, so that those not yet born can also play an effective role. If we are to understand better this "morality of *memoria*" with its narrative tradition, we shall have to explain the role of the ethically active subject in this fellowship. In the present chapter, we show how an ethically active subject always understands his actions as making present the ethical experience of his ancestors and attempts to shape these actions accordingly. These actions are at one and the same time *praxis* and *poiēsis.* This, however, does not involve the maintenance of a rigid, unvarying tradition. Rather, the tradition must become the object of a process within the community, so that one may act both in the spirit of the tradition and in keeping with the present-day context. This is the task of the palaver process.

THE SIGNIFICANCE OF PRAXIS AND *POIĒSIS* FOR ETHICAL CONTEXT

Since I have discussed in detail elsewhere the question of praxis and *poiēsis,* I limit myself here to a brief presentation of the main ideas of that essay.[1]

African ethics is articulated in the framework of anamnesis, which involves remembering one's ancestors. As a narrative community, fellowship here on earth renews the existence of the community of the ancestors. This reestablishing (*poiēsis*) in turn implies the praxis which efficiently continues the remembrance of the ancestors and gives a new dynamism to the earthly fellowship. Consequently, ethical behavior in the Black African context always involves reestablishing the presence of one's ancestors; for one who takes the anamnesis seriously is challenged to confront the ethical rules drawn up by the ancestors, in order to actualize anew the "protological foundational act" which first called the clan fellowship into life. This ethics is not, however, to be equated with an uncritical acceptance of the tradition, as the following examples show.

Marriage and Sexuality

If the remembrance of the "protological foundational act" in *poiēsis* and praxis is essential, then we can begin with marriage and sexuality, which are decisive for the further development of life—including ethical development.

The Understanding of Marriage in the African Context

John S. Mbiti has correctly observed that marriage in Black Africa resembles a dramaturgy in which each person plays an active role, not content to be a mere spectator. Hence marriage is an existential task to which all are summoned. One who refuses to play his part will be reproached by the entire community, since this negative attitude is understood as a contempt which contradicts the good law of the ancestors.[2] It is precisely this attitude that leads to the anamnetic *poiēsis.* Like many realities in the African context, marriage must be seen in the light of the tension between life and death, in which life ultimately conquers death.[3] This, however, presupposes that each person, thanks to his indefatigable involvement, looks on himself as one who "makes history" through the *poiein.*

Marriage is one of the fundamental elements which strengthen and reestablish the community;[4] it signifies an anamnetic solidarity with one's ancestors. Moreover, it is a *communio* with one's ancestors which ultimately achieves a communicative fellowship that transcends death. All this also implies the idea of fertility and the transmission of life, and this not only concerns the survival of the individual but also embraces the entire fellowship: the living, the dead, and the unborn. In this sense, begetting and giving birth reestablish the legacy of the ancestors: "Do this in memory of me." Each one who continues the transmission of life through the covenant of marriage narrates the biography of his ancestors and writes his own autobiography,[5] thereby conquering death on the level both of the individual and of the community. Each child who enters the world keeps alive the memory of the ancestors and makes it present. At the same time, the birth of a child is a sign that gives the future generation the chance to survive: the newborn child is a sign that those not yet born are called to a visible existence in which they will play a vigorous role in *poiēsis* and praxis within the community. Thus, children represent both the unborn and the ancestors. In relation to the ancestors, they are a genuine *memoria,* while they are *nuntii* in relation to the unborn, whose arrival they proclaim.

When so much weight is attached to the birth of a child, it follows that the worst death is to die childless. This makes it necessary to discuss and justify anew the problem of the celibacy required of Catholic priests and religious women. To speak of "discussing and justifying" is not a plea to abolish celibacy; but it must be clarified how it is possible to integrate the African view of the ethics of fellowship into the new Christian context. A new argument on behalf of celibacy would speak not only of children but also of marriage as a covenant and as the place where the human person is realized in his totality—for, as has been shown above, the human person is constituted in his entirety only in a union of the two genders. This uniting in marriage likewise reestablishes anamnetic solidarity with one's ancestors and with the coming generation. Hence, married life is a high and demanding ideal. One who attempts to attain this ideal must pass through many, often painful experiences, which finally bring him to maturity. This allows us to grasp the African attitude to celibacy: an unmarried person is inexperienced and immature. Moreover, as has been pointed out, he withdraws from the anamnetic solidarity with his ancestors, by destroying rather than establishing the community.

Certainly, much in this view must be differentiated, complemented, or even sometimes corrected in the process of dialogue with modern Christianity. At the same time, it presents a number of challenges to the modern Western view of the world, which is often unnuanced and disregards local cultures. The African understanding of marriage questions the Western understanding, where marriage lived individualistically and considered as nothing more than a private contract between two persons, without consideration for the community so that marriage is no longer a *poiēsis* which establishes fellowship by means of its praxis. This results in a different understanding of sexuality than in Black Africa, where marriage makes visible the communal dimension of sexuality.

Sexual Life in the Context of the Community

African communities are interested in the sexual lives of all their members, since sexuality is not a private matter. The goal of sexuality is to keep together the community entrusted to us by our ancestors and to bestow ever new life on this community. It follows that the community must prepare young people for a responsible sexual life (and sexual pleasure), psychologically and physically. Psychologically speaking, young people are to become so mature that they learn to refuse every abuse of sexuality; physically, wise women and men teach them the correct relationship with their own bodies. This takes place above all in the period of initiation, which is the best school for self-control and is oriented to the future of the community. In many ethnic groups, the entire clan fellowship is interested in the wedding night; discreet questions aim to discover whether the newly married couple are satisfied and happy with their sexual life, since it is on this—not only on the ability to beget or give birth—that the future of the marriage, and hence the fate of the entire community, can depend.[6] A further indication that sexuality aims at more than just procreation is the fact that in many regions particular events are to be sealed or celebrated by sexual intercourse between the spouses, for example, the marriage celebrations of one's children, the appearance of a child's first teeth, and also funeral rites. The goal of the sexual act is to strengthen the bond between the family and clan community in all three dimensions mentioned above. From this perspective, sexuality in the African tradition has succumbed neither to unbridled license nor to the consumer mentality: it aims at building up the community. One must not lose sight of this background, when one encounters practices that are foreign to Western Christianity, for example, the idea that sexuality is a form of hospitality. As stated in chapter 1 above, the tradition in some cultures in Black Africa is that when a friend comes to visit, the husband gives the guest his wife for the night, as a sign of friendship. Among the Masai, the period of initiation plays an important role in the sexual community: companions in initiation (i.e., men who were in the same initiatory group) are allowed to have sexual intercourse with the wives of other members of this group. Here too the basic idea is the cohesion and renewal of the community.

Undoubtedly, none of these practices can pass unquestioned today. But at the same time, one must be aware of the underlying value at which the practice aims. Thus, to take another example, masturbation must be evaluated otherwise than in the Christian context; in some cultures, it is a normal part of the preparation for marriage and life in fellowship. In some African traditions, initiation includes the proof of sexual maturity, including masturbation; but this does not mean that the practice is to be condemned. The decisive factor in the evaluation of this action is above all the subsequent marriage, which is meant to be lived in harmony and concord. And all of this in turn serves to make visible the anamnetic dimension of the community, which is thought of in holistic terms. Thus, sexuality is not evaluated with regard to procreation, nor in keeping with the individualistic-personalistic pleasure principle: it is the community that legitimates sexuality.

I have already shown that one must reason similarly with regard to homosexuality. Let us take up the problem of modern prostitution. What has been said makes it perfectly clear that since sexuality is not a private affair, it can never be exchanged for money or other goods. The African tradition had succeeded in giving sexuality a humane dimension that erected a strong barrier against the life of a prostitute. All young people were prepared by taboos and self-discipline for their later sexual life, and almost all women were given the possibility of contracting a marriage and thus having a legitimate sexual life, since they were materially well provided for. Indeed, under polygamy a woman even had the possibility of an economic autonomy which made her financially independent of her husband.[7] This means that we need a more nuanced view of polygamy. At any rate, it is incorrect to say that traditional polygamy resulted in economic misery for women, especially since traditional African society was unacquainted with social classes such as "poor" and "rich," "beggars" and "non-beggars." On the contrary, it has been noted that precisely the prohibition of polygamy in modern times has driven many women to prostitution, since it was no longer possible for them to contract a marriage with a man who had already married according to the Western model. After the grave damage inflicted by Western industrialization on the structures of African life, illiterate single women without a profession cannot survive financially.[8] And it is precisely at this point that the "symbolic language" of sexuality, its dynamic and humane character, is replaced by the anonymous power of money. Sexuality no longer serves for communication with one's fellow human beings; it is no longer the *poiēsis* which allows the reestablishing of the community in its triple dimension, since it is no longer the anamnesis of the world of the ancestors. It becomes banal, something to be bought and sold.

Let me repeat the point: one certainly should not accept African practices uncritically. Nevertheless, the African pattern of ethical justification confronts Western ethics with a number of questions from which it should not shrink. The attitude that sexuality is not an individual possession, but attains its full dignity only in the community, challenges Western ethics to consider the African perspective and revise its usual arguments, allowing it to be enriched in the process.

The same holds for the natural-law ethics adopted by the Catholic Church. The *Catechism of the Catholic Church,* although intending to address the multicultural world, continues to employ natural-law arguments in the area of sexuality. For example, it sees the gift of fertility in marriage as based on the *inclinatio naturalis.* The *Catechism* emphasizes: "Fecundity is a gift, an *end of marriage,* for conjugal love naturally tends to be fruitful" (*Catechism* 2366). In the area of divorce, the *Catechism* retains the concept of contract, although it also speaks of a "covenant." However, it employs both concepts in the same passage, whereas in the African understanding of marriage and sexuality, as we have already seen, a marriage is based on a covenant—since it is this covenant that embraces all three dimensions of the African community. Let me repeat: a moral theology that rigidly argues on the basis of natural law becomes irrelevant since it fails to recognize the dynamic and anamnetic character of African ethics, which is realized through communitarian and communicative action.

If we turn to art in Black Africa, we find the same principles that have been expressed so clearly in the area of marriage and sexuality.

The Anamnetic Dimension of Choreography and Art in General

Dance and art are the commonest expression of the Black African's experience of transcendence, an experience that cannot remain on an abstract, theoretical level, but leads to concrete consequences on the level of ethical behavior.

Dance Is More than Talent and Folklore

Within the framework of the idea of *memoria,* dance is no mere choreography in which human beings reveal their ability and talent. Rather, it is a language that intends to communicate the deeper dimension of the total reality of life. To see a kind of folkloristic beauty in African dance is to fail to grasp the depth of the transcendental experience which is expressed by the person dancing. This is because the human being in Africa dances his own life.[9] In fact, all the existential events are danced: birth, marriage, and death, but also the new moon, political events, and so on. The various genres of dance express various hidden religious dimensions. For example, the dance can tell about pain and suffering, about joy and sadness, about love and thankfulness. It is always a cantatory, narrative *poiēsis,* which makes the message from beyond the grave a present reality in solidarity with the entire fellowship.

For example, when one dances death, the dead person is "danced through," or danced into life. This means that the dead person is formed anew and fetched back into the fellowship. The Bahema in eastern Congo say: "We have danced him or her out of the earth," or: "We are going to dance him or her out of the earth." A *poiēsis* cannot be more clearly expressed; but this *poiēsis* always results in a new praxis. In the case of the dance of death, this means a new relationship to the dead, who are once again among us. Modern abuses make it important to recall that the dance is meant to lead to consequences in praxis, for like the popular songs dealing with specific events in the manner described above, the dance too can criticize or correct an unacceptable state of affairs in the community. This critique employs a language that makes possible a better communication, full of life, by reminding people of the *poiēsis* which, thanks not least to the experience of contact with their ancestors beyond the grave, gives them hope for the future, so that the three-dimensional fellowship is not destroyed.

If one compares traditional dance in Africa with modern dance, one finds a certain emptiness. Dance no longer embodies the richness it traditionally possessed, but it degenerates more and more into folkloristic presentations—it is sometimes even put on show for tourists. Often it is employed for the support and glorification of politicians, who want their dictatorial power to be praised as "service of the people"; this strips it even more of its *poiētic* function.[10] When dance is misused in this way, it can no longer be the anamnesis of the ancestors which continually summons their descendants to awaken the community to life. The same is true of objects of art.

Artistic Objects and Their Ethical Message

Objects of art belong to the sphere of the nonverbal communication, which permits the communication of the experience of transcendence in the African world. Mulamba-Mutatayi's study of the Bakuba is very instructive here.[11] This study is exemplary for the understanding of art in Black Africa in general. The author studies the carvings and masks of the Bakuba in the Democratic Republic of Congo. Since the carvings of this people (like those of other peoples) do not correspond to the well-known

Western rules for art, "admirers" schooled in Western-classical terms tend to express a negative judgment of them. For example, the statue of a king displays a striking lack of proportion: the head can take up a third of the entire statue. This nonverbal language can be understood only when one recalls the importance of a king for community life. He is such an important person that he is compared to higher beings. Since the head has a very significant role to play in the sphere of wisdom, intelligence, and spiritual forces, this part of the body must be especially prominent.

Another characteristic of the statue of the king among the Bakuba is that the eyes are only half-open. This signifies that the person portrayed is now beyond the grave in the fellowship of his ancestors, while at the same time remaining present in the fellowship of those left behind on earth. Thus the deceased king continues to care for the fertility of the community, protecting it and ensuring its prosperity. His broad shoulders and muscular form transmit the same message. All this is intended to show that the human being is more than the material universe, which he must transform. In a similar manner, the emphatically round belly and the prominent breasts emphasize the profound significance of procreation and fertility, for which the human being carries an inalienable responsibility.[12] And here we must emphasize that, while the king protects the fellowship and ensures its prosperity, at the same time each member of the community is called on to continue the work of the king and thus unwearyingly to shape the community and establish it anew.

In a very explicit manner, the Negro-African masks display a summons to ethical behavior, as we see in the significance of the Bakuba masks. To begin with, these masks are the incarnation of the invisible, pointing beyond death to make visible that which is indescribable, that which no human word can perfectly express. This act of making visible refers also to the ethical sphere, for some masks draw attention to the moral order so that the life of the individual and of the community becomes receptive to transcendence.

The masks play an important role in moral instruction, especially in the initiation rite. They recall the ancestors and their foundational act which made the community life possible. Attention is drawn here to many practices and rites, but especially to ethical demands as well. One can summarize as follows the fundamental attitude that lies behind all this: it is only by preserving and handing on (in a critical spirit) the protological act of the ancestors that life in the comprehensive sense of the word is guaranteed for the earthly fellowship, which remains both stable and dynamic.

In order to indicate the various challenges posed by the masks, we must consider the individual categories of mask. The Bakuba masks show this very clearly and can be taken as a typical example of the Black African worldview,[13] particularly since their most strikingly evident traits can be found among other ethnic groups too.[14] Mulamba-Mutatayi distinguishes three genres of mask—*Mwoshambooy mu Shall, Ngaadi Mwaash,* and *Bwoom.*[15]

MWOSHAMBOOY MU SHALL. This is a royal mask which portrays *Woot,* the first ancestor, and has many functions, especially in the initiation rites. It recalls the order laid down by the first ancestor and the promise he made. The gestures, dance, and other rites carried out in connection with the mask help to attain the ideal that was realized by the first ancestor. This mask presents the perfect ideal on the ethical, political, and spiritual levels, for the instruction of later generations.

NGAADI MWAASH. This is a feminine mask which portrays *Mweel,* the sister and wife of Woot. It recalls the first woman of the Kuba ethnic group and symbolizes the one who gives birth to the whole of humanity, thus expressing the idea of a fertility that is both biological and spiritual. But the mask aims to do more than simply offer something traditional as a model to be imitated: it is at the same time a harsh criticism of the protological act of the first king, who became the ancestor and founder of the Kuba people's community by means of an ethically disgraceful act, viz., through incest. Because of this monstrous deed, the two masks *Mwoshambooy* (king) and *Ngaadi Mwaash* (consort of the king) are never allowed to appear together. This makes it clear that the two masks intend to proclaim an ethical requirement and message, namely, the prohibition of incest. His descendants are not to imitate the foundational act of the king, who married his sister; this does not, however, dispense later generations from showing continual gratitude to the primal parents for the life they received from Mweel and Woot.

In this precise context, the mask *Ngaadi Mwaash* emphasizes the dignity of the mother queen and her position within the kingdom: she is quite simply the symbol of the feminine, without which the man cannot be perfect. Thus, she ultimately recalls the idea of fertility for both genders, both in the biological and in the spiritual sense. This brings us back to the idea of *poiēsis:* the mask recalls the foundational act, which must always be borne in mind, if the community is to prosper. It is always very important to note that this *poiēsis* is no mere repetition of the tradition, but is always a critical engagement with it, so that the error of the past can be corrected and the descendants set out toward a better future than their ancestors. The following mask too points in this direction.

BWOOM. This is an imposing wooden mask which often appears in the initiation rite and in the ceremonial dance. As the representative of the people, it is the counterpart of the king; the fundamental idea behind its appearance is that without the people, the king deserves neither his name nor his kingdom. If the people are indispensable in this manner, then the king is obliged to rule in dialogue with it. Thus, the mask *Bwoom* intends to proclaim that the contribution or participation of the people is necessary for political and social equilibrium. This in turn means that a king or chief is legitimate only when he is fully acknowledged by the people. This is why every dictatorship must be rejected; only a dialogue between power and the people can promote fellowship, and only so is justice done to the protological act of the ancestors, who bequeathed the charge to actualize the fellowship creatively again and again.

To sum up: these remarks have attempted to make it clear that even today, Black Africans seek and have the experience of transcendence through nonverbal communication. This has been shown above all in the description of the masks, which mediate the meaning of life to the human person by pointing to that which is unutterable and invisible—usually, this embodies the ancestors and their protological foundational act. The masks narrate anamnetically the mighty deeds and promises of the ancestors; this anamnesis also implies the moral order, which is noted but need not be adopted in an identical or uncritical manner. The masks can also challenge people to shape the moral order anew and correct the ancestors' errors by means of a new interpretation of the past. Only this critical interpretation of the tradition allows people to have a genuine experience of transcendence, which in turn makes possible a communicative fellowship; only then is it possible to hand on to others in a meaningful way the experience of transcendence and of the past.

This makes plain once again the difference between African and communitarianist ethics, especially when one recalls what MacIntyre writes about the ethics of virtue. We have seen above that despite its community dimension, communitarianism has individualistic traits with regard to ethical decisions. There exists a further difference from the African anamnetic thinking. Its orientation to the tradition does not prevent African ethics from being innovative. In the nonverbal communication, the community conducts a nonverbal palaver which challenges the participants to reflect and to adopt a critical position vis-à-vis the ancestral tradition.

If attention were genuinely paid to the innovative elements in the African tradition, it would scarcely be possible for dictatorship—so common in the black continent—to exist, since oppression in all its forms is incompatible with the anamnetic solidarity which recalls the duty of continually realizing the three-dimensional fellowship anew. This must be done dynamically, lest the fellowship perish. Within a tradition understood in this way, it is never permissible to infringe human rights. The anamnetic solidarity is concerned not only with infringements of human rights in the present; it includes equally the injustice done to those who lived in the past. This naturally also involves the guilt of the ancestors: solidarity requires that this be expiated by their descendants. In other words, every member of the African community is aware of the summons to accept responsibility for the deeds of his ancestors. At the same time, one must be willing to confess the injustice that has been done in relation to these ancestors.

Jewish history in the Nazi period has shown clearly how relevant this anamnetic thinking can be; though it is regrettable that this is mostly restricted to the tragedy of the Jewish people, without including the histories of the suffering of other groups and peoples. In this specific context, the exploitation and destruction of numerous peoples, the slave trade and the uprooting of cultures in the colonial period are seldom recalled as injustices that must be expiated. The Western world tends to think individualistically and refuses to admit to its past. Despite all the differences from African ethics, one must agree with MacIntyre when he observes: "From the standpoint of individualism I am what I myself choose to be . . . I may legally be a citizen of a certain country; but I cannot be held responsible for what my country does or has done unless I choose implicitly or explicitly to assume such responsibility. Such individualism is expressed by those modern Americans who deny any responsibility for the effects of slavery upon black Americans, saying 'I never owned any slaves.'"[16] MacIntyre adds that one can encounter a similar attitude in English persons in relation to Ireland, or in Germans in relation to the history of Nazism.[17] It is one of the ironies of humanity that precisely those who commit themselves actively to the defense of human dignity and rights sometimes themselves acquired the privilege of being able to resist oppression thanks to the very history of oppression in which they were participants! O. Höffe remarks pointedly that the first declarations of human rights were drawn up precisely by those "White Anglo-Saxon

Protestants" whose freedom to engage in an intensive study of law and constitutional issues was due to the work of their slaves.[18] Historically speaking, however, the oppression and infringements of human rights in the case of slaves were almost completely forgotten, although the very fact of the presence of those slaves' descendants among us is a constant reminder of past injustice.

The individual *qua* individual cannot master the task of expiating all this and avoiding future infringements of human dignity. Rather, the entire community must participate in sociopolitical, economic, and indeed even ethical life. This takes place and is realized by means of the African palaver.

The Palaver between Communitarianism and Discourse Ethics

We have drawn attention several times to both common ground and differences between the palaver model and either communitarianism or discourse ethics. We shall now treat these in greater detail, though it is not my intention to give an exhaustive discussion of the various models.[19]

Our primary object of study here will be the African palaver process. Interestingly enough, this maintains a critical distance from both of the Western models, while also exhibiting a relatedness to them. First, we must enquire into the basic structure of the palaver in the African context, in order to establish the common ground and the distinctive characteristics in relation both to discourse ethics and to communitarianism.

The Palaver as Process for Discovering and Justifying Norms

Obviously, this cannot be a detailed analysis of the structures of the palaver, but only a summary presentation, which will indicate the problems connected with discovering and justifying norms in African ethics. It is important to note that there exist various genres of palaver, covering various areas of life; there is no necessary uniformity among their modes of procedure.[20] This will be made clear by some examples of these genres, which are important for the present study.

The Palaver in the Praxis of Healing

When a comparison is made between the palaver and a process such as discourse ethics, the dominant conception is usually of a kind of discussion with arguments *pro* and *contra.* However, the healing palaver proceeds by means not of arguments but of dialogue. There is most certainly a communicative community here, but this is not argumentative; it must be called a community of healing dialogue.

In order to understand the deepest meaning of the palaver, one must recall the function of the word in Black Africa. The word possesses such tremendous power that it can either create or destroy the community. This means that the word signifies life or death—it is medicine or poison. But it depends on the speaker whether the word brings life or death.

As we shall see in greater detail in part 2, chapter 3, Africans hold that when one hears the word, one also eats it and drinks it. Thus it is important how the word is digested, so that it may be invested anew in the community. But in order to test the word and see whether it possesses the power to give life, its innocence must be demonstrated publicly in the palaver.[21] Precisely this life-giving dimension is decisive for the healing palaver, which is ultimately based on the fact that illness in Black Africa always has a community dimension. Since the community is always both visible and invisible, this dimension is not limited to the living; and the invisible community in turn is not limited to the dead, but embraces the entire "supraterrestrial" world, including not only the spirits but God himself. Mostly, however, illness concerns the earthly community and its dead. In concrete terms, the cause of an illness lies primarily in interpersonal relationships. It is always a sign that something is wrong in the community, in its two dimensions of the living and the dead, and this means that the reestablishing of the broken interpersonal relationship cannot be a matter for doctor and patient alone: it demands the participation of the entire community. This is why a palaver is indispensable. Admittedly, this palaver begins with the dialogue between the doctor and the patient, provided that the latter is still capable of conversation. By means of questions and replies (which may likewise take the form of questions), the doctor challenges the sick person not only to supply information about his illness but also if need be to give an opinion about it. He may, for example, trace his suffering back to his own incorrect behavior vis-à-vis a deceased member of the family. In this case, the sick person confesses his guilt and accepts his own responsibility. He is also willing to be reconciled with the family member whom he has hurt. It may also be that the cause of the illness lies with other family members. In such a case, their confession is necessary, in order for a healing relationship to be established.

We must therefore emphasize that a palaver is always necessary. Even when it is a case of tensions vis-à-vis dead family members (as in the first example), a palaver among all those concerned is necessary, to clear up the conflict. From the perspective of Western rationality, for example, in discourse ethics, which has its starting point in a symmetry, a mutual exchange will appear impossible here. From the perspective of the African conceptual world, it must be underlined that the palaver can take other forms than the purely verbal: the communicative community implies also nonverbal forms of dialogue. Thus, a patient who relates his concerns at the grave of his deceased mother and asks her for forgiveness is not carrying on a monologue; the grave is a symbol which represents the deceased woman herself, and this nonverbal presence summons the patient to "unpack" the burden of all his problems and thus come out of his shell. In other words, the hidden presence of the deceased person makes the grave so living that its existence takes on the character of speech. Something similar may be said of the ancestral tree, which is a place of communication between the community on earth and the community beyond the grave.[22]

Where the illness of a patient does not directly concern the dead, but rather the members of his earthly community, these too must take part verbally in the palaver.[23] In this case, the doctor who is giving the treatment, the patient, and the others involved in the conversation form a communicative community, which endeavors to achieve the physical and psychological healing of them all by means of confessions of guilt. Thus, the dialogue of all these persons with the doctor is meant to lead to a new beginning in the community, in the way they deal with one another. One may rightly affirm that African communities in the process of healing attempt to bear the illness in common, as brothers and sisters, and to "suffer it through to the end." The patient is not left alone in his or her suffering.[24] The word and rites of reconciliation are the real therapy and medicine. This explains why in some ethnic groups the male or female healer undertook preventative measures once a year, for example, by inviting an entire village community together with its sick persons to expose themselves to a thorough examination of conscience. By means of questions about the various spheres of life in the village community, the doctor led those present to an awareness of their own responsibility for many tensions in their mutual relationships. This reestablished harmony in the village. They also became aware that the sick were themselves responsible for their condition, to the extent that they had incurred guilt vis-à-vis their neighbors.[25]

Let me once again emphasize that this healing process is an important palaver genre, even when the behavioral norm is established asymmetrically, through both verbal and nonverbal communication. This is the first difference between the palaver model and the procedure in discourse ethics. The latter, which makes its fundamental principle the argumentative power of reason, has clearly no place for a reconciliation that does not necessarily find expression by means of arguments and need not come about through an explicitly verbal and rational assent.

This healing procedure can be developed in Christian praxis to find its fulfillment in the sacrament of penance. From a Black African perspective, confession is a sacramental palaver in which the dialogue between priest and penitent certainly includes a healing dimension. Just as medicine should never be administered in silence, so it is "un-African" to administer the sacrament without an accompanying word; on his or her part, the penitent is summoned to share actively in the realization of what is received. Let us mention an example: the Eucharist is the high point of palaver and healing. The entire liturgy proceeds in the form of a dialogue, and an accompanying word is spoken also at the decisive point in time when the host is "administered" like medicine, a word to which the one receiving the sacrament says "Amen." Even this brief dialogue between the one who administers the sacrament and the one who receives it is an eminently important palaver element which brings about healing, since it effects the reconciliation of the one who receives the sacrament with himself, with God, with the fellowship of all human beings, and indeed with the entire creation. The last-named dimension becomes apparent in the fact that the matter of the Eucharist is the fruit of human labor, that is, fruit of the creation. It is not for nothing that African theologians point out that if this matter is to be a symbol that actually speaks to people in their culture, it must have an African origin. Here at any rate it becomes exceedingly clear that the palaver model takes the human person seriously in his total reality, without reducing him to his rationality or the rational-logical understanding.

The Family Palaver

Another palaver genre concerns family life. The word "family" is much more comprehensive here than in the West and embraces more than the nuclear family of parents and their children. Naturally, a palaver can also take place within a narrower family circle such as a nuclear family, for example, when the parents exercise their educational duty by calling their children to account for misbehavior: they do this by means of a clarifying conversation which permits an exact insight into the question at issue.

But a family palaver in the true sense of the term usually concerns a larger circle, since the questions involved concern *de facto* the existence of the nuclear family as a whole, or one member of the extended family. The one who is acknowledged as head of the family invites the representatives of the extended family to the palaver meeting, though this does not prevent other family members, who were not officially invited, from taking part. This palaver does not aim exclusively at the resolution of conflicts. It takes in all the questions that can contribute to invigorating the vital force of the extended family of the living and the dead. Its agenda is varied: it may, for example, include the division of an inheritance, or the elaboration of strategies for a common course of action that will provide a better future for the family, or the contraction of a marriage, the deposition or installation of a family chief, family conflicts, the conduct of war, and so on. In all these cases, the attempt is made to deal with the problem so comprehensively that it is not necessary to have recourse to a judicial authority outside the family; the extended family has a miniature judicial authority of its own, which seeks to counsel the palaver community aright. This group is composed of members of the same family circle.

Since, as I have indicated, the main aim of the palaver is to keep the family together and give it a new vital dynamism, the anamnetic dimension is very significant if the whole enterprise is to succeed. This presupposes the participation of the elders and of wise persons who have sufficient experience of life and who know the entire family history well. The elders are charged with recalling again and again the events of the family's past, so that these may suggest a similar solution for the question under discussion, or perhaps a nuanced and partly new solution. This makes it clear that the anamnetic dimension is not in the least a brake on the future of the community. The past is significant only when it proves to be the bearer of life for the present and the future.[26]

This mention of anamnetic thinking underlines once again one of the most important characteristics of the palaver, viz., the invisible community which must necessarily be included in the conversation. People in Black Africa do not see this merely as an "advocatory" speaking on behalf of the dead (as in discourse ethics); rather, they believe that the dead are truly present, thanks to the rites and statutes which they have laid down and to the words of their testimony. The recollection of the ancestors is not merely something that "is" but something that actually "speaks" to the descendants. This "speaking" allows the voices of the ancestors to be heard anew and presents their great concerns, which can be summarized as "life in fullness." The voices, concerns, and experiences of the ancestors that are expressed in a palaver are not, however, to be understood as immutable commandments or prohibitions. They only request and challenge the participants in the palaver to ask themselves seriously what path will augment life in the future. The fact that the participants are absolutely obliged *both* to consult the ancestral tradition *and* to confront the new questions that arise in a new context makes it once again clear that the main point of a palaver is not fidelity to the tradition but saving the family community. Thus, a palaver about a marital conflict will not attempt to save the "institution of marriage" in keeping with the literal will of the ancestors, but rather to act under the changed circumstances *in the spirit* of the ancestors; nor does one save the married couple alone, since what is at stake is the well-being of all the members of the marriage covenant, which embraces both the extended families, the husband's and the wife's.

The palaver, which sometimes lasts for several days, usually ends with a celebration, or at least with an informal get-together; the form of this concluding celebration will depend on the kind of question discussed. Where a conflict or quarrel is brought to an end, the celebration will be linked to a rite of reconciliation, as the example of the Bahema in the Democratic Republic of Congo clearly shows. If the palaver community has succeeded in convincing two persons who are in love but are close relatives that the incestuous marriage which they desire is prohibited, a rite of expiation is prescribed for the crime (viz., the cohabitation of two relatives). In this rite, the entire village of the extended family of the man (who usually bears the larger share of guilt) is to be sprinkled with the blood of a he-goat, to purify it. Along with other obligations imposed by the palaver community on the guilty persons, this blood serves to reconcile the entire family of the living and the dead. If the palaver was held to deal with a situation free of conflict, the conclusion may be celebrated with a shared drink or a meal in common, where the ancestors are not forgotten.[27] In all these cases, even where no conflicts or tensions are involved, the palaver cultivates a healthy, harmonious relationship within the community. Where there are tensions, peace is re-established and promoted; where there are no conflicts, the palaver is very effective in bringing people together so that they learn the art of listening to one another, tolerance, and a new style of relationship. Thus the palaver has always a medicinal, therapeutic character, besides its function as an ethical authority.

The family palaver is supremely important for the establishment, consolidation and further development of family ethics. The viability of the tradition is examined, so that all the ethical norms can be either confirmed or changed. The ethical norms confirmed or newly established and justified in the palaver obligate everyone, and this means that every individual member and the whole family (in the widest sense of the term) are responsible for keeping these norms. If however the family community is not able to achieve consensus in one particular question, it is also possible to appeal to a higher authority and continue the palaver on an extra-familial level.

The "Suprafamilial" and Administrative Palaver

The best-known palaver procedure concerns the life of a larger group than individual families or clan communities. This palaver has an official, political character and is often (though not invariably)[28] linked to a trial before a court. Where (as has been indicated) this involves a case which the family palaver has failed to resolve satisfactorily, it is a kind of court of second instance. It may, however, involve a completely new case, which the public, suprafamilial palaver treats directly, as the first instance.

Apart from those immediately concerned, the participants in this palaver meeting are the members of the village or regional council of elders, who are delegated by the various communities to be counselors of the king or chief. As with the palaver genres presented above, however, all who can make a contribution to the resolution of the problem are admitted to this meeting too and have the right to join in the consultation. There is no methodological difference between this procedure and the palaver genres that we have already analyzed; at most, a few additional points could be mentioned, though even these are present in all genres.

One difference is the person of the president. In the healing and family palavers, it is the healer or the family elders who preside; in the public palaver, the king or chief or a member of the council of elders presides. Here too it is forbidden for the president to behave arrogantly or in an authoritarian manner. He must be able to discover the element of wisdom in every person, man and woman, who speaks, without being content with a merely logical-rational argumentation. This is why poetic speeches are important contributions to the solution at which the palaver aims. However, beautiful language is not enough—more attention is paid to the message that this language communicates. In this context, we must draw attention to the great importance of proverbs, fairy tales, parables, and the use of symbolic language. The symbolic language can of course be found in all three forms, viz., proverbs, fairy tales, and parables.[29] The message transmitted in these three forms has an ethical character. Particular attention must be paid to the proverbs, since these are used most frequently and intensively, not only in the palaver but also in daily life.[30] Their common usage does not prevent them from playing a very important role in the palaver, where they give a precise, concentrated, and pregnant expression to existential questions and solutions. In the palaver procedure, proverbs seem to be the most appropriate instruments for communication among the participants. The knowledge involved here is not to be understood in a Cartesian sense as the presentation of compelling proofs, but rather as "a kind of *commercium* between one existence and another."[31] O. Ndjimbi is right to observe here that proverbs in Africa are concerned with the protection of life; they lose all argumentative force when they fail to serve the foundation of existence and the development of life.[32] This is why their *sapiential* character must be emphasized; they are not to be regarded in an abstract or juridical manner. One must agree with Scholler's remark that judicial proverbs in Africa "indicate standards, i.e. principles or rules of experience in the manner of sapiential adages, rather than laying down concrete legal rules."[33] But this makes the adages very important, since they are able to formulate even a harsh truth in such a way that it is accepted. This means that they serve to support a purely rational argumentation.[34]

We should also note that a proverb is not automatically accepted by the palaver community. Despite its sapiential character, it can meet with objections, if it fails in a given context to take in the whole truth. We have also pointed out above how one proverb can be supplemented or refuted or contradicted by another. This, however, presumes that the members of the palaver community are well acquainted with the world of proverbs, for otherwise the judgment might go in the wrong direction and offer a misleading solution. The participation of experienced persons—mostly members of the council of elders—is therefore very necessary, since it is these who are most capable of immediately confirming or supplementing the proverbial wisdom, or correcting it by means of further proverbs. Supplements and corrections also take place by means of the recollection of the events of the past; and in a nonliterate society, it is the oldest, experienced persons who know the history best.

As I have said, not only proverbs but also fairly tales and parables are often employed in the palaver process, especially since these frequently function as vehicles for proverbs. A humoristic tone has an important function in the palaver: it serves to reduce the tension now and again between proponents and opponents and helps to avoid conflicts that could hinder a neutral and correct judgment. In some places it is customary to interrupt the palaver from time to time with songs, dances, pantomimes, allegories, narratives, and so on.[35] This calms down participants who have become too excited, creating a peaceful atmosphere in which the discussion can be brought to a close. This is yet another proof that the African palaver takes the human person seriously in his totality, including the religious dimension. This is why every palaver process—the family palaver and the suprafamilial—concludes with a ceremony of reconciliation in which a privileged place is accorded to the deceased members of the community. Here too we can see the therapeutic element for the entire community, even though this is not therapy in the strict sense, but rather the avoiding or ending of the tensions that can make community members sick.

Let us make one more point about the argumentation. I have mentioned nonverbal forms of dialogue above in connection with "the palaver in the praxis of healing." Such forms belong basically to all the palaver models and are therefore found in this third genre too. Africans consider even silence or a look to be an important element of the palaver argumentation. "That which is not uttered" in the palaver (not "that which cannot be uttered"!) deserves particular mention. Many realities are packed in words so well that they end up veiled or only hinted at; at first sight, such statements can even come close to lies. The art of the palaver consists in setting out on a journey of exploration. For example, a woman who feels that her husband is neglecting her might complain as follows: "He refuses to buy me clothes and furnish my house . . . I have nothing at all at home." Only when her husband counters with an argument demonstrating that the house of his wife is not at all empty will she go one step further in her statements and specify as follows: "I'm not talking about things in the house—but I don't have any nice clothes." Once again, a counterquestion is posed, to drive the woman into a corner, for example: "But you are wearing beautiful clothes, aren't you?" These questions bring the whole truth to light, when she replies: "I bought these beautiful clothes myself." Only now do we know what the point at issue is, only now do we have the precise accusation against her husband. This argumentation has nothing in common with the discourse of Western rationalism; it takes the shape of a "chain logic" which is assembled only gradually and requires many questions and counterquestions.[36]

The discourse that comes into being in this way can be compared with a cable consisting of many threads. Each thread, taken by itself, is weak and cannot bear weight; but taken all together, they form a very strong cable.[37] There is more to a discussion than logical arguments alone; the hermeneutics of discourse play a role that must not be underestimated. This is fundamental in the African palaver,[38] where the arguments are conducted not for the sake of logic but for the sake of communication, in view of the life lived in interaction within the community.

In conclusion, let us emphasize the especial importance in the palaver of this life in interaction. The task of promoting life together is genuinely incumbent on all, including first of all the kings or chiefs as links between the ancestors and those now living. Chiefs can be called to account by the people if they incur guilt in any way. In other words, the palaver is conducted without respect of persons, with impartiality as the guiding idea. This confirms that African political life kept dictatorship far from the people: a chief who had incurred guilt was deposed by the people in the palaver.[39] A fundamental reevaluation of this valuable tradition is an urgent necessity in contemporary political discussion in Africa. We shall return to the question of how far this model is valuable also for the process in which norms are established and justified.

The Essence of the Palaver

We have already seen a number of differences and points of contact between the palaver and both discourse ethics and communitarianism. This will be examined more closely in the following section. Once again, however, it is not my intention to offer a systematic presentation of these two theories; I refer to already existing studies.[40]

Differences from and Points of Contact with Discourse Ethics

Like discourse ethics, the palaver presupposes a number of fundamental principles which serve as a basis for the public discussion process. We must first mention Jürgen Habermas, who has adopted the norms proposed by Robert Alexy, since he sees in these a possibility or condition for the success of a "discourse."[41] The basic rules of the palaver are not formulated as systematically as in Habermas, nor are they so emphatically logical, but one can discern in the palaver process too—at least implicitly, as a kind of silent presence—some aspects of the rules of discourse ethics. Rules for the palaver are not in fact formulated, just practiced. Habermas gives some examples of rules for discourse: "Each person can call any affirmation into question"; "Each one may contribute any affirmation to the discussion"; "Each one is allowed to express his attitudes, wishes and needs."[42] There can be no doubt that the palaver proceeds according to these rules, though without specifying them explicitly,[43] and there is equal clarity about the following rule: "Every subject who is capable of speech and action may take part in the discussions."[44] Indeed, the Ashanti in

Ghana say explicitly that everyone has the right to participate directly or indirectly in drawing up the laws.[45] This is why one speaks of "laws" in connection with the palaver: it is taken for granted that this plays an indispensable role in the elaboration of all the laws that regulate the community.

The Ashanti rule makes it clear also, however, that the palaver, unlike the discourse process, broadens somewhat the circle of participants, since it speaks not of *every subject who is capable of speech and action,* but simply of *everyone.* Besides this, the palaver allows an indirect participation, which would be no participation at all from the standpoint of discourse ethics; the latter would see a so-called advocate's argumentation here. The expression "everyone" in the palaver regulation refers not only to the invisible community of the ancestors, but genuinely to *everyone,* such as the handicapped, who perhaps cannot express themselves in speech but nevertheless are capable of communicating by means of symbolic actions. For an argumentation on the basis of discourse ethics, such actions are devoid of significance, but they can be decisive for the palaver, for example, in therapy.

The sections on the various palaver genres have drawn attention to another difference between the palaver and discourse ethics, viz., the religious dimension: one cannot conceive of the palaver process without God and the world of the ancestors. Thus, the first rule of the palaver among the Ashanti states that the gods and the ancestors watch over the world and together guide all the powers of the universe.[46] The formulation aims to point out that the human person cannot construct the meaning of his life on his own; this meaning goes beyond him and can come only from a transcendental world. This is the basis of the entire endeavor to establish correct moral precepts.

The text of the plebiscite on reform of the Swiss federal constitution in 1999 shows that even a modern Western state does not dismiss this attitude to morality as something obsolete and naive. The preamble began as follows: "In the name of God the Almighty! The Swiss people and the cantons . . . give themselves the following constitution."[47] The *invocatio Dei* at the beginning of a constitution, even in a secular state, is meaningful, since it shows that no matter how skillful its elaboration may be, any constitution ultimately comes up against boundaries; our human existence is necessarily limited. The *invocatio Dei,* which cannot be reduced to a matter of law, recalls that not everything has been said about human existence by the mere fact of establishing what is right; rather, human existence must always yearn for something still greater, something infinite, if it is to find perfect fulfillment. This is precisely how we are to see the foundational principle of the African palaver, where God and the world of the ancestors are considered the highest norm, providing every discourse with orientation—not uncritically, yet indispensably. In general terms, the heart of the African palaver procedure is not the instrumental reason, which can so easily become an instrument of domination. Rather, the human person, positioned within the tension between life and death, must *excavate* the truth existentially and sapientially through the total active commitment of his own person. The word "excavate" is meant to emphasize that the palaver does not limit itself methodologically to the discursive element (*ratiocinatio*), but makes use of all the realities of human existence, since it envisages the human person *holistically.*

We must also emphasize that this palaver rule among the Ashanti not only speaks of God (or gods) and the ancestors, but also includes the entire cosmos in the palaver process: it states that those who have responsibility in the government or the community must see to it that all the regulations and modes of conduct among the Ashanti remain in harmony with the laws of nature and with the ancestors.[48] This principle of Ashanti society certainly applies to most ethnic groups in Black Africa. The human person is a part of the cosmos and cannot become and remain his own self unless he attempts to structure his life in this context. This is because there exists an interaction between the cosmos and the human person, to which Placide Tempels has drawn attention in his penetrating study. He compares the world of forces among the Bantu with a spider's web: if one touches a single strand, the entire web shivers in sympathy with it.[49] E. Mveng underlines the point that the human person appears within the ordering of the world as a synthesis of the entire universe, as it were a "microcosm" within the "macrocosm."[50] Indeed, the human person combines in himself the heavenly world, the world of spirits, the sun, moon, and stars—in short, he is spirit, animal, plant, stone, fire, water and wind. Finally, he is heaven and earth, that is, the entire universe.[51] This helps us to grasp why the healing praxis cannot do without cosmic elements. Not only plants but also such things as minerals, pieces of wood, bones, and hairs of animals are employed in carrying out the healing palaver.[52] The human person will attain harmony and peace in daily life only when he constantly remembers that he belongs together with nature and with the whole cosmos, and when all his contacts with the cosmic elements are characterized by the spirit of partnership.

All this has made the differences between discourse ethics and the palaver unmistakably clear, but there is still one distinctive element of the palaver that must be emphasized, viz., the dimension of guilt or sin. This is an obvious fact, since the palaver often concerns the question of reconciliation. Among the Ashanti, the problem of sin is explicitly defined as the basis of the palaver, when it is stated that grave offenses against the will of the ancestors or the gods are sins. Punishment and expiation are prescribed for such offenses, and these are imposed without exception.[53] This important ethical aspect has in practice no significance within discourse ethics; even where it does touch on this problem, the intention is to declare that discourse ethics is incompetent to deal with it. The following observation by Jürgen Habermas is typical: "Moral desperation demands an answer to the fundamental ethical question of the meaning of life as a whole, the meaning of my identity or ours. But it is not philosophers, but rather those immediately concerned, who are responsible for the ethical-existential self-communication of the individual and for the ethical-political clarification of a collective self-understanding."[54] In his view, the pluralism of existential projects and forms makes it impossible for philosophers "to take it upon themselves to provide *universally binding* instructions about the meaning of life."[55] They must withdraw to the reflective dimension of "an analysis of the procedure" involved: in other words, the philosopher must be content with *formalistic* principles, which can then be applied to concrete existential forms.[56] One does not need philosophy in order to experience or learn what moral and immoral conduct is, since this conduct is antecedent to "all philosophy." Habermas sums up: "Thus, moral theology is able to clarify the moral point of view and to justify the universality of this perspective, but it makes no contribution to answering the question: 'Why be moral at all?', irrespective of whether this question is understood in a trivial, an existential or a pedagogical sense."[57]

Sin—as this finds expression through the palaver—concerns the ethical (not the moral) sphere and the question of existential projects and forms; this is why it does not belong within the competence of discourse ethics. The palaver, as we shall see clearly in connection with communitarianism, is concerned not only with universal, formalistic principles but also with the concrete structuring and success of human existence. This means (to employ the vocabulary of Habermas's discourse ethics) that the palaver embraces both morals and ethics—otherwise, one will be speaking of the human person *atomistically*. In order to remove all possible misunderstanding, we must note here that when the palaver procedure speaks of guilt or sin, this is not to be understood in the sense of Ernst Tugendhat, whom Habermas has criticized as follows:[58] "Tugendhat understands moral shame and guilt as reactions to the loss of one's own value—ultimately, my self-respect is put at risk when I behave in an immoral manner. One who offends against moral norms not only exposes himself to others' contempt, but also despises his own self, since he has internalized this sanction."[59] This means that morality is based on mutual respect, which can of course be universalized. Habermas also criticizes the "instrumental" dimension of the principle of self-respect, which Tugendhat demands: "respect for the other becomes an instrument, since the true goal is respect for one's own self."[60] In other words, the outcome of Tugendhat's thesis is that "each one can respect *himself* only when he is respected by persons whom he himself does not despise."[61] Tugendhat goes on to justify his thesis largely on the basis of the community: one feels moral shame and guilt thanks to one's membership in a community. This means that the self-understanding of one's own person is so tightly woven together with one's societal identity that one can esteem oneself only when a "decisively important authority in the community" confirms that one enjoys the status of community member. Since one regards oneself as a member of this community, the sanction here is "fear of being excommunicated from a community" with which one identifies.[62] Habermas also emphasizes that societal membership now takes on the same position Tugendhat had earlier attributed to self-respect: the idea of the community is antecedent to self-respect, since it is only the community that makes it possible for each member to have a sense of his own worth, and it is only in this way that mutuality between the individual members is possible.

Habermas asks at this point whether "the meaning of every 'moral obligation' can still be found in the 'internal sanction,'" when this same obligation demands a reciprocal or mutual acknowledgment. Thus, the question is whether the feelings of shame and guilt would not in fact be secondary, derived ultimately from the "reciprocity of the structures of acknowledgment within the community."[63] Habermas accuses Tugendhat of "confusing genesis and validity." For it is impermissible to infer from "the fact that an authority in the conscience is formed in the process of socialization by means of the internalization of external sanctions" that moral obligation is due to an internal sanction of "loss of one's own worth, rather than to the non-coercive coercion of the good reasons which give moral insights a convincing force."[64] Habermas's penetrating analysis of Tugendhat's theory concludes that this ultimately understands "the validity of moral norms" in a cognitive sense, which, however, cannot be deduced from internal sanctions. It is indeed true that moral rules in traditional societies are linked to "religious images of the world and to collective forms of living"; individuals must identify with the substance of these existential forms as concrete, "established" morality, and this teaches them to live up to their status as members of a "settled community." But all this changes in modern societies, where the moral norms are detached from specific contents (which can exist only in the plural). According to Habermas, all we find in modern societies are moral norms based "on a societal identity which has become abstract." This means that membership is no longer in *particular* communities, but in *one* community. The validity and sphere of application of the morality generated in this situation can only be "universalistic and egalitarian"; in relation to the substance of its norms, it is purely *formal.* Thus, the understanding of morality is no longer noncognitive.

Habermas's analysis goes on to show that Tugendhat returns to Kantian inter-subjectivism when he speaks of the "enlightened perspective" which he considers determinative of a valid assent, and when he speaks of the tenable "kernel of all moralities" which must be reduced to "the natural or rational basic stock of norms" without which there would be no community; this means that his empirical premises are invalidated.[65]

Habermas concludes this examination, which has been presented at length here because of its importance for African ethics, by saying that the justification of moral norms is guaranteed only in the theses defended by discourse ethics, with cognitivism as its main characteristic. Habermas has clearly demonstrated that not even Tugendhat can detach himself so easily from this explicitly Western tradition. But it is precisely here (as I have already pointed out) that we find one of the main differences from palaver ethics. Let us return to the problem of guilt and sanctions. For Tugendhat, the issue at stake is the self-respect that leads one to respect others, or to fear a sanction that would amount to excommunication by the community. Such an ethic may appeal to the community, but it remains individualistic, and it is difficult for such a morality to see guilt and sanctions as a constitutive element in a community ethic, since these are not the elements that lead to the establishing and justifying of norms. On this point, Tugendhat and Habermas agree: guilt and sanctions are not constitutive of morality: for Tugendhat, this is because one's own "ego" is put at risk, and for Habermas, because they are excluded from the sphere of formalistic principles. In the palaver procedure, however, guilt and sanctions are not something secondary, but belong essentially to the process whereby norms are constituted. Since African ethics does not split the human person dualistically into "cognitive" and "noncognitive," or "reason" and "feelings," the active subject can develop and live a healthy morality only in the endeavor to be capable of action as one who is totally a person and totally related to the community. Guilt and (if need be) sanctions are one dimension of this: not only as presuppositions of the endeavor, but as essential elements that lead to reconciliation. Only one who is completely healthy is able to understand, to justify and to live morality. It is therefore not enough to say: "The general structure of those relationships of acknowledgment which make possible at one and the same time one's self-understanding as a person and as a member of a community is presupposed in communicative action, and remains present in the communicative presuppositions of moral argumentation."[66] For more is involved in African ethics than a presupposition or an auxiliary—*ancilla rationis et intellectus.* Rather, all the stages in the establishing of morality and the discerning of norms are equally important and imply one another.

Habermas criticizes the principle of self-respect, which justifies respect for others in view of the goal of self-respect. African ethics is not concerned about respect for one's own self: the community occupies center stage in such a way that the individual members must always bear in mind and aim at a growth in quality of life for all members. This is why the guilt of individuals affects all, and sanctions (which can also be assumed by the community) intend to supply a new vital force to the entire community. It is not strange, therefore, that the philosopher Tshiamalenga-Ntumba unceasingly endeavors to base African ethics on the idea of the community, with his starting point in the Baluba of Kasai in Congo-Kinshasa, where each one is called *Muntu-wa-Bende-wa-Mulopo,* that is, "human-being-from-Bende-from-God." This means that each human being comes from Bende, while Bende comes from God. But what does "Bende" mean? Tshiamalenga explains that it has two meanings, viz., "those who are his [i.e., God's], those he created in his own likeness" and "the absolutely Other." This absolute Other belongs to God alone, and his descendants are inviolable. Ultimately, Bende is presented as the origin of all human beings, indeed of everything; this undeniably emphasizes the unity of the human person with the entire cosmos, something to which I have frequently drawn attention above.[67] The most important point here is that the expression "Bende" lays emphasis on the unity of humanity as a whole—with no exceptions; and this means that the whole of humanity is an extended family in Black Africa. All are siblings.[68] In this extended family of brothers and sisters, the "we" comes first. This is why one can speak in Black Africa of "jamaa-language" or "extended family language," where everything is related to the "we," not to the "I." Tshiamalenga presents a typical example: among the Luba, one who has a family member in a coma can say, "I am in a coma!" What this person means is that one "of us and with us," or a part of our family, that is, of our own self, is in a coma. Behind this lies the following conception: "Each time a grave is dug, something of all of us, something of the extended family of humanity, is buried. . . . No one lives for himself alone, no one dies alone. No one feels alone and abandoned, for everyone is our brother or sister."[69] If this relatedness to the "we" is not to crumble and decompose into a plurality of "I"s, a primal harmony in the community and a primal trust in each other are necessary.

Tshiamalenga sees relatedness to the "we" as the basis of all trust, especially since he links the "primacy of the 'we'" and the transcendental pragmatics of discourse ethics. He speaks of a "community of argumentation related to the 'we.'"[70] Primal trust is "the primary and original fundamental attitude of the human person,"[71] since the absence of trust in interpersonal relationships would amount to the destruction of the human family. He goes on to ask how this fundamental trust could be justified in philosophical terms; in his view, only transcendental pragmatics can "give a self-reflective, irrefutable answer." He formulates this answer as follows: "The human person differs from the animals in that he is capable of language, argument, and dialogue. However, a genuine dialogue can take place only when the dialogue partner *can trust* that there is basic willingness on both sides *to aim at* a true *consensus which can genuinely be affirmed by the unlimited real-ideal community of argumentation.*"[72] Tshiamalenga's thesis is that this real-ideal community of argumentation is necessarily "related to the 'we.'" The consequence of this is "that all interpersonal trust must a priori and necessarily presuppose the primacy of the 'we' in the real-ideal extended family of humanity, within which the argumentation takes place."[73] He sees the true humanity of the human person in trust, when it is understood in this way: "The human person is a human person only when he can also be trusting and 'bestow' trust in a fundamental manner."[74]

Tshiamalenga's thesis intends to go beyond what he calls the "traditional African view in terms of transcendental anthropology and theology of the extended family of humanity, related to the 'we.'" The traditional trust is indeed based in a transcendentally postulated universal relatedness of all human beings, conceived in anthropological and theological terms. But Tshiamalenga sees the "transcendentally and pragmatically postulated trust, which is anticipated in every genuine dialogue," as one of the presuppositions necessary for every dialogue partner, if he is truly to be a dialogue partner.[75]

I find the philosophical concept sketched here very attractive, but one must ask whether the author has not adapted his thesis rather too much to the Western theory of discourse ethics. It seems to be important for him to establish an ultimate basis (in Karl-Otto Apel's sense) for African ethics.[76] African ethics need not at all costs be derived from transcendental pragmatics. On the contrary, its nature is existential, although it does not in the least lack the transcendental dimension, as the entire palaver procedure shows. I find the most questionable aspect in Tshiamalenga that this trust is based on the primacy of the "we," since life seems more fundamental than trust in African ethics. This presupposes not a community based on trust, but one based on life—and life must be antecedent to trust. I hold it to be unquestionable that African ethics is a community ethics; but it acquires validity only where it provides the individual and the community with the meaning of life, that is, where it allows life to flourish.[77] Where no life exists, one can speak neither of community nor of trust. I am not really convinced that the basis of ethics in Africa is this trust in the community or the "extended family of humanity, related to the 'we.'" Nor is this ethics always articulated exclusively within a community of argumentation in the sense intended by discourse ethics. As has been indicated above, norms also come into being in an "asymmetrical" manner.

Tshiamalenga's thesis, which adheres very closely to Apel and Habermas, moves within a discourse where no attention is paid to guilt and forgiveness. Forgiveness is not necessarily based on mutual communication, as where the perpetrator "asks for forgiveness" and the victim "grants forgiveness"; it can also come about "asymmetrically," when a victim pardons a perpetrator who has not asked for forgiveness. This dimension is extremely important in African ethics. For example, the Bahema of Congo-Kinshasa call someone "noble" when he does not "bear grudges," or when he refuses to seek revenge and instead grants pardon even when his enemy does not ask this of him. This is also the general function of the initiation rite in Africa. It prepares young people for life in all its many facets, teaching the "initiands" to survive the heavy, dark periods in their lives. One example is learning to yield in a conflict, even when one is in the right, in order not to endanger peace. Ultimately, this means forgiving, even where one's enemy cannot understand such a gesture and scorns it. Only one who is faithful in the face of all unfaithfulness is a truly "noble person" who takes thought for the growth of the vital force of the entire community.

The significance for life in common of pardon that had not been asked for is well illustrated by a fairy tale among the Bahema. The narrative concerns Lokpariba, who guarded his maize field against elephants and was killed by them. His son Lokpari wanted to avenge his father, but he had no spear to go hunting with. He borrowed the spear of his uncle (his father's brother) and went to guard the maize field. He succeeded in killing a giant elephant, but the spear remained stuck in the beast. When the victorious guardian of the maize field returned home and told his uncle proudly how he had now avenged his father (and his uncle's brother), the uncle asked to have his spear back; he did not want to exchange it for other (even better) spears, and rejected every offer his nephew made. Lokpari was so desperate that he took his life in his hands and ventured into the elephant village in disguise, where he presented himself as a member of the elephants' family. The beasts gave him many pearls, and he was also given the spear which had remained stuck in the dead elephant. He gave this back to his uncle. The little daughter of this same uncle now swallowed one of the many pearls that Lokpari, at great risk to his life, had received from the elephants, and he demanded that his uncle give him this one pearl—no other, no matter how costly it might be. This inhuman demand forced the uncle to slit open the stomach of his little daughter, thus sacrificing the child. This completely destroyed the fellowship between uncle and nephew: they remained enemies forever.

The point of this fairy tale, which is often told to children and young people (and to adults of all ages), is that Lokpari ought to have forgiven his uncle unconditionally. Despite the uncle's unyielding cruelty, he ought to have been reconciled to him. The hardness of both their hearts, and the nephew's yearning for revenge, not only led to the death of the little daughter, but totally destroyed the entire existential community.

This fairy tale shows that ethics in Africa is not necessarily based on mutual trust! Nor do we find here what discourse ethics calls an "ultimate impermeable barrier" of the argumentative discourse, so that failure to understand the arguments would amount to "mental illness."[78]

We may sum up by emphasizing once again that palaver ethics allows the human person to be seen holistically, eschewing a dualistic outlook that would admit people to the discussion only on the ground of their ability to engage in arguments. To the extent that discourse ethics makes reason the criterion for mutual communication, it invites contradiction when it speaks of an unlimited communicative community. On the other hand, since the palaver model is not bound in every respect to reciprocity and verbal communication, it displays traits that can also be found in communitarianism.

Differences from and Points of Contact with Communitarianism

I have already pointed out a number of differences and points in common between African ethics and communitarianism. A brief summary is therefore sufficient here; I shall discuss some points more specifically and in greater detail. The first common ground between African ethics and communitarianism seems to be the strong emphasis on community, although we must not assume that their attitude to community is the same.

O. Höffe's reference to the famous work by Ferdinand Tönnies, *Gemeinschaft und Gesellschaft,* can give the discussion a fruitful orientation.[79] Höffe criticizes the North American communitarians for hardly ever mentioning Tönnies, although they continuously use the word "community" (without providing a clear definition). Tönnies makes a clear distinction between *Gemeinschaft* ("community") and *Gesellschaft* ("society"). Community means that the members are essentially linked to one another, although each retains his or her own identity; this unity is based on a uniform "essential will," which aims at the long term.[80] In a society, on the other hand, the members are indeed linked as contractual partners, but remain "fundamentally" separate. Tönnies speaks here of an "optional will," which, however, can be unified only at one specific point and cannot last.[81] Tönnies gives the following description of community and society: "Wherever life in common is intimate and exclusive, with a sense of being at home . . . this is understood as life in community. Society is the public sphere, the world. One lives in community with one's own family from birth on, linked to it for good and ill. One enters society as a foreign realm. There is a community of language, of customs, of faith; but there is a society of commerce, of travel, of the sciences."[82] When this description is read in the light of the African context, we find that Tonnies' understanding of community comes close to the African understanding, although people in Africa could not assent to some of the characteristics he ascribes to society. The important point, however, is that Tönnies sees community as something organic; this indicates a fundamental unity which excludes every "atomizing autonomy" on the part of the individual, since community is characterized by harmony, religion, and customs, whereas society is manifested by means of convention, politics, and public opinion.[83] Naturally, African ethics, which deals with life in a holistic manner, will not go along with this radical separation. O. Höffe notes that even in the liberalistic theory society in this pure form no longer appears; nor is the modern world so easily dissected, since all its forms overlap.[84] Nevertheless, even allowing for what Höffe calls the "oscillating polysemy" of the concept "community/communities,"[85] we can say that African ethics is concerned more about community—though in a sense that goes beyond Tönnies—than about society in the Western sense. Höffe speaks here of civic communities, states, churches, families, neighborhoods, friendships, clubs, and associations: "It is indeed worth consideration whether one might not speak of today's humanity, in relationship to their ancestors and descendants, as a community; and not least, whether one might call all human beings who have ever lived a community, in relation to the non-human world, to nature."[86] Höffe has certainly pointed here to a weakness of communitarianism, which appears not to nuance the concept of community within the Western context in which its theory is native. From the perspective of Western sociology, it gives the impression of blending community and society together—and this is the substance of Höffe's accusation.

This objection cannot be made to African ethics. For Black Africans, the community consists of the clan fellowship in its dual dimension of the living and the dead, but it also embraces "those not yet born" and is indeed cosmic. This makes it unthinkable that the "nonhuman world" could lie outside the African community; I have indicated this above. Let us emphasize one other important aspect of the community. Höffe considers the various genres of community to be more or less incompatible with the communitarian understanding; and people in Africa find no difficulties in identifying themselves fully with all these categories. If one bears in mind the fundamental principle of *Muntu-wa-Bende-wa-Mulopo* ("human-being-from-Bende-from-God"), then it is clear that Africans understand the community as universal, in such a way that each human being *qua* human being must be seen as a member of the "we"-community, irrespective of the group or association to which he belongs. Höffe holds that the units and groups he lists cannot be classified "unproblematically in a structure, in the voluntary unity of an organically constructed social body."[87] He mentions the conflicts, rivalry, intolerance, and readiness to resort to violence that are found there; there is a lack of harmony, which ought to be the first characteristic of a community.[88] Even where we find a further characteristic, viz., a unified religion (or Christian denomination), true homogeneity has long ceased to exist. The same is true of customs, which likewise belong to the characteristics of a community.

All this calls Tonnies's definition into question; but it also makes it clear that this definition was drawn up from a Western perspective. Thus, the characteristics it lists agree only in part with the African understanding of community. Besides this, there is no general agreement that these required characteristics may never be infringed upon, or that a community loses its very essence as soon as it infringes upon one of them. The function of the African palaver is precisely to ensure harmony when conflicts, intolerance, violence, and so on, have become dominant.[89] The palaver excludes no group or association, especially in view of the fact that everything—not only human beings, but the whole of nature—is to be understood "from-Bende-from-God." Thus, Höffe's following remarks are not an objection to the African understanding of community: "Neither within the individual 'communities' nor between one community and another, nor between human beings and non-human nature, do we find unqualified love and friendship."[90] If one takes one's starting point in the theory of "Bende-from-God," then community is not a reality that exists statically once and for all, but rather something that continually comes into existence. Again and again, indeed unceasingly, new "we's" join, since the whole of humanity and the whole of the cosmos belong to one community, or better, all are moving toward a more perfect community. In this process, the palaver is an important instrument that is meant to lead to reconciliation and peace.

This shows once again that the *communitarianism* that Höffe rightly criticizes has a somewhat different understanding of community. To put it bluntly, communitarianism seems to view the individual as "caught" in a static community that cannot acquire new members who think in a different way.[91] Ultimately, both the acting subject and the community that determines this subject display a pronounced individualism.

A further point concerns the problem of the good life (*eu zēn*), which goes back to Aristotle. Here communitarianism and African ethics draw closer, yet remain distinct. This also involves the question of virtues. It is well known that Charles Taylor accuses procedural ethics of rejecting the ethics of the good life, although procedural ethics itself cannot exist without the idea of this *eu zēn.* Taylor writes: "A growth in the practical reason takes place in the framework of recourse to the good, and means that earlier distortions and fragmentary pieces of knowledge are superseded."[92] This shows that the idea of the good is "a fundamental presupposition." Only when one becomes better acquainted with the concept of the good, as presupposed by discourse ethics, will one understand discourse ethics better; and only then will this ethics display its convincing force.[93] Ultimately, discourse ethics is criticized for preferring a theory about what is correct and the "canon of rules" to an ethics that is concrete and filled out with substance; the latter must necessarily be an ethics of virtue.[94] Here we find common ground with African ethics, which sees life as the highest good at which one must aim. At the same time, however, as has been shown, this good must be ever better articulated and specified in the palaver process. It cannot be lived and attained in a "particularistic" manner; since it is life in continuous growth, it is a universal good. The aim here is both to establish the ethical principle and to give it concrete application.

As I have indicated above, Jürgen Habermas's discourse ethics is aware of this problem of the good life, but holds itself incompetent to say anything about it.[95] Nevertheless, Habermas has distanced himself to some extent from his earlier publications[96] by acknowledging the necessity of a theory of application alongside the principle of universalization: "Discourses about justification . . . cannot completely exhaust the idea of impartiality, but only in relation to the dignity of universal-reciprocal acknowledgment. The norms which are *prima facie* valid remain 'unsatisfied,' since they require further interpretation, thanks to the special constellations of unforeseen situations in which they must be applied."[97] It remains an open question in the discourses about justification, to what extent and indeed "whether the norms which are valid in relation to those situations which are adduced as exemplary and foreseen as typical, are also *appropriate* to similar situations which will occur in the *futurum exactum,* in view of the relevant characteristics of *those* situations."[98] In order to answer this question, Habermas proposes what he calls a "discourse of application," guided by the principle of "appropriateness."[99] The intention is to demonstrate which of those norms already presupposed as valid is appropriate to "a given case," and this requires a study of all the relevant "characteristics of the situation, which must be noted in as great detail as is possible."[100] The reader understands clearly that the principle of appropriateness plays the same role in the discourses of application as the fundamental principle of universalization in regard to the discourses of justification. The idea of impartiality is complete only when both principles are combined.[101] Nevertheless, although discourses of application concern concrete situations, they remain, "like the discourses of justification, a purely cognitive matter, so that they offer no compensation for the detachment of moral judgments from the motivations of behavior."[102] Even when the discourses of application take place, it is impossible to compel anyone actually to put into practice "that which is held to be correct."[103] This makes it clear that Habermas locates both the discourses of application and the principle of appropriateness in the sphere of that which is "moral."[104] In other words, even the discourses of application, with the principle of appropriateness, remain still on the level of theory, although—unlike the theory of justification—they are related to concrete matters and situations.

Karl-Otto Apel has likewise endeavored to make good the "deficit" in the discourses of justification. He has observed that the application of the formal principle of discourse ethics needs to be complemented by the ethics of responsibility.[105] Discourse ethics, which up to this point had concerned itself with the ultimate transcendental-pragmatic justification —which Apel calls Part A—is now expanded by means of Part B. This means, *inter alia,* dealing with the real historical situation in keeping with the ethics of responsibility. Analogously to the formal principle of universalization of Part A, the principle of complementarity is offered in Part B to come to terms with real situations. This means that the complementary principle is teleological, unlike the principle of universalization, which is deontological; for the principle of complementarity in an ethics of responsibility implies a strategic goal-orientated rationality.[106] Apel affirms that it is no longer possible in the case of the ethics of responsibility "to hold apart *strategic goal-orientated rationality* and *consensual-communicative rationality,* in other words, *teleological* and *deontological* ethics. Rather, there must be a genuine conversation between these two ideal-typical orientations." Apel does not understand this proposed "teleology" as the realization of the good life, for example, as individual *eudaimonia* or as the unity of *eudaimonia* and justice, as in Plato's utopian Republic; the "*teleological* orientation" of the principle of complementarity does not in the least orient it "to the substantial *telos* of the good life. Its *telos* is the removal of hindrances to the application of the pure principle of discourse."[107] With regard to the individual or collective totality of "a *form of life,*" the realization of the good life would be a matter for "individuals or concrete human communities," since this cannot be directly attained or anticipated by means of a universally valid principle. On the other hand, the principle of complementarity aims "at the realization of the conditions which enable such a communication, making it possible in a *post-conventional* form—that is, by means of *practical discourses*—to justify those norms which establish the restrictive conditions binding on all persons . . . for the realization of a life which is both good and happy." According to Apel, the principle of complementarity combines with the principle of universalization to form one single principle "of discourse-related discourse ethics," which is a genuine expression of discourse ethics since it refers a priori to the ideal of regulating all normative problems by means of practical discourses. And since it "includes the principle of complementarity," it is capable a priori of achieving consensus "in philosophers' argumentative and reflective discourse on the ultimate justification." Even when Apel's discourse ethics is expanded in keeping with an ethics of responsibility, he sees it as a *post-Kantian ethics of principles,* clearly distinct from an ethics of substantial morality. He distances himself from Neo-Aristotelianism, which he regards as an attempt to retreat behind the Kantian principle of universalization into "*commonplaces and* phronēsis."[108]

Despite this ingenious theory, Apel ultimately fails to touch the *concretum* of ethical conduct. The objection can be formulated as follows: the principle of complementarity is a theory about application that does not actually affect the application itself. In his critique, Habermas says that the principle of complementarity allows one to decide beforehand, in the abstract, something that can be evaluated only with reference to the situation and to the concrete possibilities, if the will to political action is to be achieved. Apel is led astray by "the hierarchical construction of his theory to slash vertically with a super-principle through the Gordian knot of the questions of political ethics"—although such questions are not similar to the question of the justification of the moral principle.[109] In my opinion, this critique also shows that Apel is still developing a theory about theory; he himself says explicitly that he is not concerned about the *telos* of the good life. He is still discussing "discourse in the discourse," not the translation into life of that which is justified in a discourse guided by the principle of complementarity. Apel unambiguously rejects the "commonplaces" and *phronēsis* which he calls "Neo-Aristotelian."

The terms *eudaimonia,* "the good life," and *phronēsis,* and their rejection by Apel and by discourse ethics in general call for some specifications. Since the discourse ethics of Apel and Habermas connects these concepts with Neo-Aristotelianism and goes on to reject them, the first step would be to investigate their use in Aristotle himself, and the philosopher Otfried Höffe has carried out such an investigation.[110] Aristotle speaks of the good life only in connection with "happiness," which consists *inter alia* in noble descent, wealth, successful and numerous children, a happy old age, health, beauty, strength, and so on.[111] The virtues too have their place here: prudence, courage, justice, and sobriety are mentioned specifically.[112] Aristotle, however, sees the entire human person as the subject of ethical conduct, and he emphasizes that it is not sufficient to act correctly: one must also find joy in doing what is right.[113] It is important to note, as Höffe has convincingly shown, that Aristotle does not maintain a particularistic perspective in his teaching about happiness and virtue (or indeed in his ethics as a whole), but rather a universalistic perspective. This is a "trans-human universalism," which sees morality's claim to truth not as limited to the world of human beings but as extending beyond this; it is also a "genus-specific universalism," valid for humankind without any restriction.[114] However, Aristotle's remarks about justice make it clear that this universalism does not forget the contextual aspect. In *Nic. Eth.* 5.14, he discusses appropriateness as an "occasional corrective" to justice: "Since there is a risk of arbitrariness wherever human beings rule over others, justice demands laws; but since these are universal rules, they cannot deal adequately with every individual case."[115] Höffe wishes to present the universalistic dimension of Aristotelian ethics here, against the communitarians, who wish to confine this ethics within a "particularistic context." His criticism would also be valid vis-à-vis the proponents of discourse ethics, who hold that the categories adopted by Aristotle envisage a status quo and cannot make any universalist claims in ethical questions.

A further problem that should be mentioned here concerns the good life (*eu zēn*). Discourse ethics attributes priority to that which is just rather than that which is good.[116] It regards "the ethics of goods" as something concerning existential problems, the need to find a meaning in life, and individual expectations of happiness, and such questions lie beyond the scope of philosophy.[117] As I have noted, Karl-Otto Apel argues in a similar manner. It may be true that some communitarians have seen the problem of *eudaimonia,* the good life, and *phronēsis* too narrowly, reducing this to stable, particularistic communities alone.[118] If, however, the communitarians and the proponents of discourse ethics had gone back to Aristotle himself, many misunderstandings might have been avoided.

We have already spoken of the universalistic perspective in Aristotle; let us now consider the concept of the good life. Aristotle certainly did not believe that the good life excluded the problem of justice and injustice (see *Politics* 1.2, 1253a 17). Höffe is correct to state that Aristotle maintains "the identity of the good and the just, rather than of a precedence on the part of the good," although this identity is not complete. "The good of a community/society lies in the acknowledgment of common principles concerning what is just and unjust."[119] In the final analysis, however, this means that the good life exists only where justice holds sway, and this dismisses both the communitarians (who are criticized by the liberals and by the proponents of discourse ethics) and the proponents of discourse ethics themselves. The task of *phronēsis* is precisely to deal with the existential questions of the good life, so that what is right may actually be put into practice. This *phronēsis* cannot simply be equated with a contextual thinking which is unable to go beyond particularism. Since *phronēsis* is concerned with individual cases, it is undoubtedly capable of determining that (to take one example) the suffering which may not be inflicted on one specific human person in one specific case may not ever be inflicted on any human person at all. This means that the path is not from the universal to the particular, but quite the opposite: the particular can be universalized.[120] The starting point is the experience that guides the *phronēsis* and leads to wisdom. In the tradition of Aristotle and Thomas, this *phronēsis* is not in the least naive; it is a situational moral judgment that cannot be separated from the reason. Thomas Aquinas sees *phronēsis* in connection with the *recta ratio agibilium,* or practical reason;

it is classified as "prudence," among the abilities of the human understanding.[121]

If a particular experience can be universalized in ethics in this way, there is no reason why discourse ethics should speak negatively of *phronēsis*. This is in fact a necessary complement to discourse ethics, since it can deal with the micro-ethical sphere. African palaver ethics differs from the Aristotelian-Thomistic *phronēsis* and discourse ethics at this point because it embraces both the macro- and the micro-ethical spheres. It attempts to ensure that the entire community, as well as the individual members, possess the highest good, viz., life. Unlike the Aristotelian-Thomistic and the communitarian understandings of happiness, which emphasize the self-realization of the individual, the African good life is to be realized both communally and individually.

I hope that this chapter has made it clear that African ethics is not to be categorized as discourse ethics or communitarianism, still less as the doctrine of natural law. It does indeed display obvious common ground with all these models, especially with discourse ethics and communitarianism; but the differences are equally undeniable. Both discourse ethics and communitarianism, each in its own way, emphasize the significance of the community for moral conduct, but only with reference to the positing or justifying of norms; it is then up the individual to get on with living according to these norms. African ethics is always a "we"-ethics, which does not rest content with supplying norms to the individual without then accompanying him on the path of praxis. When considered in this light, palaver ethics occupies an intermediary position between discourse ethics and communitarianism.

PART 2

Identity and the Understanding of Freedom

THE FIRST PART OF THIS BOOK PRESENTED NOT ONLY THE FOUNDATIONS of African ethics but also African anthropology. Western philosophical theories and systems alone cannot provide us access to the ethical life of people in Black Africa; we also need to study in detail their manners and customs, their religious convictions, and their understanding of the world as a whole. Only after such an intensive study can one employ Western categories such as truth/lie, freedom, conscience, and sin, in judgments that do justice to the African reality. Since Christianity has not succeeded in meeting people at the point where their deep roots lie, all it has been able to communicate to Africa up to now is a surface morality. This can be seen in the official proclamations of the church in Rome, which mostly debate problems that (apart from social questions) have little to do with the world outside Europe and North America.[1] Among the most recent examples are the *Catechism of the Catholic Church* (1992) and the encyclical *Veritatis splendor* (1993); but even as long ago as 1983, the new Code of Canon Law, which was supposed to make the fruits of the Second Vatican Council accessible and comprehensible in ecclesial praxis, simply failed to take heed of the concerns of the non-European churches. Not only juridical thinking, but its entire theological and ethical categories remain wholly Western.

Unsurprisingly, the discussion of these documents has been carried on exclusively within the European-American theological "schools," since the problems they address concern a Western cultural context. Perhaps the clearest example of this is the discussion of the moral encyclical *Veritatis splendor.* Unlike the debate aroused by *Humanae vitae* (1968), only a few specialized studies have examined *Veritatis splendor.* But where this has occurred, scarcely any attention is ever paid to questions beyond the European-American sphere. From a non-Western perspective, one has the impression that neither the critics nor the defenders of this encyclical are particularly interested in how its doctrine is received in non-European or American cultures, even when these scholars consider the problem of universality. This is shown by the choice of contributors to collections of essays on the encyclical and by the authors cited in their footnotes.[2] It is ironic that those who accuse the magisterium of an unacceptable universalism commit precisely the same mistake and thereby fall into the same trap.

This eurocentrism affects all non-European churches, but applies in a particular way to Black Africa, since the black continent is receding into the background of consciousness, even in terms of the global economy. If, however, it is true that an economy without a culture cannot exist, then Africa must resist a globalization that seeks to level down all cultures, and hence perhaps all ethical insights too, into a kind of world ethos. What applies to the economy as a whole applies even more to the church, which must avoid a false absoluteness that denies ethical pluralism.

These questions make it imperative to study African anthropology, even if only in an elementary manner. In the second part of our investigation we turn to the question of identity and freedom, since we must show in greater detail how the individual who is embedded in the community can act freely and maintain his own identity. We shall examine this ethically significant question in view of the problem of autonomy, which is vigorously discussed in the West as well. This concept is attacked by communitarianism in its critique of such ideas as the "unfettered ego." A study of the way in which leading contemporary moral theologians have adopted the Western doctrine of autonomy will enable us to investigate the problem of sin, freedom, and conscience in the Black African context. This will show us how necessary an inculturated moral theology is, if the Gospel is to be proclaimed in Africa in a way that does justice to human persons.

CHAPTER 1

Western Christian Ethics and African Anthropology

THE DEBATE ABOUT AUTONOMY HAS BEEN SO DOMINANT IN CATHOLIC moral theology since the Second Vatican Council, especially in the 1970s, that one could easily think that all other ethical questions had become secondary to or were discussed in terms of this fundamental issue. The debate was generated by Paul VI's encyclical *Humanae vitae* (1968) in which the magisterium believed it necessary to establish obligatory norms for ethical conduct based on an interpretation of natural law, as two quotations from this encyclical show.

In no. 11, we read:

> God has wisely ordered laws of nature and the incidence of fertility in such a way that successive births are already naturally spaced through the inherent operation of these laws. The Church, nevertheless, in urging men to the observance of the precepts of the natural law, which it interprets by its constant doctrine, teaches that each and every marital act must of necessity retain its intrinsic relationship to the procreation of human life.[1]

This affirmation is confirmed in no. 14, when the pope declares:

> It is never lawful, even for the gravest reasons, to do evil that good may come of it—in other words, to intend directly something which of its very nature contradicts the moral order, and which must therefore be judged unworthy of man. . . . Consequently, it is a serious error to think that a whole married life of otherwise normal relations can justify sexual intercourse which is deliberately contraceptive and so intrinsically wrong.

This papal statement develops teaching already proposed by the Second Vatican Council. Despite its openness to the world (above all in the Pastoral Constitution *Gaudium et spes*), the council insists that the Catholic Church is the "teacher of the truth" with the "duty to proclaim and teach with authority the truth which is Christ and, at the same time, to declare and confirm by her authority the principles of the moral order which spring from human nature itself" (*DH* 14). The council regarded birth control as one of the spheres where this principle was to be made concrete (*GS* 51). Although moral theologians already debated the competence of the church's magisterium in ethical questions such as the economic order or problems involving nuclear weapons, it was, as I have noted, the encyclical *Humanae vitae* that gave this reflection its strongest impetus, so that it could no longer be removed from the agenda.[2]

My intention in the present chapter is not to discuss *Humanae vita*. After recalling the discussion of autonomy in the postconciliar era, I shall inquire whether it is possible to universalize the concept of "autonomy," which bears the imprint of Western culture, and apply this to other cultures. One sometimes has the impression that classical "autonomous moral theology" sees the individual as autonomous vis-à-vis the community; this is not the case in the Black African anthropology which we shall examine here. We shall begin by describing the Western perspective, which centers on the individual as ethically acting subject; this will lead us to reflect on the position of the individual within the Black African community.

Individual Responsibility in "Autonomous" Moral Theology

Without Alfons Auer, the discussion of autonomous moral theology would be unthinkable. His book *Autonome Moral und christlicher Glaube*, first published in 1971, generated a worldwide debate within Catholic moral theology. Even the moral encyclical *Veritatis splendor,* which intends to offer a corrective to Auer's position, cannot escape his influence. A summary of both perspectives—not limited to the positions of Alfons Auer and *Veritatis splendor*—will be useful here.

The Practice of Autonomy in Ethics

The concern of the proponents of an autonomous moral theology should be clear from what has been said above. To put it briefly: since the church's magisterium claims general competence in human ethical questions, the proponents of an autonomous moral theology want to know more about what is specific to Christian ethics.

Is there a revealed moral theology, such that the church alone can claim to have the truth at its disposal and to declare and confirm universal moral principles on the basis of an essence of the human person? But not all ethical wisdom that proceeds from human nature is the exclusive inheritance of the Catholic Church; the proponents of autonomous moral theology point out here that a "baptized" reason does not automatically add to ethical knowledge. Human reason is derived from creation, which includes all human persons without distinction, believers and unbelievers, Catholics and non-Catholics. The word "creation" brings us to the fundamental Western doctrine of natural law. Autonomous moral theology, as understood by Auer, clearly accepts this tradition. Auer writes that his position is derived from Thomas's "ethics of Being," which he attempts to update.[3] Josef Pieper has given the following summary of the Thomistic thesis which determines Auer's starting point: "Every obligation is based in Being. The good is that which is in accordance with reality."[4] This means that correct ethical judgment depends on substantially correct knowledge; this knowledge must be the "criterion of what one wills and what one does." This gives reason such a central position that the ethical is understood as the yes to reality.[5] When it is objected, against the scholastic thesis *ens et bonum convertuntur,* that the primary concern of ethics is with "what ought to be," Auer replies that that which exists "appears as that which ought to be. The fact that that which is real and that which ought to be are not identical, is experienced by the ethically aware person as a moral impulse."[6] In other words, moral obligation consists in perfectly realizing what is.[7]

My intention here is not to present Auer's entire theory,[8] but simply to indicate that he argues within the framework of the natural law, where reason is decisive in interpreting reality. It is, accordingly, reason that discovers and posits ethical norms. Auer's basic concern is the communicability of ethical norms, which must be established[9] for the sake of dialogue with the world[10] or with other sciences—he speaks of a "justification in terms of the human sciences."[11] Communicability is based in the reason itself.[12] This means that one must distinguish between a "world ethos" and an "ethos of salvation";[13] the ethos of salvation does not add any substantially new directives to the world ethos.[14] There is, however, a reciprocity between the two:[15] "the vertical supports and guarantees the horizontal."[16] Josef Fuchs expresses something similar using the concepts of "categorical" and "transcendental."[17] In ethical action, the Christian intends a value which transcends the "particular-categorical" in such a way that the ethically acting person realizes himself holistically; but this

Christian intentionality does not determine the substance of the particular-categorical behavior.[18] Nevertheless, Fuchs holds that an "ethos of the *humanum christianum*" can influence Christian action. Not only does Christianity provide a "deeper" motivation for concrete (i.e., categorical) behavior by "generating humane conduct; it also determines *substantially* the ways in which we behave."[19] Fuchs emphasizes, however, that there cannot be a "fundamental" difference of substance between Christian and "humane-autonomous" morality. "The Christian's *act of faith* is the human person's act of faith and is therefore always *at the same time an act of humane morality,* the act of faith of the *human person* who is continually realizing himself ethically."[20] Alfons Auer is perhaps even less ambiguous on this point: the Christian faith exercises an integrative, challenging, and critical function vis-à-vis the "world ethos."[21]

What, then, of the competence of the magisterium to teach morality? The church must exercise greater caution in regard to the world ethos or categorical morality. In saying this, I do not deny that the church possesses the authority to teach the faithful not only in questions of the faith, but equally in questions of morality; but in the latter area, one must recall the statement of the Second Vatican Council in the Pastoral Constitution that the church "is eager to associate the light of revelation with the experience of mankind" (*GS* 33). This text goes on to call thc laity to "strive to become truly proficient" in every sphere. The council says that pastors do not possess universal competence; this does not belong to their mission. It follows that the laity must shoulder their proper responsibility "under the guidance of Christian wisdom and with eager attention to the teaching authority of the Church" (*GS* 43). It is important that the council insists here on professional knowledge, which cannot simply be deduced from revelation, even when one acquires this knowledge as a Christian in the context of faith.

The proponents of autonomous moral theology "in the Christian context"[22] argue here that the church's magisterium can no longer make the same claim to competence in the field of natural law as Pius XII (a claim confirmed subsequently in *Humane vitae*).[23] This field is accessible to reason, and the church should not disqualify the human person from making his own interpretation of the natural ethical laws, based on the *ratio.* In support of this thesis, moral theologians can appeal to Thomas Aquinas, whose teaching has repeatedly been recommended by the magisterium as a model.[24] For Thomas, it is his likeness to God that makes the human person an ethical subject. After Thomas speaks in the first part of the *Summa Theologiae* of God, he begins the second part, devoted to moral theology, as follows: "Since . . . we are told that the human person is made in the image of God . . . ; after speaking above of the exemplar, viz., of God . . . , it now remains to consider his image, i.e., the human person, in view of the fact that he himself is the origin of his works, since he has free will and the power over his own works" (*STh* I-II Prol.). Thomas makes this doctrine of the human likeness to God, derived from Genesis 1:26, the fundamental principle of his entire moral theology. He points to the dynamic realization of this principle. It is not enough to be created as the image of God: the human person, as a rational being, resembles God the more he imitates his "exemplar." Thomas writes: "The human person is considered as formed after the likeness of God in that he has a spiritual nature. He is formed in the highest manner after the likeness of God, thanks to the fact that the spiritual nature can imitate God in the highest manner" (*STh* I q. 93a. 4c). Thanks to this likeness to God, the human person participates in a special manner in the *lex aeterna,*[25] since he "can 'provide' for himself and for others"[26]—the Latin verb *praevidere* also means to "care for."[27] For Aquinas, the law has to do with reason, and this is why natural law can exist only in the human person: as a participation in the eternal law, the natural law requires insight and reason, if it is to be called "law" in the proper sense (*STh* I-II q. 91 a. 2 ad 3). Otto Hermann Pesch remarks appositely: "If the natural law has the character of law, this depends not on the *ratio* in God, but on the *ratio* of the human person. . . . Thanks to his reason, the human person gives himself the law; at the same time, this natural rational law is the eternal law of God."[28] As numerous studies have demonstrated,[29] Thomas's entire moral doctrine, and especially the tractate on the law, show clearly that the human person, thanks to his likeness to God, was given autonomy at creation, in the sense that he does not simply repeat the divine ideas but becomes the law for himself, bearing responsibility for himself in all things. Thus, it is not surprising that proponents of autonomous moral theology keep on returning to this Thomistic starting point.[30]

Naturally, one must take care not to equate Thomas's doctrine with the modern idea of autonomy. This notion of autonomy is indeed present when he speaks of the human likeness to God. Thomas develops his doctrine as a theologian, rather than as a philosopher; I believe that this has been demonstrated conclusively by research into Thomas in the 1960s,[31] and most clearly by the discussion of the plan of the *Summa Theologiae,* which includes the treatise on the law with its treatment of the *lex naturalis.* This discussion has led to agreement that the *Summa Theologiae* can only be understood in terms of the dispensation of salvation, that is, of the doctrine of *exitus* and *reditus*.[32] Accordingly, when we speak of autonomy in Thomas, we must beware of pressing his texts so far as to agree with the doctrine of Kant. With regard to ethical norms, Kantian autonomy can be understood only in terms of the categorical imperative—something foreign to Thomas's intentions. For Thomas, God himself is the ultimate justification of morality; when the human person employs his reason for ethical action this is based in the same God who gives reason its legitimation. This means that we must not equate Thomas's view with that of discourse ethics, not only because of the "good life" (which discourse ethics rejects) but also because of his discourse about justification of the principle that "good must be done and evil avoided," which resembles the formalistic principle of justice in discourse ethics but for Thomas can be understood only on the basis of God the creator.

The "theonomous autonomy" of which some moral theologians speak is *substantially* a better expression of what Thomas intends to say.[33] One of Franz Böckle's theses runs as follows: "Faith in God does not hinder the autonomy of the human person; it allows the reasonableness of reason to see its own transcendental basis."[34] Alfons Auer argues along precisely these lines. Hans Hirschi calls Auer's starting point a "teleology of creation" in which the claim that an obligation exists is based not on decision making but on knowing.[35] This should make it clear that autonomous moral theology does not contradict the Christian faith, but rather is in harmony with this faith—something that critics of this model too often overlook.

The Encyclical Veritatis Splendor

Some critics of the autonomous moral theology have suggested the need for an ethics of faith.[36] As the entire discussion in the 1970s showed, the accusation made by these critics missed the point, since the proponents of an autonomous moral theology did not in the least deny the *proprium christianum* in moral theology; their concern was only to avoid a fundamentalistic perspective, a "fallacy of faith" in moral theology.[37] The encyclical *Veritatis splendor* likewise gives the impression of having misunderstood the fundamental thesis of the autonomous moral theology which it criticizes. All the aspects of moral theology with which this text deals can in fact be traced back to the problem of autonomy, but we shall examine here only the passages where this problem is expressly considered.

By starting with the example of the rich young man (Matthew 19:16), the encyclical operates on two levels of ethical argumentation. On the one hand, it refers to the Ten Commandments (Matthew 19:17–19); on the other hand, it emphasizes the words of Jesus which urge the rich young man to go beyond the observance of the commandments (see *VS* 6–27; also 52 et al.). As is well known, moral theology assigns this second level to the sphere of the *evangelical counsels.* Auer remarks, undoubtedly correct: "Every Christian must aim at perfect love; most do so by dealing responsibly with the earthly goods which they possess, whereas others—like the rich young man in Matthew 19—are obligated by a personal vocation to give away all they possess to the poor."[38] The encyclical seems to understand this counsel (which denotes a personal vocation) as universally obligatory; but such an interpretation cannot be directed against the concerns of the autonomous moral theology.[39] The counsel remains voluntary and must not be confused with the Ten Commandments, which are an expression of the *lex naturalis.*

As for its critique of autonomy, one sometimes has the impression that the encyclical exaggerates its points and thereby misses the mark. Few moral theologians would agree that there are tendencies which "despite their variety are at one in lessening or even denying *the dependence of freedom on truth*" (*VS* 34).[40] One must also ask seriously whether there actually are any Catholic moral theologians who deny "the fact that the natural moral law has God as its author, and that man, by the use of reason, participates in the eternal law, which it is not for him to establish" (*VS* 36). The proponents of autonomous moral theology see in this critique more than a simple misunderstanding but rather an unjust criticism when the encyclical says: "Hence obedience to God is not, as some would believe, a *heteronomy,* as if the moral life were subject to the will of something all-powerful, absolute, extraneous to man and intolerant of his freedom" (*VS* 41).

The encyclical does indeed go on to acknowledge that "Others speak, and rightly so, of *theonomy,* or *participated theonomy*" (*VS* 41), but I do not believe that this statement does justice to *all* the representatives of autonomous moral theology, since even where theonomy is not *explicitly* mentioned, it is always presupposed. These theologians know that the human person must not be allowed to sink into a mere "autonomism"; they are aware, in the spirit of Thomas Aquinas, that the human person is *capax Dei.* This "capacity for God" enables the human person to transcend himself and discover the ultimate ground of his being transcendentally in God. This "capacity for God" does not allow the human person to behave like a puppet in the presence of God. As *capax Dei,* the human person is involved in a dynamic process in which he expresses his orientation to God. The human person's likeness to God may not be conceived of as something in his roots, a datum of creation that exists once and for all. It is the task of the ethically acting subject to become more and more like God, ever more perfectly his image. One who was content with a likeness to God which existed in root as a datum of creation would be burying the Lord's talent in the earth (cf. Matthew 25:14–30). This, however, means that the human person, who is meant to become ever more perfectly the image of God, cannot do so without "creative" activity, best in the ethical realm. One can become like God only by acting *freely, autonomously,* and "creatively"; this does not in any way abolish the theonomy.

It must be obvious here that the expression "creative" does not mean "a creation out of nothing, like the act of God himself." If we are to speak of responsible action, a critical encounter with experiences, laws, norms, and so on is required. This is why Alfons Auer emphasizes that when God gave the human person reason, he gave him what the encyclical calls "a primordial and total mandate" (*VS* 36) to "explore all the truths established in the world," including the ethical truths. Auer continues: "It is surely not God's intention to communicate concrete ethical directives to the human person in explicit revelatory procedures. Rather, in a critically productive encounter with his experience, the human person must discover what allows his existence to prosper and what he must renounce for the sake of this happiness."[41] The fact that the reason is a critical authority for the moral life does not mean the relativization of ethical norms. When the encyclical speaks of the "universality" of norms (*VS* 51ff.), moral theologians will not disagree, provided that this is meant in the sense of general principles—since it is always true that "One must do good and avoid evil," "You shall be just," and so on.

The moral theologian will, however, join Thomas Aquinas at this point in adding that the validity of these general principles does not always find the same expression in praxis. The more concretely one must act, the more difficult does it become to translate general principles into action. This is clear from *STh* I-II q. 94 a. 4, where Thomas distinguishes between "speculative reason" and "practical reason." The former, reason oriented to vision, is concerned with speculation, while the second, reason oriented to action, is practical. But, according to Thomas, not all persons share exactly the same truth or "rightness" in regard to what is to be done; and even where this is in fact the case, not all persons recognize this rightness in the same way. Thus Thomas's position is that, while the natural law is one and the same for all persons when considered "in general terms," there are certain individual points, "presenting as it were consequences drawn from the fundamental principles" (*STh* I-II q. 94 a. 4), which are not the same in all contexts. It must therefore be said, with regard to the natural law, that it is only in the majority of cases (*ut in pluribus*) that one and the same proposition can be valid for all persons in relation to rightness and knowledge. The general law, even the natural law, cannot a priori determine what *bonum, malum, just, unjust* mean in one specific context.[42] I believe that these reflections by Thomas allow a framework for dialogue with other cultures, even when these do not accept the binding character of the natural law; and the encyclical, while insisting on the immutability of the natural law, nevertheless emphasizes:

> Certainly there is a need to seek out and to discover *the most adequate formulation* for universal and permanent moral norms in the light of different cultural contexts, a formulation most capable of ceaselessly expressing their historical relevance, of making them understood and of authentically interpreting their truth. This truth of the moral law—like that of the "deposit of faith"—unfolds down the centuries: the norms expressing that truth remain valid in their substance, but must be specified and determined "*eodem sensu eademque sententia*" in the light of historical circumstances by the Church's Magisterium. (*VS* 53)

One must, of course, point out here that non-Western cultures are interested not only in "the most adequate formulation," but in inculturation itself, which cannot rest content with superficialities.

Veritatis splendor employs a Western doctrine of natural law; but the precepts deduced from this doctrine are based on human reason, which does not necessarily exclude errors. As Josef Fuchs says: "The individual norms concerning prohibitions, as well as the theory of the *intrinsece malum* as such—even though this is traditional, and is taught in the church—are justified only by the natural law, which means by human reflection. But human reflection cannot absolutely exclude erroneous thinking."[43] This certainly raises the possibility of comprehending ethical truth otherwise than by natural law alone. This question is not trivial, but concerns fundamental matters; it is not a dispute about pluralism within one and the same system, but rather about accepting that differing modes of thought endeavor to interpret one and the same fundamental principle of the gospel and to put it into practice. In my view, *Veritatis splendor* fails to do justice to this fact, since it asserts a priori a claim to universality *in moralibus*. Although it addresses the bishops of the whole world (see *VS*

5), it operates within the categories of Western philosophy and ethics and addresses problems that are an urgent concern for the Western world.

The pope's words might have taken on greater significance if he had urged moral theologians not to assert the absolute validity of their own views but to listen to the voices of other cultures too. This would have taken up a discussion that (for example) Latin American liberation theology has sought with regard to autonomous moral theology.[44] Marciano Vidal has given a vivid summary of liberation theology's criticism.[45] He observes that the ethics of autonomy proceeds "along lines laid down by the Enlightenment," so that criticism of the latter affects the former too. This criticism says, "'The womb of reason has brought forth monsters,' which include not only wars, the Holocaust and the injustices vis-à-vis particular classes, but also the economic and political colonialism which has promoted the prosperity of the capitalist bourgeoisie."[46] Vidal applies this general criticism to autonomous moral theology, emphasizing that this has "justified and favored" a bourgeois morality which coincides with economic, social, and political liberalism; it also prefers "a morality of assessments" of the individual subject. It elevates optimism, self-sufficiency, and "the arrogance of the Promethean reason" to a principle. In the last analysis, its goal is progress, and it is the weak who pay the price for the attainment of this goal. The danger for the ethics of autonomy is that it may lead to a self-sufficient reason without solidarity. Vidal writes: "The inflation of the autonomous subject leads to a self-enclosed reason which finds it very difficult to open itself to the transcendence of human solidarity, and consequently also to the transcendence of religious gratuitousness." This is why liberation theology demands an ethics of gratuitousness, an ethics of the poor, and ultimately an ethics of the people, where the community is the subject of liberation. Since autonomous moral theology is entangled "with the enlightened reason," liberation theology emphasizes the function of narrative, as opposed to the function of discourse: only a narrative ethics can take the community seriously as the subject of liberation. Marciano Vidal sees the messianic or eschatological element as another function lost to view in autonomous moral theology; this too can be understood as a consequence of the preference accorded to rational argumentation.[47]

This critique by liberation theology challenges autonomous moral theology to clarify and modify its position; this in turn will allow it to put questions to liberation theology. For example, autonomous moral theology might criticize liberation ethics for placing excessive emphasis on questions of faith and failing to pay attention to genuine rational-ethical reflection on inner-worldly values.[48] The liberationist view can entail a sacralization of the world which neglects the academic study of the issues involved. Such an exchange of questions can lead to a fruitful dialogue between autonomous moral theology and liberation ethics. However, as far as I can judge, liberation theology's critique of autonomous moral theology is socioeconomic rather than cultural-anthropological, and this means that the dialogue would take place between two Western philosophical systems. Only the inter-cultural approach allows us to see the problem of ethical pluralism in its true dimensions. This perspective makes it even clearer that both the encyclical *Veritatis splendor* and autonomous moral theology remain confined within their own world, that of European-American culture: it is in this world that their dispute is carried on. It is time to present the African understanding of inter-cultural responsibility in the ethical sphere.

Individual Responsibility in African Ethics

In the framework of Black African anthropology, one could further develop some of the critical points raised by liberation theology from a socioeconomic perspective. The position of the individual and the community in ethical behavior is very important here; we have already touched on this question in the first part of the present investigation, and we now return to it in relation to ethical responsibility.

In addition, we shall consider the holistic understanding of life in Africa, which does not make the clear distinction between religious and profane as does autonomous moral theology.

The Community and the Individual

As we have seen, liberation theology criticizes autonomous moral theology for failing to adequately address the question of solidarity. But it also fails to explicitly discuss the public as the subject of moral action. These questions about solidarity and the people are posed in Black Africa in terms of the relation between community and individual.

How Is the Community Related to the Individual?

The apposite observation made many years ago by Placide Tempels about the Bantu applies as well to modern Black Africa:

> The Bantu cannot conceive of . . . the human person as an independent being standing on his own. Every human person, every individual is as it were one link in a chain of vital forces: a living link both exercising and receiving influence, a link that establishes the bond with previous generations and with the forces that support his own existence. The individual is necessarily an individual adhering to the clan.[49]

The clan is first of all a kinship by blood, but (as shown above) the community as such goes beyond this relationship to embrace all human beings as "human-beings-from-Bende-from-God" (*Bantu-wa-Bende-wa-Mulopo*). Thus Alexis Kagame is correct to point out that the fellowship based on blood extends to include non-blood relationships, so that even in modern African states male politicians address each other as "brother" and female politicians from different states consider each other as sisters.[50]

This means that we must qualify Placide Tempels's thesis that the bond between the individual and the clan fellowship "affects Being in an ontological way,"[51] since this gives the impression that individuality comes as it were automatically from "Being as anchored in the clan fellowship." This would reduce the individuality, or the person, to Being as the West understands this term; and some of Tempels's remarks tend in this direction, for example, "The deceased give the offspring one of the 'names' (i.e., ontological individualities) which define the clan."[52] According to Tempels, this does not mean that one of the deceased is active here, by returning and being born again; rather, what is involved is the individuality of one of the deceased, an individuality that experiences its rebirth in the clan by influencing the child even in the mother's womb. "This influence then lasts throughout the whole life, since it is anchored in the very Being of the new human person."[53] Tempels also asserts: "Black people always see the effective cause of things as Being, the vital force."[54] If this were correct, African ethics could be reduced to the ethics of Being, since African ethical behavior would be limited to the framework of the ontological data established by his clan. I believe, however, that it has been sufficiently demonstrated that people in Africa are able to avoid both the ethnocentric and the ontological fallacies, since they are not confined to the little world of their clan community—ultimately, they understand community as a *world community* in which they can encounter every single human person.[55]

Tempels gives the impression that the Black African understanding of the person is a variant of Boethius's definition, viz., *persona est naturae rationalis individua substantia,* "the indivisibly single subsistence of that which is most universal, i.e., intellectual Being itself."[56] Contemporary moral theology no longer adopts this definition so literally; Klaus Demmer sees it as marked by "an object-oriented thinking." The modern tendency is rather to define a person in terms of self-realization, as "an ontological act (*actus primus*) with an inherent relation to transcendence. The directive thinking here is subject-oriented, seeking to investigate that normative self-consciousness which has its privileged hermeneutical *locus* from the self-realization which is related to transcendence."[57] But since this much more dynamic definition of the person takes its point of departure in the philosophy of Being, it too is very different from the understanding of the person in the African context. It must be recalled that African ethics does not define the person as self-realization or as ontological act; rather, it describes the person as a process of coming into existence in the reciprocal relatedness of individual and community, where the latter includes not only the deceased but also God.[58] This means that the individual becomes a person only through active participation in the life of the community. It is not membership in a community as such that constitutes the identity: only common action makes the human person a human person and keeps him from becoming an "unfettered ego." It is above all the African proverbs that emphasize this community dimension. For example, the Bahema say: "Even a hawk returns to the earth, in order to die there."[59] This proverb criticizes the behavior of those members of a community who avoid contact with it and want to develop themselves independently of it. One who behaves in this way ought to know that he does not become fully human, and that his enterprise will ultimately fail—and precisely when it fails, he will see how necessary the community or other people are for him, in order to become fully a person, in the true sense of the term. This is why the Bahema also say: "Human beings did not come out of a tree or a stick."[60] The meaning of this proverb is the same: one who despises his fellow human beings and behaves without consideration for interpersonal relationships and solidarity with the community strips himself of his humanity.

An adage in Burundi puts it as follows: "If one member of the family has eaten dog-meat, all the members of the clan are disgraced."[61] To eat the flesh of a dog is utterly disgraceful for the Barundi; one who does so should not think that he alone can bear responsibility as an individual for this deed, since all the members of his family and clan are involved. The wicked or erroneous conduct of one single member infringes the personal dignity of all of them, for "When the eye weeps, it makes the nose weep too."[62] Solidarity makes itself known in good things and in bad, but with different consequences: solidarity in good things is required if one is to become a person, whereas solidarity in bad things is harmful. But not only solidarity in bad things kills the whole community: a lack of solidarity has the same effect. As the Baganda say, "A lazy person kills the whole community."[63] The underlying ethical concept concerns the existential dynamism that operates only in reciprocity, that is, through the exchange of vital force. According to this model of interaction, there is a continuous flow of life between all the community members, including the deceased. Indeed, even God and the entire cosmos are drawn into this flow of life. The life which issues from God becomes a task for all human beings to accomplish: they must ensure that this initial gift of life reaches full maturity, and this is possible only when people act in solidarity. Each member must be conscious that his actions contribute either to the growth in life of the entire community or to the loss or reduction of its life, depending on whether they are good or evil. Each one who commits himself to act in solidarity for the construction of the community allows himself to be brought to completion by this same community, so that he can truly become a person. In keeping with this view, the Bashi in Congo-Kinshasa say: "Two ants are able to carry a locust,"[64] and "One bone cannot put up any resistance to two dogs."[65] A superficial reading of this proverb might suggest merely an individualism *à deux,* where each dog fights for a bit of the bone, for nourishment or survival, but the real meaning is that the two dogs collaborate in carrying out a hard task which benefits each of them. Their motivation is not egotism: by deciding to work together, they intend to give each other the gift of life. Only through mutual help can they get nourishment. Transposed to human beings, the meaning is that no one can realize himself as a person all by himself; one becomes a person only in relationship to others. This is fully confirmed by a further proverb of the Bashi: "If the pages were not numerous, this would mean that they were not clever."[66] The pages teach one another that differing human qualities ultimately benefits them all. Thus, the page is constituted by the reciprocal enrichment which is the fruit of the exchange of the qualities of the individuals. We see a similar idea in the proverb: "If an ant does not keep to its marching orders, it becomes wild and a loner,"[67] and then one can no longer call it a real ant.

We should, however, note that African logic does not necessarily imply that one becomes a person by means of concrete actions or achievements. The person is not defined as an ontological act by means of self-realization, but by means of "relations." This means that the human person in Africa is from the very beginning in a network of relationships that constitutes his inalienable dignity. Thus the question of the origins of human life, the object of such lively debate in bioethics, is posed differently than in the West. According to the Black African understanding of "person," the unborn child is already a person at the early stage of development. What Western biology calls a fetus or embryo is closely related to the community both of the living and of the dead; the embryo, which does not yet have an independent life of its own, is embraced by the love of the visible and the invisible community. Both communities continue their life in the fetus or embryo, which bears hope for the future, not only in the biological sense of extending the clan fellowship but also as regards life in general. Thus there is already interaction between the human fellowship and the unborn child, so that the embryo shares in a general manner in the growth of life. There is already a palaver at work here, thanks to a nonverbal communication which contributes to the process whereby individual members of the community, and the unborn child itself, become persons.

In this context, we must say something about the sick and the dying. Here too we see that the process of becoming a person takes place only within the framework of the community. It is well known by now that people in Africa seldom die alone and isolated. The community of relatives, friends, and acquaintances accompany their sick and dying persons until death takes them away. They speak with the dying and give them in various ways the feeling and the awareness that they are included in the *process of personal growth* even as their physical strength declines. Through this solidarity of the community in suffering and at the hour of death, in a communication that may take the form of a nonverbal "palaver," the sick and the dying find fresh courage and learn to face suffering and death with greater human dignity. At the same time, their coping with suffering and death provides instruction for the fellowship of those who accompany them; they learn to reflect on their own existence and to confront suffering and death bravely when their own hour comes. Thus, even sick and dying persons make a very significant contribution to the growth in life of the fellowship of those around them, so that each member becomes a new person.

In short, there is no end to the process of becoming a person in the Black African community. Not even entrance into the community of the deceased ancestors bestows a completed personal existence, for they too remain always dependent on the community of the living. Each day they must become persons, just like those on earth—and not least, thanks to those on earth.

The Identity of the Individual in the Community

We have already seen that the individual is not absorbed into the community;[68] only a few points require further attention. I have discussed in detail elsewhere how African names are linked to persons, and identify and determine the individuality of the members within the community.[69] The name is not transmitted from father to son, but designates the individual in his uniqueness and historicity.[70] Even when a child is given the name of an ancestor, this is not meant in the sense we know from Western society, nor does it denote a kind of rebirth of the ancestor in question. The child is indeed in a special anamnesis of the deceased person, but must develop into a person in continuity with, but distinct from, its ancestor. In other words, this is not a type of reincarnation.

The position of the individual in Black Africa is clearly expressed by fairy tales and proverbs. For example, one fairy tale concerns a leopard and a very cunning little animal called Mbepele who were good friends and lived together in fellowship. All that they did was done in fellowship and harmony. One day, however, Mbepele tricked the leopard by suggesting that they should each kill their respective mothers, since these obviously were useless. The mothers were to be thrown into a river. Both set off; each had to carry his mother on his head to the river and then throw her in. But Mbepele hid his mother. He wrapped a wooden mortar in a garment that he had smeared with red pigment, and when he threw the mortar into the water, the color resembled blood—proof that he had actually killed his mother. The leopard was convinced, and killed his mother. He believed that they were now both orphans, but in reality Mbepele continued to live happily in fellowship with his mother, visiting her in secret so that the leopard would notice nothing. Mbepele ate his fill every day, while the leopard went hungry . . . until the day came when he realized that his friend had deceived him. Then the leopard went in secret to Mbepele's mother and killed her, and from that day on the two friends were enemies.

The message of this fairy tale undoubtedly concerns the problem of the individual and the group, since it shows that the individual may not blindly follow the group. Life in community demands alertness and the maintenance of one's own individuality. In other words, the discernment of spirits must be preserved even in the context of friendship and community. If the leopard had critically posed questions about his friendship with Mbepele, he would not have murdered his mother. The fairy tale also teaches that a community into which the individual is absorbed, destroys itself. The friendship between Mbepele and the leopard was shattered precisely because the leopard let himself be dominated by his friend to such an extent that neither was able any longer to remain an individual, which would have allowed for a universally enriching fellowship.

A second fairy tale runs on similar lines. There was once a "handicapped" hen with only one leg. The family to whom she belonged had many other healthy poultry—hens, cockerels, and chickens. One day they decided to get rid of this hen, which they regarded as worthless, and send her into the bush. A short time afterwards, an epidemic broke out and all the hens, cockerels, and chickens died. There was not a single fowl left in the village, but the hen that had been exiled went on living in the bush. She had many chickens, and these grew up in the course of time. Whenever the family that had expelled her were away, she came back to their farmyard with her brood, and they ate up maize, millet, and everything in the yard. Since there were no poultry left in the village, the family found this inexplicable, but one day one of them hid himself to see what was doing this damage. The one-legged hen and her chickens turned up and ate everything as usual. Suddenly, the man leapt out from his hiding place and seized the hen and her chickens. He recognized her and was astonished that she should have so many healthy chickens. He begged her to come back with her chickens and live again in the family farmyard, but the hen said: "You threw me out once, because I was handicapped. I feel well and happy where I am now. And that is where I want to stay for good."

This fairy tale too shows that the individual has an inalienable dignity and may not be discarded as something worthless. Even a handicapped individual has a unique position in the community and becomes a person thanks to other human beings, just as these become persons thanks to the one who is handicapped. The one-legged hen who was rejected and exiled indicates that a human being can perish when the community denies him the chance to become a person. Only in different surroundings, where she was fully accepted and welcomed with love, could the hen also enrich her new home—for the fairy tale hints that the hen did not feel discriminated against in the bush; in this environment, she felt fully accepted. Despite her handicap, she was thus able to develop fully as a hen, not least by bearing so many chickens. Although this fairy tale speaks of human beings and hens, it is concerned ultimately not only with human dealings with the animal world or with the cosmos; it is also meant to emphasize the need to respect the dignity of each individual.

Many proverbs and adages in Black Africa likewise recall the dignity of the individual in the community. Since these communities must be able to count on their members if they are to survive, the position of the individual is seen perhaps most clearly in the proverbs and adages that concern the work ethos. They often underline the need for the individual to have trust in himself before turning to the community or group. For example, a Bashi proverb says: "A clever or far-seeing man increases his drink [i.e., beer] with water."[71] This means that an industrious person who never stops trying will always find a way to increase his possessions. But he must find this way and then take it. Before one helps one's family, or the community *qua* community, one must be aware that this is possible only if all cooperate in the endeavor. One who works in order to acquire possessions is also in a position to give help. In order to attain this goal, that is, to be concerned about one's own property, each one must be aware that he is not automatically entitled to the property of his relatives. Thus a Swahili adage says: "The property of an uncle [= the brother of one's mother] belongs neither to the nephew nor to the niece."[72] This means that property presupposes work that is truly one's own. One cannot expect everything from the community, for each has his own work to do. This is why another Swahili adage says: "If you want to have peanuts, get yourself a roasting pan."[73]

The Baganda emphasize trust in one's self, for example, in the adage: "What you yourself have sown is better than a 'Give me a piece of yours,'"[74] or: "You cannot quench your thirst with water for which you have gone begging."[75] One who continually begs or lives from the help of others, although he is capable of work, is not considered as an adult. Nor is such a person, whether man or woman, capable of founding a family. This is shown most clearly in the case of polygyny: a man can marry several wives only when he has the property required and is willing to share in the work, so that they are all happy. In particular, a man who lets his wives bear all the material burdens would be the object of mockery in African society. Conversely, a lazy woman would find no husband. Children and adolescents are prepared for this reality from early in life by the proverb: "You cannot drive off a leopard from your own door with the stick that belongs to your neighbor."[76]

The problem of self-reliance does not only concern the work ethos; it is involved in all existential questions, as a Bahema proverb shows: "Each one must ask his own feet."[77] Literally, this means that when danger threatens, no one else can run in your place—you must run to safety on your own. The intention is to emphasize that each one must be "his own man." Only one who tries to become a self can be helped by others to accomplish this process. This is the meaning of the Baganda proverbs

"When a hair tickles your nose, pull it out yourself,"[78] and "If a captive animal does not try to free itself from the trap, it will die."[79] Both sayings mean that no one can better assess the critical situation of a person than the one whom it directly concerns: he knows better than anyone else where the problem lies and what should be done in order to resolve it. Since he is the one most strongly affected, he should be the first to venture to assume responsibility for his own situation. Social ethics would speak here of the principle of subsidiarity, which takes priority over solidarity in the African context too, unless the individual needs help in the name of solidarity—but then, only to set him on his own feet.

This means that while African ethics does not favor individualism, it is also decidedly against passively going along with the herd. This is expressed unmistakably in a proverb: "If someone says: 'Let me leap where my brother or my friend leapt,' he risks falling deep into the mud."[80] In order that no one may simply go along with the herd, or to heal this state of affairs where it already exists, one must exercise *individual* care for each member of the community. The Bashi say: "To correct a liar, one must entrust him with a specific task."[81] The point of this adage is not falsehood as such, but rather the education of the individual to assume personal responsibility, so that he will think before acting.

In the light of what has been said here, an accusation often leveled against the African idea of community must be considerably modified. The impression is often given that community solidarity in Black Africa leads to the dissolution of individual identity. Certainly, one must not overlook the danger that the community may put the individual under pressure and force him to conform to the group; this is in fact often the case. But one must distinguish (as in Christianity) between the ideal and human shortcomings. Group conformity can be observed as a matter of fact in Black Africa, and is rightly condemned; but it is not in the least in accord with the ideal of African communities. In other words, the shortcomings are not something inherently African nor would they simply be accepted without contradiction. The African tradition possesses the dynamic power to overcome the abuses that occur under cover of an appeal to precisely this tradition. And this in turn means that the community gets entangled in contradictions and destroys itself if it disregards or disparages the identity of the individual. The individual can enrich the community only when he is made a person by its individual members, so that he in his turn can share in the process by which others become persons. No one is dispensable in this process; the individuals are not exchangeable.

Thus it would assuredly not be consistent with African anthropology if one were to employ *cloning*—to take a contemporary example—in order to make the highly touted experience of the African ancestors a present-day reality. One might perhaps fancy that cloning would allow Africans to keep hold of their important ancestors, who would now be able to hand on their wisdom and existential experience to their descendants. But such an interpretation of the African tradition would amount to an abuse, since it would mean that individuality was irrelevant in African ethics. A cloned human being can never replace an ancestor. The ancestor is one who had his own experiences, which cannot be communicated by purely biological means. The ancestor is not one who simply hands on biologically determined potentialities. According to the African understanding of the person, an ancestor is a human being who is called continually, even after death, to become a person; the living relationships which he maintains with his descendants continue to shape his identity and personality. His descendants' anamnetic experiences of him enrich them, and these point to the future; but it is not only from the future that they can be awaited. The cloned human being, who has received his inheritance by purely biological means, no longer has the possibility of dialogue with those persons to whom the ancestors are indebted for their entire wisdom and experience. From an African perspective, a purely biological wisdom and experience which are not indigenous to the community through dialogue would be a cul-de-sac. And since they have no roots in the living community, they would lead to the impoverishment of the human race.

This question about the ancestors leads us directly to the next point connected with the religious dimension in African ethics.

World Ethos and the Ethos of Salvation

As we have seen, the discussion about autonomous moral theology is essentially concerned with the distinction between a world ethos and an ethos of salvation. Alfons Auer defines these concepts as follows: "*World ethos* is the total sum of obligations generated by the ordering of the way of life of individual human beings";[82] "*Ethos of salvation* denotes the total sum of obligations through which the human person's dependence on God and his fellowship with Christ can be explicitly verified." Auer sees the emphasis here as lying not on a "turning to the world," but on an "immediacy to God."[83] Naturally, this distinction between world ethos and ethos of salvation must not be misunderstood as a "dualism"; Auer speaks of a "duality," indicating that there is no contradiction between the two concepts. The same is true of the distinction J. Fuchs makes between "categorical" and "transcendental,"[84] although Auer notes that the concept "categorical," as used by Fuchs, refers more to the *doctrine about virtues and values,* whereas "world ethos" is to be understood inductively or on the basis of the insights gained through experience.[85] It is at any rate clear that these two authors see no antithesis between world ethos and ethos of salvation; they are after all theologians and are aware that grace presupposes nature—*gratia supponit naturam, gratia perficit naturam.* Despite this relationship between the natural and the supernatural, the two realities are seen as two distinct entities, and precisely this is an important difference between the Western view and Black African anthropology. We shall set this out briefly in the following section; it allows us to infer a number of consequences for a Christian African ethic.

The African Ethic Is neither Secular nor Religious

As Africans see it, it is impossible to define the human person in purely secular or purely religious terms, since he is both at once. Where one of these two dimensions is lacking, one can no longer speak of the human person *qua* human person; and this means that one cannot speak of "autonomy" and "theonomy" in the Western sense. Let us look at some examples.

Political life concerns not only things of this world, but equally the invisible life that lies beyond death. A political administration that forgot the life of the deceased would be unthinkable in sub-Saharan Africa. We have already shown above how the ancestors belong to the points of reference of the palaver, which has a decisive influence on political life too; this is not only a matter of their experiences when they lived on earth in the past, since they are included in the palaver as living and present participants. The concluding ceremony of reconciliation necessarily includes the invocation and the presence of the ancestors. I have also frequently emphasized that the king or chief can exercise his function only in union with the invisible world. He is the link between the living and the dead, between the ancestors and his people. The installation of a king or chief is not only a secular matter, but also religious. Political authority draws its force from the support both of the people over whom it rules and from the ancestors. If a king or chief ceases to communicate the vital force, he despises the ancestors or fails to do justice to their concern, thus damaging the entire community in its triple dimension of the living, the dead, and those not yet born. In the name of the ancestors, such a king or chief must be deposed by the people.[86] In keeping with this principle, the members of the council of elders in Burundi (the Bashingantahe) were legitimated by a public consecration, so that they could exercise their office efficiently as sharers together with the king in the ancestral authority.[87]

When one bears all this in mind, it is not hard to understand why the people in many places offered at least a passive resistance to the chiefs who were installed by the colonial powers: these chiefs did not have the same rank as traditional chiefs in the tradition, since they lacked one of the most essential dimensions, viz., the religious, which would come to them both from the ancestors and from the people. A chief installed according to the Western model is completely incapable of transmitting life in full to the people.[88] One is therefore justified in asking whether today's political and socioeconomic crisis in Black Africa is not connected at least in part with disregard for the traditional exercise of authority. Contemporary political life conceived on the lines of the European-American model fragments the human person in such a way that the religious appears a completely separate sphere; politicians are concerned only with money and secular power. One significant indicator of the loss of the religious dimension is the civil wars that have flared in Africa in recent years. In the genuine African tradition, the genocide in Rwanda would be impossible. The palaver and the rites of reconciliation in the name of the ancestors would ensure that the worst would be avoided and peace re-established.

The unity of "profane" and "sacred" can be seen clearly also in the morality of marriage. It is scarcely an exaggeration to say that all the studies of marriage in Africa concur in identifying the religious element as part of the basis of the life shared by husband and wife: if God and the ancestors are excluded, a marriage cannot come into existence. This is why the invocation of the world beyond the grave plays an essential role during the entire marriage process and afterwards.[89] Precisely because marriage is understood in this way, it is considered a covenant, not a contract. It is not only a simple earthly convention and institution: it binds husband and wife into a community with an obligatory covenantal force which reaches beyond death. The Western form of marriage has led to disregard for this fact, with the consequence that African non-Christians celebrate two weddings (traditional and civil), while Christians celebrate three (traditional, civil, and ecclesiastical). People in Africa believe that only the traditional wedding constitutes a marriage. The church must be on its guard here lest the contemporary globalization process lead to a razing of foreign cultures; for Christian sacramental marriages are taken seriously only where Christianity accepts African religiosity as a component of the human person.

A third example, African medicine, makes clear the problem of the inherent interrelation of the "secular" and the "religious." I have noted above, in connection with the palaver process, that medicine in traditional Africa envisages the human person in his totality. The "vital force" of which Africans speak is not only biological but fundamentally "spiritual" too, and this is why the healing process cannot treat the spiritual and psychological as "secondary" dimensions. The "physical" illness is usually the crystallization point of the invisible dimension in the community—many conflicts in the community, among the living and the dead, lead to a worsening of health, which finally finds a "biological" expression. For this reason, there is no genuine healing in traditional Africa without rites of reconciliation, which include both the visible community and the invisible community beyond the grave—and the latter includes God.[90]

These examples from the spheres of politics, marriage, and medicine indicate an intrinsic connection between "secular" and "religious," "profane" and "sacred." This makes it impossible for Black Africans to speak of the "autonomy of the ethical" in the sense of "independence," or of a creation that must be distinguished from the religious dimension. There is only one world, which is not first profane and then religious, but both in one. Henri de Lubac has drawn attention to the presence of these ideas in medieval theology, for example, in Thomas Aquinas.[91] We cannot set out here a detailed consideration of the Thomistic idea of the "natural desire to see God"; we must concentrate on the essential points. This doctrine is based on the one history of salvation, which must not be broken; it begins with creation and finds its summit in Christ. As I mentioned, the *Summa Theologiae* is structured on the pattern of *exitus* ("going forth") and *reditus* ("returning").[92] We may simplify the pattern as follows: Thomas speaks in the first part of the cause that lies behind all that happens, and in the second part of the cause that is the goal of everything, before speaking in the third part of Christ the Redeemer.[93] Otto Hermann Pesch has summed it up admirably: "From God through the world to God in Christ—the crucified."[94] He sees the addition "the crucified" as marking the caesura at the beginning of part IIIa.[95] The *desiderium naturale* is involved in this Thomistic structure of going forth and returning, according to which creatures proceed from God and return to him as their *principium et finis* (see *STh* I q. 1 a. 3). The relationship between the human person and God is that of an *imago* to its *exemplar* (see *STh* I-II Prol.), in which it finally achieves its fulfillment. Thomas accordingly sees the yearning for the vision of God, in which the human being arrives at perfection, as a necessity of creation. He presupposes that when the human intellect seeks the *quid sit* ("whatness"), the human intellect is likewise moving toward the *visio beatifica* in which God's essence is this vision, in which God's essence is contemplated in all eternity. This, however, cannot be realized in this earthly life, but only in heaven. The decisive question is whether this created desire for the beatific vision is necessarily fulfilled; Thomas answers in the affirmative, since nature does nothing in vain, and it is impossible that a natural yearning should be condemned to frustration.[96] If one thinks this through, it means that it would be unfitting and absurd for the wisdom of God to give the human person a yearning for something unattainable. The philosophical argument in Thomas is that each thing is perfect to the extent "that it reaches its origin." The created spirit finds "its highest perfection in that which is the source of its Being" (*STh* I q. 12 a). Thomas does not, however, remain content with a philosophical justification: according to the theology of creation, the human being derives immediately from God, and is his image. This means that he acquires perfection (*beatitudo perfecta*) only when he returns to his Creator and sees him face to face.

One must beware of suggesting that Thomas reduces grace or the beatific vision to the natural sphere. On the contrary, his words leave no room for misunderstanding: "To see the substance of God goes beyond the limits of every created nature" (*SCG* III c. 52 n. 2295).[97] Nevertheless, it cannot be emphasized strongly enough that Thomas sees no antithesis between the unmerited quality of grace and the *desiderium naturale,* since God realizes every creature and leads it to perfection in keeping with its capability and "potentiality."[98] Thus we must say that grace presupposes nature. Grace already possesses a certain "receptivity to nature."[99] Even sin cannot completely destroy this *susceptio* (*De Malo* q. 2 a. 12).

In view of Thomas's basic conception, it is certainly wrong to employ the so-called *potentia oboedientialis* to explain the doctrine presented here, since this does not correspond to Aquinas's teaching about the "natural desire to see God." The *potentia Dei absoluta,* which leads to the *potentia oboedientialis,* means that God awakens an utterly unsuspected potentiality in a creature, allowing it to attain a goal undreamed-of in its own nature, as, for example, would be the case if God were to raise a stone, a plant, or an animal to eternal vision in bliss. According to Thomas, however, the beatific vision is not a wholly undreamed-of potentiality in the human person, and he consequently rejects the designation of the justification of a sinner as a "miracle" (*STh* I-II q. 113 a. 10c).[100] The reason for this is that the soul is *naturaliter gratiae capax,* that is, capable of receiving God by grace thanks to its own likeness to God. This means that the search for God is something based in the creation itself, in order that grace may finally bring this search to fulfillment.[101] Despite its natural yearning, the soul cannot attain grace by itself; but as soon as God gives grace, this corresponds to a natural capacity imprinted on the soul at creation. Here too the human person remains a human person. As Thomas Deman puts it, "He is perfected in his human nature when he attains justification."[102]

Thomas Aquinas's fundamental thesis is similar to Black African anthropology. If one adheres consistently to Thomas, it is possible to avoid a two-storied moral theology which sees the natural and the supernatural as two separate levels. The Second Vatican Council points in this direction, when the Pastoral Constitution *Gaudium et spes* speaks of the *integral vocation of the human person* (*GS* 11), a sign of the conviction that one must see the human person holistically—the one who is called to share in the divine life is the same one who engages in honest endeavor for the promotion of earthly realities in his life here on earth. It is always the same human person who seeks to attain to the one God, and this is what Thomas teaches when he presents the beatific vision (thanks to the *desiderium naturale*) as the one natural goal of the human person.[103] Alfred Vanneste is, however, correct to point out that some of Thomas's formulations are ambiguous.[104] He speaks of a "double bliss or happiness of the human person" (*STh* I-II q. 62 a. 1)[105] and emphasizes a "double mode of truth" (*SCG* I. 3 n. 14).[106] A "new additional light" is required to grasp the truth of faith, which surpasses human knowledge (*In Boet. de Trin.* q. 1 a. 1).[107] A further example is the treatise on virtues in *Summa Theologiae* part IIa, which makes a clear distinction between divine virtues and other virtues that lie within one's natural capacity. Thomas also speaks of "acquired" and "infused" virtues.[108] Vanneste has pointed out that the use of *duplex* in Thomas is so ambiguous that we already find in his writings all the material that was later to be used for the dualistic distinction between the "natural" and the "supernatural."[109] Thomas was the one who established the separation, by speaking on the one hand of natural knowledge and natural action in the human person, while on the other hand emphasizing the supernatural faith and *caritas,* for which the human person requires the "additional light" and the *auxilium superadditum naturalibus.* Although Thomas does not fall back into Pelagianism here, he does make the natural independent of the supernatural; he also makes faith a *scientia infusa supernaturalis,* which has as its object those truths that have nothing to do with human experience and must be considered, in the logic of this "system," as having fallen directly from heaven.[110]

Vanneste has attempted to show that later Thomistic theology developed Thomas's *duplex* theory into the dualistic doctrine of the "natural" and the "supernatural," and he may be correct; but such a sharp distinction does not accord with Thomas's fundamental thesis. His doctrine of the *exitus/reditus* structure of the dispensation of salvation makes it very unlikely that Thomas was the father of this dualistic doctrine that divides the human: where he does speak of *superadditum naturalibus,* he asserts that this is not something *against* human nature. His question is always how the human person can attain the natural "capacity for God" and the "natural desire to see God"—thus, the *superadditum* does not make him a "superman" but fulfills him. Eberhard Schockenhoff is correct to note, in his study of virtue in Thomas:

> An interpretation which does justice to Thomas in the whole breadth of his theological-ethical questioning must assume that both modes of the *virtus moralis*—that acquired by the human person through his own effort and that gratuitously bestowed on him by God—are also substantially . . . indispensable, and irreplaceable in their own proper order . . . , if the success of human conduct in all its dimensions is to be interpreted appropriately.[111]

Since the human person has only one vocation, the supernatural dimension is no appendage, but belongs essentially to true humanity. This is made perfectly clear by the doctrine of *beatitudo,* in which Thomas speaks of "perfect" and "imperfect" bliss: true human bliss consists in seeing God (the beatific vision).[112]

From a Black African perspective, one can agree with Thomas's fundamental thesis, since it sees the human person not dualistically but as a unity; nevertheless, his methodology is completely different from that of African ethics. As I have often stated, the latter finds its starting point not in nature or in Being but in the community, which is life-giving in both its visible and its invisible dimensions. This invisible dimension is clothed in words in another manner, so that African anthropology does not quite know what to make of Thomas's *superadditum.* This is not only ambiguous in principle, but also in fact, as Vanneste emphasizes. For example, in the discussion about autonomous moral theology, only a thorough study of Thomas can guard against the risk of seeing Christ as introducing a completely different dimension that would be discontinuous (*superadditum*) with the human dimension. In African ethics, by contrast, the question does not arise since one can speak of human beings only within a total picture embracing secular and religious/sacred.

There is, then, a fundamental agreement with Thomas here. Nevertheless, his treatise on human law seems to take a very secular path. We find a striking formulation in *STh* II-II q. 140 a. 1c: "Human laws are ordained for certain earthly good things." It follows that the goal of the state is the common good, involving the temporal order: peace, order, and so on.[113] Since Thomas locates human law in the sphere of *mundana* (earthly things), Otto Hermann Pesch is correct to say that he does not "theologize" this law;[114] thus there is no *civitas Dei* for Thomas, and he argues "a-theocratically." One example of this is his interpretation of the Old Testament legal statutes, which need not continue to be valid in the name of the old covenant; even though these statutes appeal to God, today's political goals are very different. The decisive point is thus not the order of salvation but the concrete societal-political order, the common good in the present.[115] Aquinas's refusal to theologize human law can also be seen in his affirmation that human law and the state cannot prescribe attitudes (see *STh* I-II q. 96 a. 3 ad 2; q. 100 a. 9). Even in external matters, the state does not have unlimited power to compel obedience; its law concerns disciplinary measures (see *STh* q. 104 a. 5c).[116] Ultimately, the state is not to become the guardian of morality, since it does not have the power to use the law to punish everything—here Thomas is thinking especially of the *forum internum* (see *STh* I-II q. 91 a. 4c; q. 98 a. 1c). If, therefore, the state can allow some things, this is not evidence of its approval of them, but rather of its powerlessness (see *STh* I-II q. 93 a. 3 ad 3). Thomas makes this principle concrete by means of the example of simple fornication, which must go unpunished even though it is sinful "according to the divine judgment." This is because "the human law does not demand the heights of virtue from the human person, since such virtue is characteristic only of a few people and will not be found in the great mass of persons on whom human law must necessarily be imposed" (*STh* II-II q. 69 a. 2 ad 1; see also q. 78 a. 3 ad 2). The punishments of human law have medicinal character and must be applied only in the case of a corruption that could inflict grave damage on the common good (see *STh* II-II q. 108 a. 3 ad 2).

It is not the task of the present study to set out Thomas's treatise on the human law in full detail, but only to show that he did not adhere rigorously here to his fundamental thesis of the uniform vocation of all human beings—since this point shows us most clearly the difference between Thomas and the holistic Black African anthropology. African ethics does not distinguish between law and morality in such a way that the secular realm (or politics) and religion fall apart.[117] Additionally, internal attitudes and the external actions are so woven together that the law, which concerns the common good, is relevant to both. Both the attitudes and the actions are to be understood on the basis precisely of this interweaving of "secular" and "religious"; they cannot be separated. In other words, the common good also concerns the community beyond the grave, and this includes the relationship to God.

At this point, we must indicate briefly the cultural perspective that would permit the development of a Christian-African ethic.

Basic Characteristics of a Christian-African Ethic

I offer here only a rough sketch of the problem, since I have discussed many aspects of it elsewhere. A Christian-African ethic ought not to lose sight of African attitudes about life and community: in both Christianity and traditional African attitudes, the ancestors and God are involved, since the ancestors share in the life that comes from God and hand this life on to the community. As I have shown, however, the ancestors do not exercise absolute control over the vital force of their descendants. They need their descendants in order to live beyond the grave in continuous interaction with the earthly community.[118] It is precisely in this way that the anamnetic dimension of African thinking plays its full part.

A comparison with the Christian faith will show that this fully confirms the holistic thinking of Black Africa, in which the secular and the religious are not torn asunder: there is only one vocation of the human person, a vocation with God as its goal. This means that African anthropology, which envisages the earthly (secular) and the religious (sacred) together, does not require a distinction between world ethos and ethos of salvation leading to the mutual autonomy of the two. Christian faith does not mean a quantitative *addition* to African anthropology, but it is *qualitatively different,* although it points in the same direction.

For example, in the case of the idea of the ancestors, a Christian theology will attempt to discover the significance for African anthropology of Jesus Christ as the proto-ancestor. With its starting point in Paul's model, where Christ is the firstborn of those who sleep, or the second Adam (more than the first Adam), African theology shows that the proto-ancestor precedes all the other ancestors in such a way that these receive all their life-giving force from him. This, however, does not add on the proto-ancestor to the existing ancestors in the manner of Thomas's *superadditum.* He is simply at the origin of what those who live in the African tradition have always lived and experienced. The proto-ancestor opens up for them a qualitatively different dimension of their sphere of action, and this means that they need not abandon their fundamental ethical insight that the human person can become fully a human person only by combining the secular and the religious in his thinking, and behaving accordingly. Jesus Christ, the proto-ancestor, develops the primary concern of the African tradition in a radical way; where Africans have introduced many practices under an erroneous appeal to the life that comes to them from the ancestors, the proto-ancestor opens their eyes to the true life and corrects abuses and misunderstandings. One could present many examples here, but a few must suffice.

The best-known case in African ethics is that of a childless marriage. According to the tradition, one may not continue in such a marriage, and infertility justifies either a separation or polygyny. Married couples who have no children are often exposed to contempt on the part of the community, which undermines their entire married life; all this happens in the name of life, and with an appeal to the ancestors. Where sterility leads to contempt for the married couple, the proto-ancestor points to the true dimension of life, since it is precisely the weak to whom he wishes to give the fullness of life. Childless couples are the weak ones in society, and these must be protected and supported, so that they too may have the life of the proto-ancestor in fullness.[119]

Similar considerations apply to handicapped children, who were killed among *some* ethnic groups who saw them as a threat to the life of the community. This was not counted as evil, since the ancestral tradition intended thereby to ensure a growth in life for all. Here too the view of Christ as the proto-ancestor corrects this view by imparting the true "definition of life," which is perfectly in accord with the intention of the ancestors. The handicapped are not a threat; on the contrary, caring for them and loving them will give the community the fullness of life. Jesus' saying about the man born blind discloses perfectly the idea of the African ancestors, who are not in favor of death but commit themselves actively to the promotion of life in the full sense. Jesus, the proto-ancestor, sees the work of God in the man born blind: "Neither he nor his parents sinned; but the work of God must be made manifest in him" (John 9:3). From the African perspective, the works of God and the fullness of life are one and the same, since God himself is life.

Finally, let us consider African anamnetic thinking, which is likewise developed through the theology of the proto-ancestor. The community of those who believe in the risen Lord is in the highest degree an anamnetic community, with the remembrance of Christ at its center. This does full justice to the great concern of the African communities for memory of their ancestors. This memory is not simply the recollection of past history and cannot be detached from the religious element. In order to be a genuine *memoria,* it must belong both to earth and to heaven. This anamnetic discourse, uniting those on earth with those beyond the grave, is supremely important when the palaver attempts to discern what is right. As an anamnetic community, the church in Africa will continue the traditional palaver all the more insistently, since the anamnesis of the African communities is extended and *qualitatively* changed in the anamnesis of Jesus Christ, the proto-ancestor, in order that it may perfectly attain its highest goal, viz., the fullness of life. Specifically, the Christian church will understand itself as a palaver church in which the word of God (i.e., the Bible) is read and discussed in community. The community's reading and discussion will reflect on all the problems of daily living, in order to find a solution that is no longer either that of the "world ethos" or that of the "ethos of salvation" but *both in one.* One should not be too quick here to suspect a latent fundamentalism. African communities have always seen the human person as a whole and have considered his action as the expression of one single vocation to community with the ancestors beyond the grave, without thereby falling into fundamentalism; this has been shown in our presentation of the palaver process. Further, Black African ethics, precisely because it sees the human person holistically, has never put forward ethnocentrism as an ideal; this too we have seen clearly in the doctrine of *Muntu-wa-Bende-wa-Mulopo* ("human-being-from-Bende-from-God").[120] The principles of human dignity and universalism, so fundamental to African ethics, are taken up into Christian faith in the proto-ancestor, so that they may unfold their vitality to the full. The positive element in African ethics and tradition finds in the Christian faith a unique support against the dangers of ethnocentrism which are immanent in this same ethics.

If we now turn to modern political life, we find it likewise possible to unite African tradition with faith in Jesus Christ the proto-ancestor, since political power can be understood in this tradition only in the light of the link between those on earth and those beyond the grave, a perspective developed further (and even more urgently) by the Christian faith. I have expressed this elsewhere as follows: "Ultimately, the exercise of a function and the possession of public power must be related to the model of Jesus Christ. . . . The modern Black African can walk in the footsteps of Jesus Christ only if he sees in him not a tyrannical *kyrios* but rather the proto-ancestor whose testament is an appeal to his descendants to work untiringly so that inhumanity may be overcome."[121] We can put this even more clearly: in the Black African tradition, a chief or king is assessed according to his success in transmitting to the people entrusted to him the life that comes from the ancestors—but a Christian will expect modern politicians to fulfill their duties in ways that do not contradict the fullness of life promised by the proto-ancestor, Jesus Christ, and this expectation is completely in accord with the ideal of the African ancestors. This means, in keeping with African tradition, that the modern state must be so organized that an unworthy politician will be deposed by the people as a whole, both in the name of the ancestors and with an appeal to the proto-ancestor, Jesus Christ.

This attempt to interpret the African tradition and the Christian faith shows that one cannot speak here of world ethos and ethos of salvation in the sense of autonomous moral theology; rather, as the Second Vatican Council says, "Christ the Lord, Christ the new Adam, in the very revelation of the mystery of the Father and of his love, fully reveals man to himself and brings to light his most high calling" (*GS* 22).[122] This "most high calling" is not to be understood as if there were another, lower vocation as well; for the council emphasizes precisely the integral vocation of the human person (see *GS* 11). Since ecclesiastical praxis in the so-called mission territories failed to pay heed to this and acted in accordance with a dichotomy between "world ethos" and "ethos of salvation"—and still continues to act in this way—such practices as the Petrine privilege with regard to the moral theology and canon law of marriage were introduced. If papal authority is invoked to dissolve a non-Christian or half-Christian marriage *in favorem fidei* ("in favor of the faith"), a two-decker marriage is introduced, natural and supernatural, or lower and higher; and this signals to Africans that their valid, profoundly religious marriage is not taken seriously; the Pauline privilege tends in the same direction (see Code of Canon Law 1143).[123] If the church (as theology has always taught) recognizes in principle the legitimacy and validity of non-Christian African marriage, the introduction of this *duplex ordo* ("double ordering") is incomprehensible and is in fact a contradiction of the Second Vatican Council, which underlines the "integral vocation" of the human person. From an African perspective, this *duplex ordo* in the moral theology of marriage leads to a dilemma: if the church itself divorces a divinely willed marriage deeply rooted in the African religiosity which is to be evaluated positively, how then can the church proclaim that divorce is forbidden? For ultimately, the God of revelation is the same as the God of African tradition.

These brief indications show how urgent a new consideration of the problem of the natural and the supernatural is in Black Africa. If one wishes to elaborate a non-dualistic moral theology that preserves the understanding of the human person in the African tradition, it is necessary to stop teaching the theology of grace in the traditional Western form.[124] Only when this treatise, and theology as a whole, is presented anew in keeping with the pattern of African thought will moral theology be original. What I have written here is only a stimulus to further work in this field.

CHAPTER 2

Sin and Freedom of Conscience

AFRICAN ANTHROPOLOGY AS PRESENTED IN THE PRECEDING chapters implies an understanding of sin, conscience, and freedom that differs from the Western one, where the individual occupies a central position; this is confirmed by the debates about democracy, human rights, and so on in Black Africa, since these realities have failed to establish themselves on the European-American model, where individual freedom plays such a great role. The same is true of fundamental issues such as conscience and sin, where—according to the classical moral theology of the tradition—individual responsibility is an essential factor. The dominant globalization tends to produce a uniform image of the world in almost all spheres, and this makes a palaver-like debate about all these themes all the more urgent. In the ethical discussion, Hans Küng's "world ethos"[1] is a disputed thesis among moral theologians and philosophers.[2]

The following reflections take up an earlier, somewhat more detailed study of the topic,[3] with the intention of continuing the debate begun there. Our starting point is the understanding of conscience in classical Catholic moral theology and the concept of sin that this implies. We shall go on to explain the problem of conscience and sin in the African context. We must then investigate to what extent individualism and community must be complementary to do justice to human dignity.

Sin and Conscience in Classic Catholic Moral Theology

The doctrine of the conscience, systematically developed above all in Roman Catholic scholastic theology and philosophy—see the handbooks of moral theology—is not, of course, limited to Catholicism alone. Rather, the idea of conscience is culturally determined (despite all methodological nuances) and has determined ethical reflection in the West as a whole.

We shall first present a short summary of the classical Catholic teaching, before discussing challenges to this understanding by the so-called new moral theology.

Catholic Teaching on the Conscience

The debate about conscience, at least in Catholic moral theology, mostly involves emphasizing the *subjective* ethical responsibility of the individual human person, usually with recourse to, especially Thomistic, doctrine. Although Thomas wrote no treatise on the conscience, his teaching seems to exercise a continual attraction since it clearly expresses the function of the conscience as ultimate moral authority. Aquinas based his doctrine of *synteresis* on the conscience. Since this doctrine is very well known, I shall merely recall its basic outlines here.

Thomas sees *synteresis* as the fundamental principle of ethics, not as *actus* but rather as *habitus* (see, e.g., *STh* I q. 79 a. 12c). The human person possesses an intuitive knowledge in the speculative and the practical spheres. Since this knowledge is *habitual* in the speculative sphere, it must also be *habitual* in the practical sphere, where the *synteresis* exercises the same function as the principles of the speculative intellect.[4]

He speaks in this context of the *principia in se nota,* which correspond to a natural disposition. Thus, the *synteresis* is congenital to the human person (see *De ver.* q. 16 a. 1 ad 14), and Thomas declares: "As the contemplative reason draws inferences with relation to that which can be contemplated, the practical reason draws inferences in reference to that which can be put into practice. Just as nature gives us fundamental principles for that which can be contemplated, so it must also give us fundamental principles for that which can be put into practice" (*STh* I q. 79 a. 12c). Hence the *synteresis* is infallible, since its function is to stimulate to that which is good and to protest against that which is evil (see ibid.).[5] It is the *synteresis* that tells me: "One must do good and avoid evil," and it is infallible here, especially since its participation in the divine intellect is a datum of creation. Thomas quotes Psalm 4:7 from the Vulgate: *Signatum est super nos lumen vultus tui, Domine,* emphasizing that the human person has the divine light in himself (see *STh* I q. 84 a. 5c; I-II q.19 a. 4c; q. 91 a. 2c). He must orientate himself by means of this light, above all where human reason breaks down (see *STh* I-Iiq. 19 a. 4c). This doctrine is decisive for Thomas's understanding of conscience, since it is on this that individual decisions depend. Even today this is the context in which the ultimate authority of the conscience is discussed. Conscience translates into action the *synteresis* about what is good or bad. Thomas states clearly that "the entire force of the conscience to examine or give counsel depends on the judgment of the *synteresis,* just as the entire truth of speculative reason depends on the first principles" (see *De Ver.* q. 17 a. 1 ad 1).[6] This is why he emphasizes precisely the obligatory force of an erring conscience that obeys the commandment of the higher principle (i.e., the *synteresis*) (see *Super Rom.* c. 14 *lect.* 2 n. 1119–20). Since the *synteresis* has its immediate origin in God and is bestowed on the human person at creation, the situational conscience too proceeds from divine inspiration (*De Ver.* 1. 17 a. 1 ad 6: *ex divina immissione*). Thus one who obeys this conscience *bona fide* does not sin. It must, however, be remarked that Thomas's doctrine about the erring conscience is very nuanced (see *STh* I-II q. 19 a. 5–6).

When he speaks of the *conscientia erronea* which must be obeyed, he presupposes that the acting subject has done everything in his power to avoid ignorance: failure to know something that the acting subject is obliged to know does not excuse him from sin (see *STh* I-II q. 19 a. 6c [*quam scire tenetur*]). This means that reliable information is necessary, but complete information means more than solitary study: the logic of Thomas's approach also implies a communicative community. I believe that the Catholic debate about the conscience, above all in regard to assenting to the teaching of the magisterium, has centered too much on the individual's knowledge; this is true both of those who attack the so-called autonomous moral theology and of those who defend the individual conscience as the ultimate authority. The primary concern of both groups is not a communicative action within the community, but a definition of the *truth,* whereby the discussion of "objective" and "subjective" plays an extraordinarily important role.

Both positions assume the Thomistic or scholastic doctrine of *synteresis* and the dignity of the individual human person.[7] If conscience is derived from *synteresis* (which is considered as divine inspiration), and the human person as God's likeness and as person is willed by God "for his own sake both as a species and as an individual" (*De Ver.* q. 5 a. 3),[8] then one must respect the autonomy of informed moral decisions. Thus it is possible for the individual to follow the judgments of conscience against a whole community or against the church's magisterium. I have discussed elsewhere the dilemma when both partners in a dispute—for example, the individual ethically acting subject and the magisterium—lay claim to it.[9] We may note that even the opponents of an autonomous moral conscience can appeal to the same kind of arguments as their opponents. Since they too see the basis of the conscience in God, they hold that one may not deal arbitrarily and autonomously with it—the conscience is seen as a given, pointing us to the transcendent dimension.

Theo G. Belmans refers in this context to Thomas's teaching in *STh* I-II q. 19 a. 5 ad 2, where the ordering of the reason is compared to the command of a proconsul who is the vicegerent of the *imperator* (emperor or general). One who disobeys this command insults the emperor or general himself. Belmans adduces an even clearer quotation from St. Bonaventure, who calls the conscience "God's herald" and "messenger": it possesses obligatory force, since it acts in the name of a higher commander, viz., God.[10] It is striking how Belmans repeatedly speaks in this very polemical study of principles: "objective" and "subjective," or "good and evil." He never mentions the community in which the ethical subject is located and which allows him to experience intersubjectivity, the exchange of views that leads to the formation of conscience. The main point for Belmans seems to be the solitary discovery of an already existing, eternal principle.

Although Cardinal Joseph Ratzinger is much more nuanced and cautious than Belmans, something similar can be said of his proposal to replace the scholastic concept of *synteresis* with "anamnesis."[11] The word *synteresis,* derived from the Stoic doctrine of the "microcosm" and introduced into the medieval discussion of conscience, has remained unclear, thus hindering the development of the doctrine of conscience. Ratzinger writes:

> Without entering into disputes in the field of the history of ideas, I should therefore like to replace this problematical word by the much more clearly determined Platonic concept of anamnesis. Not only is this linguistically clearer and philosophically deeper and purer; above all, it is in harmony with essential motifs of biblical thought and with an anthropology developed on the basis of the Bible.[12]

Ratzinger links his thesis about anamnesis with Paul's affirmation in Romans 2:14 that the Gentiles are a law unto themselves, although they do not possess the law. If the conscience is understood on the basis of anamnesis, it involves a *primal recollection of the good and the true.*[13] Through conscience, the human person discovers the divine in himself, or better: the conscience recalls the human person to his own origin, which alone bestows solidity on his existence. This is how Ratzinger defines the task of mission: "The Gospel may, indeed must, be proclaimed to the Gentiles, since they are secretly waiting for it (cf. Is 42:4). Mission is justified when those it addresses recognize, in the encounter with the word of the Gospel, 'Yes, that is what I have been waiting for.'"[14] This recalls the patristic teaching of the *semina verbi,* or Tertullian's *anima naturaliter christiana.*

What is then the function of the pope when he gives ethical directives for Catholics? The Petrine ministry consists in instructing the anamnesis which belongs to our very Being. Ultimately, this is a teaching function, and Ratzinger offers the following summary: "The *true meaning of the pope's teaching authority* is that he is *the advocate of Christian memory.* The pope does not impose something *ab extra*; rather, he unfolds and defends the Christian memory."[15] This view is identical with the doctrine of the encyclical *Veritatis splendor.* Both reject the idea of a *creative* conscience (see, e.g., *VS* 54, 56), since what is involved is God's voice in us (see *VS* 58; *GS* 16). This, however, creates the impression that in order to realize himself the human person need only recall the thoughts that God has already thought. It appears that if one presses Cardinal Ratzinger's idea of "anamnesis" too far, its total aversion to every "creativity" leads to a fundamentalism in matters of faith. Moreover, it is unclear how such an idea can do justice to the doctrine that the human person is made in the image of God, for this cannot mean merely that the human person *discovers* the fact that he is made in this image—it must surely mean above all that he activates and *perfects* himself. He shares actively in the process whereby the image of God is perfected in him. The human person is not only the image of God in the sense of an already existing reality: he must become this image in a continuous work of construction, behaving not like a puppet but as God's partner whose action *shares in the divine creativity.* As the image of God, the human person has the task of interpreting anew that which already exists. If this interpretation is to be comprehensive, it cannot be done solipsistically by a solitary subject who endeavors to discover a noncontextual, abstract truth. Cardinal Ratzinger is right to criticize the reductionist concept of an excessively individualistic conscience, but he does not sufficiently distance himself from an understanding of conscience in which the community has no place. At any rate, he gives the impression that the word "conscience" means "a sharing in the knowledge of the truth."[16] However, the Latin word *conscientia* emphasizes a relatedness to the community.[17]

As I have repeatedly emphasized, and as we shall see even more clearly in the following section, this communal emphasis is better in keeping with the African understanding of the conscience, where the community—especially by means of the palaver—plays an important role. In connection with Ratzinger's thesis about "anamnesis," African tradition is also familiar with a "*memoria*-conscience."[18] Unlike the Platonic anamnesis, however, it does not endeavor to rediscover the past and the world beyond the grave, in order to preserve this at all costs. The African community is *anamnetic* in the sense that it reflects on the words and deeds of the ancestors, in order to interpret these anew in today's community. Thus conscience is a living creative *memoria*. This conscience has both a communitarian and an individual character. Precisely because the Western understanding of conscience begins primarily with the individual rather than with the community, it is understandable, from the African perspective, why the so-called new moral theology proposes such an extreme interpretation of the rights of the individual conscience.

Situation Ethics

While the debate about conscience has died down, the mentality which gave rise to it remained. This is seen in assertions that "morality is a private affair; each person must follow his own conscience; one need not justify one's ethical decisions to other people; and so on."[19] Such statements are associated with situation ethics, which wished to liberate the human person from the clutches of a legalistic-casuistic moral theology that was unable to do justice to the uniqueness and historicity of the individual person.[20] These reflections have solid philosophical and theological foundations. In what follows, we shall indicate some of the principal ideas that are significant for posing questions in the African context.

Philosophical Orientation

Jean-Paul Sartre, whose existentialism elaborated a doctrine about the human person rather than an ontology, must be mentioned in this context. Sartre understands existence as the de facto existing and acting of the human person, who achieves his identity through action. Existence precedes essence in such a way that the human person not only possesses full freedom, but is absolute freedom. This, however, means that all true Being can be posited only through the absolute act of the human person. All nonexistential Being evokes nausea in the human person.[21] Since God does not exist, the human person is regarded as the criterion and absolute author of all things; this is why it is quite natural for Sartre to put the following affirmation on the lips of Oreste in *Les Mouches* (*The Flies*): "There is nothing more in heaven, neither good nor evil, nor anyone to give us orders, because I am a human being, Jupiter, and each human being must invent his own path."[22] Oreste's words affirm unambiguously that he alone is the norm and criterion for his existence. In other words, there are no given values. One who trusts an objective value lives "dishonestly": honesty means the unconditional acceptance of one's own will and one's responsibility as subject, since the human person is condemned to freedom. "It is only human freedom that creates values—his creative arbitrariness which finds expression in a particular situation."[23] This is a logical consequence of Sartre's thesis that human freedom is not something added on to nature, but is constitutive of the human person's very Being.[24] Jean Marie Aubert correctly observes that the only evil acknowledged by Sartre's atheism is the rejection of the perfect existence which realizes itself through free decisions. An action is considered good only if it is begotten in freedom—its substance is irrelevant to the evaluation as good or evil.[25]

The logical consequence of this thesis is undoubtedly the absolutization of the individual to such a degree that he requires no external law or community of any kind in order to become himself. We can apply to Sartre what Theodor Steinbüchel wrote many years ago: "Situation ethics is born of the ethos of existential philosophy, which no longer sees the human person as existing in the security of a tidy world-order, and wishes to show him his naked existence 'free of all illusions.'"[26] Ultimately, this means that the human person is "de-substantiated," so that one can no longer speak of an "essential consistence" in him. He is entrusted to himself in a solipsistic manner, and he alone must define himself in every unforeseeable situation. This ethics concentrates therefore on the "present," that is, on "the limitation of the existence of the truly living, particular human person by that which is independent of the self, cannot be derived from it, and is inexplicable." Steinbüchel is right to note that this means the collapse of all the categories of value and abiding virtues of which ethics speaks. "There is no longer any moral 'principle' from which to derive commandments and values that provide goals to make the human self perfect."[27] If we read this affirmation in the context of the problems connected with the conscience, we see that the human person who is confronted each time with a unique situation must take his solitary decision in such a way that it does justice to the present state of his existence in this particular and unique moment.

The position for which philosophical support is offered here can be found in a similar manner among theologians.

Theological Perspective

Some theologians place a similarly one-sided emphasis on the individual's responsibility in ethical behavior. They do not hesitate to adopt the theses of situation ethics and to defend them consistently. In view of the comparison we are making between African and Western anthropology, three representatives of situation ethics seem typical and significant, viz., Søren Kierkegaard, John A. T. Robinson, and Joseph Fletcher.

SØREN KIERKEGAARD. Kierkegaard's ethics is based on faith. He never wearies of emphasizing that faith is the paradox that "the single individual is higher than the universal—yet . . . in such a way that the movement repeats itself, so that after having been in the universal he as the single individual isolates himself as higher than the universal."[28] In comparison to natural thinking, faith seems absurd to the one who acts in the light of faith. A typical example is Abraham, who, when God commands him to sacrifice his only son, does not hesitate to obey. Abraham acts in the power of the "absurd," and this confirms that he, as an individual, is higher than the common run. Kierkegaard speaks here of a "teleological suspension of the ethical." With this deed, Abraham "transgressed the ethical altogether, and had a higher *telos* outside it, in relation to which he suspended it."[29] This transgression is a purely private action; its goal is not the saving of a people or the idea of the state, or even reconciliation with angry gods. Obedience to God's will is Abraham's only motivation in doing what this God commands him; thereby he gives the proof of his faith that the same God expects of him.

Abraham's temptation consists in the fact that precisely the ethical factor seeks to hold him back from doing God's will; but it is only this will that can place Abraham under obligation. "Duty is simply the expression for God's will." One who thus suspends the ethical through obedience to the will of God exists as an individual "in contrast to the universal." But as long as one holds fast to faith, this cannot be sin.[30] According to the logic of this thesis, *sin* would consist in obedience to the ethical dimension.

L. Monden notes correctly that Kierkegaard sees in the absurd a leap of faith that reflects an unconditional trust which is the personal gift of oneself to God. This presupposition allows one to relativize and transcend natural ethical conduct. Natural conduct belongs to the world of sin, which is *condemned* by grace and *emptied of value.* The law is incapable of providing norms for the dialogue with God; this dialogue provides norms for everything, and God can summon the human person immediately and individually. This divine invitation becomes the norm and "triumphs over the generality of the moral law." The example of Abraham shows most clearly how religious absurdity can triumph over human rationality, provided that one does not withdraw oneself from the will of God.[31]

Although later theologians, especially in Protestant ethics, no longer argued in the same way as Kierkegaard, he influenced or inspired their thinking. Richard Egenter notes:

> One theological root of situation ethics (above all from the time of Søren Kierkegaard onwards) is the Reformation understanding of God's omnipotence and of the fragility of human nature, weakened by original sin. Where God's will is understood (as in Karl Barth) only as the unique claim which he addresses in each situation to the believing Christian, a decisive significance must be attributed to the situation, as the "locus" of this divine claim. But even when the necessity and theological significance of universally obligatory structures is acknowledged, the Reformation understanding of the divine governance requires that in individual cases, the demands made by the gracious divine omnipotence can cancel a universally binding norm (cf. Emil Brunner).[32]

We may therefore say that the debate about the so-called new moral theology in recent years in fact continues a debate begun by Kierkegaard, even if the arguments differ.

JOHN A. T. ROBINSON. The Anglican bishop John Robinson became famous above all through his book *Honest to God,* in which he accuses traditional moral theology of supernaturalism: "To this way of thinking right and wrong are derived 'at second hand' from God. They are the commandments which God gives, the laws which he lays down."[33] A moral theology conceived in this way is timeless, since it comes directly from heaven. It defines some things a priori as evil; these are always sin, and "nothing can make them right," not even differing social and cultural contexts. Robinson adduces Catholic moral theology as a typical example of this kind of supernaturalistic thinking, "magnificent in its monolithic consistency." He warns against the attempt to base morality on the ten commandments or the ethical teachings of Jesus. The Sermon on the

Mount ought not to be elevated to a law, as if Jesus had imparted specific commandments that were universally binding: "The moral precepts of Jesus are not intended to be understood legalistically, as prescribing what all Christians must do, whatever the circumstances, and pronouncing certain courses of action universally right and others universally wrong. They are not legislation laying down what love always demands of every one: they are illustrations of what love may at any moment require of anyone." Robinson emphasizes that the Sermon on the Mount does not lay down infallible norms.[34] Its substance is not a law about what one must do in all circumstances, but: "This is the kind of thing which at any moment, if you are open to the absolute, unconditional will of God, the Kingdom (or love) can demand of you." This is the precise opposite of supernaturalistic ethics, where only principles count which command and dictate heteronomous norms to the human person. Nevertheless, to be fair to Robinson, we must point out that he does not see "theonomy" as a kind of heteronomy. He interprets Paul Tillich's concept of theonomy as a position in which "the transcendent is nothing external or 'out there' but is encountered in, with and under the *Thou* of all finite relationships as their ultimate depth and ground and meaning."[35]

Robinson holds that when the principle of theonomy is applied to ethics this is the basis of moral judgments, although it may not be exalted to a universal norm. It is, quite simply, a unique and unrepeatable relationship in which one encounters "the claims of the sacred, the holy and the absolutely unconditional," and these are the only claims one must accept. For Christians, this means the unconditional love of Jesus Christ, who must be recognized as the ultimate ground of Being, of every relationship and every decision. This means that the Christian's behavior must be governed by love alone, following the commandment and example of Jesus. "Life in Christ Jesus, in the new being, in the Spirit, means having no absolutes but his love, being totally uncommitted in every other respect but totally committed in this." Understood in this way, love is "a built-in moral compass" for our ethical behavior, able to provide orientation in any given situation.[36]

This standpoint does not permit one to judge a priori that some actions are definitively wrong. Premarital intercourse or divorce cannot be called "wrong or sinful in themselves. They may be in 99 cases or even 100 cases out of 100, but they are not intrinsically so, for the only intrinsic evil"—according to Robinson—"is lack of love." One must indeed acknowledge that laws and conventions offer protection to love; but ethical norms necessarily remain related to specific situations.[37] And love will succeed in "*applying* these standards to the changing situation."[38] Christians need not be afraid of changes, for God is not only "in the rocks" but also "in the rapids." A Christian must have the courage and the freedom to swim along with the current.[39]

To sum up: the ultimate basis for ethics is love, for love alone makes an action good or bad. The human person hears in this love the summons of the unconditional, expecting an answer of love. Ultimately, it is a question of encountering a personal God in Jesus Christ, not an abstract, objective law.[40] Although Robinson has a different starting point from Kierkegaard, the similarity is undeniable; Robinson too holds that there is ultimately an inner, theonomous law which summons me personally and to which I give or refuse my assent. Thus morality is a private matter between the acting subject and God. This line of thought is developed perhaps even more radically by the American theologian Joseph Fletcher.

JOSEPH FLETCHER. As I have indicated, Joseph Fletcher's thesis builds on Robinson's. Here too, it is love that determines the whole of morality. Only love is "always good and right, intrinsically good regardless of the context."[41] Thus love alone is the norm and the goal of ethical conduct. Love is the end which sanctifies all means, so that one may say: "Only the end justifies the means; nothing else." Fletcher cannot understand why Christian moral theology has unanimously accepted without protest the proposition that "The end does not justify the means." In his view, every action that does not serve an end that justifies it, is sheer arbitrariness. Since the end which justifies is love, Fletcher agrees with Robinson that it is impossible to determine what is good and what is evil, since "good and evil are not properties, they are predicates or attributes. And *therefore* what is sometimes good may at other times be evil, and what is sometimes wrong may sometimes be right when it serves a good enough end—*depending on the situation.*"[42] In other words, good and evil are not inherent in an action, but lie in the circumstances, which must be evaluated in accordance with the principle of love.

This means—against the view of traditional, classical Catholic moral theology—that there is no *intrinsece malum.* Fletcher applies his basic principle to concrete questions, in order to make it clear that intrinsically evil actions are excluded a priori. For example, if someone asks whether adultery is wrong, the answer can only be: "I don't know. Maybe. Give me a case. Describe a real situation." Questions such as whether one may tell lies to one's wife, engage in industrial espionage, or fail to pay one's taxes can be answered only with another question: "Have you a *real* question, that is to say, a concrete situation?" Other examples are premarital intercourse, breach of contract, or calumny. All these concepts are abstractions without substance; and this means that one must always ask whether in some cases these categories could be good, from the perspective of *love.*[43] This shows us how radically situation ethics calls into question the traditional moral theology where the central position belongs to the objective law, as the criterion for ethical conduct. Hans Rotter is correct to emphasize that this criticism on the part of situation ethics can still be heard today.[44] The church's magisterium quickly recognized how fatal the thesis of situation ethics can be, and it rejected this thesis very clearly.

The Position Taken by the Catholic Magisterium and the Evaluation of Situation Ethics

Pius XII and the Holy Office were the principal spokesmen for the response to situation ethics by the official church magisterium. The Holy Office condemned situation ethics on 2 February 1956 (*Dignitatis Humanae* 3918–21), but one should also mention here Pius XII's discourse to the World Federation of Young Catholic Women on 18 April 1952.[45] The pope gives a detailed presentation of situation ethics and examines the questions it raises; in particular, he draws a comparison between situation ethics and Catholic moral teaching. He admits that situation ethics is right to demand that one bear in mind the uniqueness of each situation in evaluating ethical conduct, but claims that this concern is not at all foreign to traditional Catholic moral theology:

> Catholic ethical doctrine has always discussed in great detail this problem of the personal formation of the conscience, after evaluating the case that is to be decided, and this entire doctrine offers valuable help in the theological and practical decisions of the conscience. One need only refer here to St. Thomas's unsurpassable expositions of the cardinal virtue of prudence and of the virtues linked to this. His treatise displays an understanding of personal conduct and relevance; this embraces all that is correct and positive in situation ethics, while avoiding all its confusions and errors. Thus, the modern moral theologian need only continue along the same lines, when he wishes to study new problems in depth.

This long quotation is very important for the further development of our discussion of the African understanding of conscience, since it clearly shows how Western Catholic moral theology too emphasizes the individual dimension in ethical conduct. Despite the similarity and consensus, however, it must be admitted that this papal text does not really grasp the true concern of situation ethics, which is not interested (as Catholic ethical teaching suggests) in defining the particular circumstances in which exceptions to the law are allowed, nor in the prudent application of one particular law to one particular situation. Rather, situation ethics contests the very assertion that objective laws and norms can provide an answer in a specific situation. Classical Catholic moral theology holds that the law can be interpreted broadly, without thereby being abrogated (consider, for example, *epikeia,* which Thomas calls a virtue), but the new moral theology holds that the only criterion is the goal, not the law, which can be ignored completely if love is salvaged as the sole ethical principle. On this view, laws and norms are only aids to decision-making; they cannot determine "existential situations," since these are unique and unrepeatable. Ultimately, however, this means that laws and norms do not offer any ethical relevant information applicable to these varied, unrepeatable, and unique situations, since moral theology is not a train journey where all the stations are known and determined in advance! In short, the new morality's criticism of traditional moral theology is that it emphasizes the fundamental helplessness of the human person vis-à-vis a law that is conceived as absolute (even though it sometimes allows exceptions) and is incapable of giving the ethically acting subject information about good and evil.[46]

Clearly, situation ethics (above all in its theological variety) draws our attention to the ethical responsibility of the individual and to the role of individual conscience. One must nevertheless ask whether a fundamental rejection of every objective norm does not ignore the danger of individual arbitrariness. If one is too quick to appeal to the individual conscience, this could lead in concrete situations to absolutize one's own private opinion in such a way that it becomes a law unto itself. The traditional doctrine of the conscience reminds us here that ethical judgments depend on "objective" truth. The individual does not establish this truth for himself: it exists antecedently and must be given a place in his reflections.[47] We are also reminded that a person is not able to realize himself in isolation: he is oriented toward an "I/Thou"-relationship which involves a "we"-relationship in a larger community, and this in turn means that the question about the knowledge of good and evil cannot be answered without recourse to our interdependence and interconnection. Thus, a Christian ought not to make any ethical decision without bearing in mind the ecclesial fellowship of those who believe in Jesus Christ.[48] In general terms, it does not matter how the individual understands a given norm but also how others expound it, and how one can do justice to the experience of others on which it is based.[49] Norms can originate only in the interpersonal, historical and social context.[50]

Although the Western doctrine of conscience has a communal dimension, from an African view it does not genuinely contemplate the action of the community.[51] Even when the interpersonal and ecclesial dimensions are emphasized, this is more a matter of "noting information received" rather than involving a debate in the sense of discourse or palaver ethics. Besides this, the subject who takes care to acquire correct information is alone in taking the decision which then counts as the ultimate authority. As I have noted above, this emphasis on individual responsibility, which must prevail even against the community, finds its extreme interpretation in situation ethics. Even the Second Vatican Council, whose teaching is adopted by the encyclical *Veritatis splendor* (45ff.) defines conscience as "man's most secret core, and his sanctuary. There he is alone with God whose voice echoes in his depths" (*GS* 16). This point is very significant also for the kind of theological situation ethics we find in Kierkegaard; this doctrine is the ultimate source of the appeal to conscience as ultimate authority, sometimes going so far as to absolutize this very appeal, which we hear in our days.

In the next section, we shall briefly present Black African anthropology, which has somewhat different emphases. Precisely for this reason, it can be significant for dialogue within the church.

Sin and Conscience in the African Context

I have offered elsewhere a detailed discussion of the problem of conscience in Black Africa;[52] I shall not repeat those observations here. Instead, I wish to make a somewhat closer connection between the question of conscience in relation to the African concept of sin. I shall first discuss the existential perspective on conscience and personal responsibility for sin and then the communitarian dimension of the responsibility of the individual conscience.

The Internalization of Ethical Norms

I hope that what I have written so far makes the position of the individual in ethical conduct clear. But perhaps it has not been sufficiently emphasized that this ethical dimension is internalized in a *personal* manner.[53] Some scholars have maintained that Africans are so obsessed by the idea of community that they feel guilty only when "caught" in some wrongdoing; one logical inference from this would be that Africans do not look on evil thoughts as sin.[54] If this were correct, it would mean that a lie was not a sin as long as the individual reckoned that his lying was profitable, or was extricating himself from an unpleasant situation by means of a clever untruth. However, the palaver process has shown us clearly that even private, secret actions and inner thoughts can become the object of a trial before the African public. The therapeutic palaver, in which the patient should reveal all actions and thoughts to the doctor or midwife who is treating him or her, no matter how hidden, leaves no doubt about the significance of internal actions in African ethics. The evidence of the palaver is corroborated by several other facts. I pointed out earlier that African ethics locates the seat of ethical conduct in the inner organs of the human person.[55] The *heart* occupies the primary position here. The heart is not only seen as linked to love and hatred; virtually all the virtues and vices (or sins) are brought into relation to it. Self-control, courage, bravery, truthfulness or honesty, and all the opposite thoughts and actions proceed from the heart.

Among the Bahema and Walendu of Congo-Kinshasa, not only fear or timidity but also lies are rooted in the heart. A person with "two hearts" is one who, for example, lacks spontaneous "generosity"; he is basically niggardly. This can, however, also mean that he lacks openness, that he is untruthful, that he is suspected of murder, and so on. Here we wish above all to emphasize the dimension of truth. Like other ethnic groups, the Bahema and Walendu see truth as one of the qualities of the heart, since the heart is linked to intelligence, memory, and will. It is the heart that either wills something or does not will it (*mathi jîrî, mathi jîrînza*), just as it is the heart that forgets or remembers something (*mathi vivi, mathi nori[nga]*). Again, it is the heart that thinks (*mathi dy'ari*) or produces something creatively (*mathi nori*) and speaks (*mathi rîpo*). Hence, the function of the heart goes beyond the realm of emotions or feelings alone to embrace even the "intellectual" dimension. Hence, wisdom and prudence are not understood on the basis of their rational character: they proceed from the center of the person, that is, from the heart. The Bahema and Walendu express their conviction that the heart is centrally significant for all human conduct by calling one who is not wise, or one who is mentally backward, "heartless" (*ngathi*). From this perspective, the Protestant tradition was quite right to render the "*Holy Spirit*" in Kilendu[56] as *Blothi,* i.e., "good heart"; the Catholic tradition translates this term with *Güke,* a word derived from *Le-Gü* (liver). The Protestant translation is certainly preferable, when one thinks, for example, of the gifts of the Holy Spirit, which correspond precisely to what the Bahema and Walendu attribute to the heart as seat of the ethical dimension and of human qualities or vices.[57]

I have underlined the "ethic of the heart" among these two peoples, the Bahema and the Walendu; but this is not limited to these groups. All African peoples give the central position to the heart when they speak of the interiorization of ethical norms. The Banyarwanda in Rwanda, the Barundi in Burundi and the Bashi in Congo-Kinshasa call the heart "the human person's little king," thereby expressing the essential dependence of human existence as a whole on the heart. According to the Batetela of Congo-Kinshasa, one who incurs guilt has a dirty heart. For the Bashi, the heart of a stranger is like an impenetrable forest: that is, he is unpredictable since his motives lie hidden in his heart. The Bashi make the decisive importance of the heart even clearer when they say: "An intimate embrace is not enough to transmit warmth to another person"; that is, the exterior has no significance, if it does not correspond to the interior.[58]

The Gikuyu of Kenya speak likewise very clearly about human intentions, for example: "There is no difference between a thief and one who desires."[59] This means that there is not only a material, "physical" theft; even the thought of taking something unjustly and without permission from another person, in secret or in public, is disgraceful and sinful. In order to avoid theft, one must first fight against the thought and the desire, so that the evil is throttled before it has the chance to grow.[60] Another Gikuyu proverb points in the same direction: "One who does not possess a goat does not yearn for meat."[61] This means that one who does not own a goat ought not to try to obtain meat illegally or immorally; one should not entertain a wish that cannot be realized morally or within the law. "Practice self-control, do not let yourself be led astray by the desires of your heart."[62] According to the ethical ideal of the Gikuyu and many other ethnic groups in Africa, a strong individual personality displays self-control both internally and externally; the latter dimension is essentially dependent on the former.[63]

If one considers all these facts, it is no exaggeration to say that the heart plays a role in Africa similar to its role in the Bible. One of the decisive texts is Matthew 15:17–20, where Jesus says: "Do you not see that whatever goes into the mouth [into the human being] passes into the stomach, and so passes on? But what comes out of the mouth proceeds from the heart, and this defiles a person. For out of the heart come evil thoughts, murder, adultery, fornication, theft, false witness, slander. These are what defile a person; but to eat with unwashed hands does not defile one."

This is precisely what the Bahema mean when they say to someone, "*Nitsonga sani che,*" "The interior of your mouth is dirty." This designates a person who injures others by means of words alone: curses, angry words, insults to someone's honor, disrespectful words, and the like. The meaning is that words of this kind have not been digested, and do such damage to the heart that they emerge through the mouth, disfiguring it totally with their filth. Thus, the internal dimension of ethical conduct extends to other human organs too, such as the stomach. If a word is undigested, it can have destructive consequences for interpersonal relationships; if a word is properly digested, it contributes to building up the community.[64] As I have said, Alexis Kagame has drawn attention to yet another organ, viz., the liver, which plays a decisive role among the Baluba with regard to the morality of ethical conduct. In general, however, among most ethnic groups (including the Baluba), the heart is central to the evaluation of the ethical acceptability of human conduct.

It must, however, be emphasized here that the human person is not divided into various sectors, corresponding to his various organs; ethical actions are not attributed exclusively to the liver, the heart, and other organs. Rather, the whole human being as a person is involved. I believe that this can be shown even better with regard to physical actions. For example, a hostile look can make someone ill, or lead rapidly to his death; but Black Africans speak here not of the "look" but of the "eyes" as evil. Naturally—as even non-Africans can grasp—it is not the eyes as such that are evil but their employment to achieve evil ends which is the issue.

This is easy to understand, but other convictions and practices connected to African ethics are often a closed book to the uninitiated. Everything that belongs to the human body—including everything it excretes—has a very high ethical relevance. Hairs, nails, blood, spittle, footprints, shadows: these are elements that permit one to manipulate or injure another person, or to acquire information about what someone is doing. Africans are convinced that the ethical identity of a person can be established by biological, physical, or chemical elements that can be traced back to the "bodiliness" of that person; traditional Africans believe that there is a kind of ethical DNA that can provide the required information about the individual ethical constitution. One may laugh at such an attitude, or dismiss it as naive or primitive, but the fundamental thesis remains (and this is all that interests us here)—namely, that the human person, even in his ethical living, can be understood only as a unity and holistically. One cannot separate external actions from internal conviction.

We can go further than this. The entire being of the human person, including his physical existence, is ethically "impregnated." For Africans, this is a matter of the vital force, which becomes totally "good" or "evil" through virtues or sins and manifests itself as such. Let me emphasize once again that this way of thinking does not lead to dualism. This, however, makes it very difficult to distinguish between taboos (which Western thought understands as applying only to the external sphere, leaving the internal sphere untouched) and those genuinely ethical actions where morality is involved. Laurenti Magesa has studied the example of guilt and the feeling of shame, and has demonstrated that the distinction cannot be applied to African ethics.[65] He disagrees with John Bradshaw, who classifies shame under the heading of "being" and guilt under the sphere of "feeling." "Shame has to do with being, and differs greatly from feeling guilty. . . . Guilt says I've *done* something wrong; shame says there *is* something wrong with me. Guilt says I've *made* a mistake; shame says I *am* a mistake. Guilt says what I *did* was not good; shame says I *am* no good."[66] In the African conception, there is no separation between "being" and "doing"; consequently, one may say that the human person *is* what he does. If action defines the being of the human person, it is also true that the human person's action is defined on the basis of his being. For example, if someone is a sorcerer, everything in him and in his actions is connected with sorcery—sorcery has corrupted him through and through. The same is true of the goodness which transforms the entire being of the virtuous person. This explains why everything connected with a human person reveals his essence and his ethical character, and why every biological element in him, and everything that has been in contact with him, can be used either to hurt him or to heal him.

This, however, makes it clear why it is a mistake to assert that African ethics is unconcerned with the internalization of actions. If one bears in mind the interaction between internal and external, one is cautious in the evaluation of "taboos," for even these cannot be separated from the whole person, who knows and feels himself to be infected in the innermost depths of his being. The contemporary discussion in Western ethics about ethical and nonethical or pre-ethical values does not interest African ethics to the same degree. For African ethics, so-called nonethical or pre-ethical values are not only significant but also constitutive of the person, since the person identifies himself with all his actions, whether he is conscious of these or not. Only the community, the ultimate basis of value, allows one to understand actions and persons that are defined in this way.

The Community and the Individual Conscience

As these observations make clear, Africans truly internalize ethical norms, such that one can speak here of a personal conscience and an awareness of responsibility. These are not, however, "privatized" in the sense of an "ultimate authority" that could be invoked, in extreme cases, against everyone else.[67] The African view has no place for a more or less "dictatorial" conscience that could appeal (in the manner of situation ethics) to an inner illumination or place its trust exclusively in its own insight. The palaver process clearly shows that ethical responsibility is the common work of the community; as we have often remarked, the individual can realize himself as a human person only in and with the community. This likewise means that one's personal conduct—indeed all that one does—affects the entire community of the living, the deceased, and the unborn. Through his conduct and his actions, the individual has an effect on the entire cosmos.[68]

For this reason, the individual cannot avoid reflecting on how his ethical actions affect the community. Ethical norms are not created by the individual *ex nihilo;* rather, the individual must identify with something that already exists. Morality is understood in African communities as lived experience which must be realized above all anamnetically. This means that one cannot avoid or pass over the experiences of one's ancestors, who established the ethical norms based on wisdom arising out of the community. John S. Mbiti is correct to note here that morality imprints itself on the human conscience only by means of a lengthy process of reflection that includes observing how neighboring peoples behave. When all these experiences are criticized and digested, they are normatively established in a moral code that becomes the inheritance of the entire community, including those not yet born.[69] In this community, it is assumed that the values, rituals, taboos, and practices that have already been tried and tested preserve the community's life from disintegration; moreover, they ensure the growth of the total life force. Mbiti rightly observes: "African religious beliefs, values, rituals and practices are directed towards strengthening the moral life of each society. Morals are the food and drink which keep society alive, healthy and happy. Once there is a moral breakdown, the whole integrity of society also breaks down and the end is tragic."[70] (The last point does not apply to Africa alone.) This is why communities in Africa are very much interested in individual ethical conduct.[71] And the individual's growth in wisdom depends on the ethical health of the community as a whole.

This is true not only of ordinary members of the community: even a king or leader of the people is subject to the same principles. Elochukwu Uzukwu has made this clear by pointing out that among the Manja people of the Central African Republic, the chief's totem is a hare, which, thanks to its long ears, is supposed to hear better than the other animals.

The Manja see the ability to listen as the main characteristic of a chief. He must have long, big ears, which bring him close to God, the ancestors, and the divinities; and these same ears link him to everything that is said within the community. He has the final word when decisions are to be made, but not as a matter of private opinion: he will speak only after having heard and digested everything that has been discussed in the community. The Bambara of Mali have a similar idea, when they speak of the "immensity" of the word which is so great, so wide and comprehensive that it embraces the whole of humankind. This means, however, that the word is too great and wide for one single mouth; no one can take control of the word on his own.[72] The word is sacred and is so significant for the entire community of humankind that it may not be monopolized by any one individual, even by a chief. The word is essentially an instrument of communication, allowing various members of the community to share their experiences of life with one another; this makes it possible for them to share life, so that all may have life in fullness. This brings us back to the palaver: one of its tasks is to form the individual's conscience so that it may serve the community. The norms established in the palaver reflect the experience of the community and represent a continuous summons to the individual, in his ethical conduct and decisions, to interpret the norms on the basis of the community. One may therefore say that the palaver process does not come to an end when the community discussion is over; rather, there is a continuous dialogue with the community, whose voice can be heard in the norms that have been laid down. We find here a point of comparison between the African world and the world of the Old Testament. The Ten Commandments derive their life-giving force not from the written words, which are "cold" letters (so to speak), but from the living God who inspires them and whose voice "resounds" in people's ears and communicates life in the "ten words." If one looks at African ethics from this perspective, one will easily recognize that the traditional statutes link the personal conscience both to the community of the ancestors and to the community of one's contemporaries. At the same time, in view of the community of those not yet born, this conscience is projected into the future. This is because ethics is concerned with life, and in the African understanding (as we have so often recalled) life is articulated "three-dimensionally." One who acts ethically must think holistically, in terms of the community, and may not exclude anyone, even those as yet unborn.

We must also emphasize that this thesis about the interaction between community and norms is not limited only to commandments and prohibitions of the (mostly Catholic) tradition of *manuals,* that is, the *praecepta positiva* and *praecepta negativa.* It applies equally to those norms known as taboos, which we are commonly told do not obligate the conscience. Although there are various degrees of taboo and although their legitimation appears unconvincing to enlightened Westerners, the traditional African understanding links all the prohibitions by taboo to the protection and furthering of life. The basic question we are investigating is not whether the legitimations of these taboos correspond to reality but what basis they have in African ethical reflection. The fundamental reflection remains the same: even if the prohibitions by taboo should resemble superstition and fail to correspond to objective reality, this does not deny that the acting subject always sees these prohibitions in connection with life, and consequently with the community. These are not external acts which leave the internal conscience untouched, nor is the motive mere dread or fear of punishment; rather, the ethical dimension itself is at stake, for disregard of the taboo ultimately harms the community, which must be respected in all contexts. It follows that the subject, when confronted with the taboos, must necessarily inquire into the negative consequences (real or perhaps only imagined) that breaking the taboo would entail for human life and even for the entire community. On the other hand, not all taboos are simply naive or magical (as one might suppose at first glance). I have discussed this point in detail elsewhere,[73] but I should like to present one example of what I mean.

It is forbidden among the Bahema of Congo-Kinshasa for a young man to sit on his father's chair during his lifetime, since this could lead to the father's death. The superficial observer sees here a baseless taboo, since the supposed consequence cannot be proven. If one penetrates the customs of the Bahema more deeply, however, its legitimation makes rational sense: the taboo is connected with the inherited tradition, and ultimately with respect for one's father. The son is solemnly introduced into his inheritance only after his father dies, and this now gives him the right to sit on the chair of the dead man. To sit on his father's chair while the father is still alive amounts to wishing his father's death; a son who would do so is capable of actually killing his father, in order to succeed him as quickly as possible. In order to prepare a boy for proper conduct, the tradition has therefore developed a brief formula: "Your father will die if you sit on his chair." Only with the passing of time will the child understand this and internalize its meaning.[74] One could mention many similar examples.

At any rate, it must be underscored that even when it is difficult to discern the significance of a taboo, all taboos ultimately help to support ethical values.[75] For example, sexual taboos that forbid intercourse at particular times intend ultimately to lead the married couple to awareness of each other's dignity during the sexual act; besides this, they encourage (especially the husband) to practice and learn self-control, which is one of the goals of the initiation rite. If the taboo leads them to discover a deeper dimension of sexuality, then the goal which was formulated in these general terms becomes concrete. The prohibition of intercourse during menstruation is based on the assertion that the man could become sick or impotent, since he fails to respect the blood that is lost, and thereby is in conflict with life.[76] The woman too must adopt a particular behavior in this time, so that no one is harmed. But the real meaning of the taboo is the appeal to take life seriously and respect it, not only in the biological sense but as comprehensively as possible. We may sum up by saying that many taboos function to protect the individual and group morality. They draw attention to its basic principle, namely, life, and lead slowly to an interiorization or deepening of the moral norms, which amounts to a formation of the conscience. This leads the individual to accept a deeper ethical obligation and guarantees the good of the community.

What applies to taboos applies equally to magic and sorcery. These practices are often condemned, but magic and sorcery have positive functions that serve the good of the community. More is involved than irrational fear and superstition. Underlying belief in magic and sorcery is the conviction that invisible powers are at work in the world and that it is impossible for reason to explain their actions.[77] Even where unjustified and exaggerated fear does exist, belief in magic and sorcery has led to ethical behavior within the community. Where people believe their conduct cannot remain hidden from a neighbor who is a sorcerer, so that their lives are at stake, ethically significant communal norms are strictly observed: theft, falsehood, adultery, insults of one's neighbor, and the like are carefully avoided. The magicians and sorcerers themselves are not necessarily exempt from such dangers, for they know that their power could be destroyed by even more powerful persons, for example, those with medical knowledge. They too must avoid evil. It is also possible to treat them medically, rendering them completely harmless. All this makes magic and sorcery a factor promoting equilibrium among relatives, neighbors, and all the members of the community.[78] It is also important to note that every individual has the potential to become a sorcerer: the power of evil slumbers within him and can awaken at any moment. This power is the chief enemy of life and finds expression in envy, jealousy, hatred, wrath, desire, or pleasure in evil, etc. One who does not exercise self-control, but allows these dispositions to grow unchecked, becomes a sorcerer. Thus, the idea of sorcery is an abiding ethical admonition intended to preserve the community from harm.[79]

This is further confirmation of our basic thesis of the interrelation among conscience, norm internalization, and communal norms. Morality cannot be privatized; one is not moral on one's own, merely for the sake of self-realization. Rather, it is by definition an interaction among all the members of the community. It is always a *give and take,* for its goal is that all may have the fullness of life, and this ideal can be mastered only in common. Ultimately, this means that one becomes a human person only by means of other human persons, as a proverb from West Africa says: "Life means sticking together—on your own, you are an animal."[80] Another proverb from Kenya says: "One who eats alone, dies alone (i.e., lonely)."[81] To die alone and lonely is the worst fate that can befall a person in Black Africa, since this means that he is totally extinguished: it is the community that guarantees one's identity. We have already discussed this question in detail in the first part of the present book. Here, we must examine another question, viz., the issue of individual freedom. If the decisions of conscience are dependent on the community, to what extent can one still speak of individual freedom?

This problem too has been discussed elsewhere,[82] and the present study clearly shows, in connection with the palaver procedure, how community and individual find expression, and how the individual retains his own identity, despite the communal dimension that he must always bear in mind. Here, therefore, we shall repeat and summarize only the most important points.

Africans never understand freedom independently of the community. I have often underlined the continual interaction between individual and community: the freedom and even the existence of the individual depend upon the freedom and existence of the community and visa versa. By contributing to the community *qua* community, the individual gives himself freedom. Africans understand freedom not only in the sense as freedom "from." It is at the same time freedom "for," but most importantly of all, it is freedom "with." Freedom does not only exist for me: it is for everyone, since I myself am free only when everyone is.[83] Here once more, we find the fundamental principle of African thinking: *I am because we are, and because we are, I am too.* This principle can be expressed by means of the principle *cognatus sum*: "I am related, therefore I am." A genuine relationship will always tend to grant others genuine human existence, and this includes freedom.[84] We may gain the impression from what has been said that the individual exists one-sidedly for the sake of the community, but Africans hold that the community is not allowed to crush the individual members. On the contrary, the community is obliged to grant them the space necessary for the unfolding of their personal existence.[85]

If we apply all this to the individual conscience, we may say that a conscience as ultimate authority (in the Western sense) does not exist. It is, however, possible to have one's own experience after a palaver, which in its turn will ultimately benefit the community. In other words, even where the conscience makes individual decisions, it must always have communitarian aspects, and must never lose sight of the good of the community.

It cannot be denied that a conscience which emphasizes the community in this way poses a number of questions that need to be discussed. We shall take this up in the following chapter.

CHAPTER 3

Critical Observation: The Challenge of Inculturation

AFTER THIS DETAILED DISCUSSION OF THE RELEVANCE OF AFRICAN cultures, above all with regard to the importance it assigns to the concept of community, we must now ask critically to what extent this tradition further developed. One who attempts to do theology in an African context is often confronted with critical questions on the part of Westerners who suspect that he is ultimately engaging in a "romantic" idealization of the culture, with insufficient attention to its dark aspects. The following observations seek to do justice to this concern, at least in part, by presenting clearly the negative elements in the African tradition and then asking whether these are outweighed by the positive elements. Finally, we shall also pose critical questions to the church's magisterium, and show the necessity of a dialogue between the church's authority and African tradition, if the process of establishing norms is to be fruitful.

Community and Structural Sin

My intention, in emphasizing the positive elements in the African community, was certainly not to canonize the ancestral tradition, since one must distinguish between the *ideal* and its *realization.* It is precisely this ideal that reminds the ethical subject that he often fails to live up to what is required, and that he is not entitled to be content with mediocrity. This ideal also demands that we speak of African sins: we must ask how these can be overcome, so as not to lose sight of the ideal.

Limits to the African Tradition

The significance attached to the community sometimes leads to the institutionalization of practices that make no real contribution to individual or group development. The criticisms below are meant only as examples. They do not pretend to deal exhaustively with the problems.

1. One urgent problem that has been much discussed in recent years is that of female circumcision. While it is true that this practice should be interpreted in the context of the religion of the community, and that it has its traditional place in the initiation rite, which aims to integrate both boys and girls into the clan fellowship, female circumcision, which is still carried out in some ethnic groups as the high point of this initiation (though in fact it is often completely detached from the traditional context), is exceptionally brutal. Unlike the circumcision of boys, female circumcision is a mutilation that carries to the point of absurdity another aspect of initiation, viz., the preparation for sexual life and also for sexual pleasure.[1] More and more voices, especially those of women, are raised today against this established tradition,[2] and one cannot continue such a practice without being guilty of oppression. This is a structure that despite its somewhat well-meaning intentions must in the final analysis be described as torture and consequently unjust.

In the traditional context, the circumcision of boys and girls was seen as one of several physically demanding and intellectual-spiritual exercises intended to teach young people that life consists not only of joy but also of suffering. The human person always lives in the tension between life and death. In circumcision, the conclusion and high point of the initiation rite, they were to learn to bear pain, so that they would be able to endure life's dark hours. Only this background can make sense of why Mzee Jomo Kenyatta defended the circumcision practice of the Gikuyu when the missionaries condemned it. He argued that the missionaries rejected female circumcision as barbaric only because they were unacquainted with the precise anthropological justification for this practice and reduced its entire significance to the biological and medical level, ignoring the factors that made it socially and psychologically meaningful.[3] When the missionaries urged the abolition of female circumcision, they had to be told that this would destroy the entire life of Gikuyu society.[4] Mzee J. Kenyatta's book attempts to justify this practice as something fundamental and non-negotiable for the Gikuyu.[5] This reaction shows the deeper meaning that female circumcision is thought to have among the

Gikuyu and in other ethnic groups, which are not willing to abandon the practice.

Nevertheless, the lifelong sufferings of circumcised women must prompt the question whether the significance these ethnic groups attach to circumcision, leading them to experience it as vitally important and as a source of meaning, could not be attached equally well to other symbols and practices without destroying the very core of their culture. Moreover, if Mzee J. Kenyatta is correct to say that it is forbidden for men from the Gikuyu tribe to marry women from ethnic groups which do not practice female circumcision,[6] this practice entails not only oppression and physical injury, but also an unacceptable discrimination which is ethnocentric. From the New Testament perspective, one must also ask how it is possible to reconcile this prescription, which displays contempt for human beings, with Jesus' criticism: "You abandon the commandment of God and observe human tradition" (Mark 7:8).

Another New Testament text speaks explicitly of male circumcision, as practiced in Judaism. This Pauline text, however, certainly does not justify female circumcision, especially given the grave harm the African practice inflicts. The law which Paul is discussing is not bad and his intention is not to condemn the law *qua* law, but rather to show that the Christ-event is incompatible with literal fidelity to the law that human beings have made: "In Christ Jesus, it is not important whether one is circumcised or uncircumcised, but only that one has the faith which is active in love" (Galatians 5:6). The Jewish circumcision law does not entail injury to human dignity; but the same cannot be said of female circumcision in Africa. It follows that the Christian faith must criticize this tradition and reject it unambiguously.

2. When speaking of the negative elements of African culture, we must also mention the problem of polygamy. This African tradition should *not* be considered automatically unjust and derogatory to human dignity, since the ideal could certainly preserve and promote a woman's dignity. Traditional polygamy has certainly protected women from prostitution.[7] Studies by cultural anthropologists have also shown greater stability in married life in those African societies which practice polygamy.[8] There is no lack of respect for women, where polygamy comes about with the permission of the first wife or even at her initiative. Mzee Jomo Kenyatta describes how among the Gikuyu the first wife urgently pleads with her husband to marry a second (third, fourth, . . .) wife, if she sees that this would help him. This lengthy, sincere pleading, expressed

voluntarily, attests to her love and concern for her husband. Besides this, it is the first wife who proposes the new wife, although she will tell her husband that he should look at the new wife and woo her.[9]

Nevertheless, we should note that polygamy today has virtually ceased to be interested in the ancestral ideal of many ethnic groups, in which the first wife held the most important position. The older and much more demanding form of polygamy is being replaced by a new form, which in reality no longer deserves the name of "polygamy" as the African tradition understands this term. This new form almost completely ignores the first wife. It is not interested in the unity of the extended family, for often the first wife does not even know about the existence of the second (or third) wife. This means the total disappearance of the covenant character of marriage, which was essential in traditional polygamy. This form of polygamy usually destroys both the nuclear family and the extended family. Some men appeal to ancestral tradition in justification, but this is a hollow pretext.

Even where the traditional ideal is observed, one must still ask whether it is compatible in modern Africa with the dignity of women. Among Christians, one must ask about its compatibility with the gospel of Jesus Christ. These urgent questions pose an inescapable challenge to African ethics: what does inculturation mean here?

3. A further cluster of problems concerns sorcery, which we have touched on above.[10] The sorcerer and sorceress who attempt to harm other people must be distinguished from the medicine man and woman who endeavor to protect them, and indeed the whole of society, from evil (both physical and intellectual-spiritual).[11] Sorcery is not simply "irrational," as is sometimes supposed in the West and by the Christian churches. Behind the visible element of magical thinking and practices there always lies something *not put into words.*[12] Belief in sorcery and magical practices is in fact the "commentary" and exegesis of an existential situation that is embedded in a broader system of social organization.

Traditional African societies have structures which prescribe certain interpersonal relationships which risk becoming inviolable ordinances: as soon as the conduct of a member of the family or clan calls the tradition into question, this person is suspected of being responsible for negative events in the life of the other members—illness, natural catastrophes, death, and so on. These suspicions and suppositions may not be based on the actual conduct of the alleged evildoer; they may have their origins long ago and may encompass the history of the entire family or clan fellowship. In other words, the tensions between two families or two clan fellowships can be handed on in such a way that they remain alive in the memory of succeeding generations.[13] Hence, it is possible that someone may be suspected of being a sorcerer merely because he belongs to a clan fellowship that has been regarded historically as suspicious or evil. Likewise, one may be a "sorcerer" simply because one's parents were sorcerers: some people are sorcerers without their active participation and even without knowing it.[14] The very presence of such a person disrupts the community and poisons human relationships by leading to tensions. In this context, we must also mention the problem of elderly persons in many ethnic groups. In the long term, their existence could be felt to be a burden, resulting in conflicts with the younger generation, who accuse elderly persons of being responsible for evils such as illness and other accidents and then call them sorcerers. The same can apply to a childless woman: she is suspected of harming children or even killing them. Clearly, the intention is to accuse her of jealousy, by alleging—often without the slightest evidence—that she envies other people's children.

We may sum up as follows: it is not possible to make ethical judgments about the idea and the practices of sorcery if one is ignorant of their individual, familial, and social background. The basic concern everywhere is with preserving an order of things laid down in tradition, which is disturbed by wrong attitudes, tensions, unforeseen events, or external social changes. The last point is especially important in modern Africa: the violence inflicted by what can only be called an assault on Black African culture has had serious social consequences. Modern Western lifestyles colonialize the lives of African people, destroying the equilibrium of the traditional ordering of life and depriving them of existential security. A member of the traditional community who enters this new, Western system cannot count on the support of his ethnic group or clan fellowship, since he represents a threat to them. Many community members fear that a son who works together with the "whites" or adopts the Western lifestyle will no longer honor the traditional African ordering of life. The elders of the community fear their sons will be corrupted by the Western lifestyle and lose respect for them. It goes without saying that this generates tremendous tensions within the community. This son's misfortunes will be interpreted from this perspective, both by him and by the members of his family. Both sides lack peace. If they are to recover harmony in their lives, they must be reconciled in accord with African tradition. On this view, all misfortunes involve someone who does not wish the family well; this person must be placated by an act of restitution.[15] In this way, one who is plagued by misfortune and illness hopes to be set free; this hope is, however, not always justified.[16]

In questions concerning sorcery, one must emphasize that here too the central point is its significance in the total life of the community, whose growth is hampered by individual deviation. The magical practices are intended to allow life to flourish in keeping with the established order. At the same time, however, we must point out that many practices do not aim at enhancing life, but have their roots (as we have just seen) in jealousy, envy, rivalry, and so on.

4. We must extend this argument to the problem of retaliatory actions, which occur frequently in Black Africa. In keeping with the principle that life is the highest good, it follows that whoever kills must himself be killed. This is not only a question of murder (i.e., an intentional killing); it seems that only the "material" dimension of the act counts here. Thus it can happen even today that a driver who, despite all his care, runs over a person is lynched on the spot by an enraged crowd. The underlying attitude is that one who kills a person, even unintentionally, inflicts harm on the clan fellowship of that person, which is deprived of some of its vital force by the death of a member; in a sense, the killer is a sorcerer, without being aware of this. It is believed that a retaliatory killing can make good the damage inflicted. The "sorcerers" (in the broadest sense of the word) who are involved in such cases are considered a threat to life, so that they must be "removed" from the community by death.

Among a number of ethnic groups—not among *all* Africans—the birth of twins is interpreted in a similar way.[17] It is believed that twins are abnormal and could bring misfortune to the community; they introduce confusion into the established order of creation. For this reason, they are rejected, or even killed, in some areas; their parents too are discriminated against and must submit to particular rites of purification.[18] Not only twins are thought to bring misfortune, however. The same fear is felt in relation to certain illnesses or physical changes. In Rwanda it was the custom to kill the *impenebere,* girls whose breasts regressed during puberty. This was done in the name of the community life, which could be harmed by such inexplicable phenomena. In other words, the atrophy of these girls' breasts made them involuntary enemies of life, like sorceresses who were unconscious of being such.

5. Another mistaken development in the African tradition is an exaggerated understanding of community, which severely limits the exercise of individual freedom. The clearest example is marriage. Despite the ideal presented above, where the community is obliged always to ensure the individual's free and full development, deviations in this sphere, in fact,

make a free consent to marriage difficult. Pressure from the group or the family can be so strong that an equally strong personality is required on the part of the candidates for marriage, if they are to prevail and be able to marry the wife or husband of their own choice. This means that the community sometimes breaks the rules of the palaver and imposes its own will on the children.

We must also recall here the problem of childless couples, which we have mentioned above. They can be exposed to community contempt to such a degree that their marriage breaks down.

6. Finally, we should not forget the modern "sins" of contemporary African society, which are committed precisely in the name of the traditional community. For example, one can observe almost everywhere today those who live a socially parasitic existence which was not found in *this* manner in the genuinely African tradition. It is, however, interesting to note that these people appeal precisely to the same tradition, that is, to the mentality of the extended family or to African hospitality. Above all in the big cities, there are increasing numbers of people who live free of charge with relatives, friends, or acquaintances for years on end and scarcely trouble to make a contribution to the domestic economy even through small tasks such as fetching water. This is indubitably an abuse of African hospitality; understood correctly, hospitality in Africa does not mean exploiting one's host. Rather, one who is a guest is allowed to rest for at most two days—on the third day he must start working. Julius Nyerere is right to underline that traditional Africa was unacquainted not only with the capitalist or the large landowner but also the social parasite who laid claim to hospitality without doing anything in return. The tradition would see such an existence as a great disgrace.[19] Nyerere continues:

> It would be good for those of us who talk about the African way of life, and are rightly proud of maintaining such an important element of this lifestyle as the traditional hospitality, to recall the Swaheli proverb: *Mgeni siku mbili; siku ya tatu mpe jembe:* "Treat your guest as a guest for two days, and give him a hoe on the third day!" Probably, the guest himself would ask for a hoe even before the host would have to give him one, since he knew what was expected of him and would have been ashamed to spend any longer lazing around.[20]

Today, where many people have lost this feeling of "shame," African society must rekindle it in them. State and church have the essential task of education in view of responsibility and solidarity in work. But how is all this to be done?

Mistaken Developments

The practices and attitudes listed above are no longer acceptable, despite their appeal to African tradition. In many cases, they are today considered incompatible with human dignity and contradict the ideal of the Christian message; further study of the African tradition also shows that they contradict the ideal of the ancestors, who aimed (and aim) by means of their statutes and traditions at the *fullness of life.* This is the ultimate basis even of those practices which may no longer be maintained today. This means that a more precise study of the African tradition makes it imperative to abolish the deviant forms and abuses of it.

If we take the example of female circumcision, we must note that, as I have remarked, one of the goals of female circumcision during initiation was to prepare girls for a life which requires courage: they must stand fast even in critical existential situations, in order that the community might not be deprived of its vital force. Today, based on knowledge of psychology and medicine, and the testimony of women concerned, we know—unlike the ancestors who introduced this practice—how terrible and harmful the circumcision of girls is. It is a crass contradiction of what the ancestors wanted, viz., a harmonious, healthy life for all. If the ancestors were alive today, their experience would forbid them to prescribe such a practice.

Today one who wishes to bestow life in fullness on African communities must find new paths in all those areas where traditional practices prove to be problematic. The basic underlying concern of the tradition must be preserved while at the same time taking the modern context into account. The African palaver culture could help here, since we know that not all ethnic groups have the same methods of initiation. This means, to continue with the example, that while female circumcision is not practiced universally, initiation rites everywhere intend to prepare young people, including women, for a hard life. In the endeavor to preserve the value of African initiation, one must hold a palaver to discuss thoroughly the various initiation practices south of the Sahara, in order to discover the best method to safeguard women's dignity. The church and its theologians cannot excuse themselves from this task, since it is not enough to declare a particular practice incompatible with the gospel or with human dignity; nor is it enough for outsiders to demand the abolition of female circumcision, since this will only generate aggression among those ethnic groups which see this practice as the realization of a deeper concern, viz., initiation into the correct way to deal with suffering and death. The Christian message must undoubtedly criticize the culture in such matters, but this can succeed only if it takes the positive concerns of the tradition seriously and points to a more promising alternative—for example, on the basis of the central position which the cross has in Christianity.[21]

These remarks about female circumcision apply *mutatis mutandis* to the problem of polygamy or of childless marriages. This question has been touched on briefly above,[22] and we add the following observations here. Polygamy too was institutionalized by our ancestors in the name of life, so that, for example, a childless *man* was given the possibility of having descendants. The traditional polygamy was not merely negative, from a purely social perspective, since it could certainly provide protection to women.[23] From today's perspective, taking the dignity of women seriously, we see that the fullness of life—at which the ancestors aimed—can no longer be attained by means of polygamy. The ancestors themselves would be the first to resist this practice today, because it no longer corresponds to their ideal. Modern life is fundamentally different from that of the tradition. For example, it was normal, perhaps even necessary, to have a large number of children in the social context of earlier times; this compensated for infant mortality and provided a source of labor and security in old age. Besides this, the education of children was the task of the extended family, since geographical factors made contact with other members of the clan fellowship much easier. Family bonds are still solid today, but living conditions make education of children in common more difficult, since modern lifestyles often require family members to live far apart.

Above all, families must consider carefully how many children they wish to have. One factor here is the modern school system: for even where solidarity in education still exists, this is a much more demanding matter than in the tradition. If children are to continue an effective system of family solidarity as adults, they need an education that equips them to deal with modern life—but this does not come gratis. One who has many children, who are unequipped to meet the demands of modern life, ultimately condemns them to death, since he robs them of their vital force. This means that he is acting against the original intention of the ancestors, who wanted life in fullness for the community and all its members.

The same applies to women who are *compelled* to live in a polygamous marriage. One should employ the traditional palaver culture to permit these women to express the extent to which they suffer under the polygamous marriage which is forced upon them. It is usually the husbands who initiate such a marriage, and this contradicts the *ideal* of traditional polygamy, which was much more demanding than the modern version.[24]

One voice representing many is that of Georgette Odi Assamoi, whose "shout" deserves to be quoted in full, in order to make the point clearly:

> Has there been any attempt to investigate even slightly the heart of African women when they are confronted with polygamy? Has anyone tried to imagine what happens in the heart of the wife of a polygamous man when he is lying legally in the arms of another woman, her fellow-wife? Has anyone tried to imagine the inner feelings of this woman who has spent her young years with a man who is as old as she is, but now quite legally shares his bed with a girl no older than the first wife's children—while she herself is getting older, exposed to the fears of the menopause, spending her nights alone with no one to share her nightly terrors?[25]

This text is a dramatic appeal to the male-dominated community to thoroughly revise its position on polygamy. The palaver culture must help all participants, including women, to examine their consciences; this means that the admonition about polygamy will not be limited to the men but in some cases applies to women also. The "secondary wife" in the situation which Odi Assamoi laments may not be entirely innocent. On the contrary, many women consciously enter into marriage with a man who is already married, although they know what this will mean for his wife. In such cases, we must conclude that women share the responsibility for the suffering of other women, their "sisters." This question too, which is often overlooked in the discussion about polygamy, should be discussed openly in a palaver culture.

Another negative element that urgently needs correction is undoubtedly the African attitude to sorcery. The concern for life becomes most evident in this sphere. The fundamental intention of sorcery is to draw attention to evil, which can totally destroy human relationships, and hence the entire community; this positive intention should be interpreted anew in a Christian ethic, so that exaggerated beliefs in sorcery can be corrected by its understanding of evil. The way to do this is not to deny or ignore the existence of sorcerers and sorceresses.

As I have said, sorcery aims to destroy the traditional order, leading to tensions within the community. Unkindness plays a central role here: these tensions are maintained by hatred, jealousy, greed—in short by the evil that lies hidden in the human heart. This, however, means that ultimately everyone is a potential sorcerer. As soon as the evil breaks out, it "eats up" human life. Belief in sorcery, which sometimes leads to attacks against innocent persons and often casts unjustified suspicions, was originally intended to protect life, broadly understood. Doing justice to the original safeguarding function of sorcery must be emphasized so that people are persuaded to love and commit themselves to universal peace.

This means the dismantling of envy, hatred, lustfulness, all kinds of discriminations, baseless suspicions, and so on, so that all may live in harmony, free of strife. Only in this way can one expect the life in fullness which the ancestors promised.

In Christian terms, it is sin that makes a person a sorcerer or sorceress. Faith in Jesus Christ leads one to fight against sorcery, since the exalted Lord has become the supreme healer, who never destroys life, but gives it in fullness. Healing from "sorcery" by Jesus Christ never happens automatically, independently of the human person's own contribution: it presupposes a willingness to be reconciled with one's enemies. Here too, we find points of contact in the African tradition itself; as we have seen, the expression of conflicts in the palaver always ends with a rite of reconciliation. Christian ethics can take this up and develop it, appealing to its own message of reconciliation. This would be a decisive challenge to the practice of killing those who unintentionally kill others. Here, the tradition must be corrected, to make it clear that life does not grow by means of retaliatory measures: only reconciliation, as the path to forgiveness, can promote life in fullness.

One must argue in the same way against the practice of killing twins. As we have seen, this killing—or at least the negative attitude to the birth of twins—aimed at protecting the life of the entire community. But alongside this attitude, we find in many other ethnic groups a positive acceptance of twins. These groups do not believe that twins represent a threat to life but see them as a blessing and a sign of God's omnipotence. The twins themselves are treated with great respect, since they embody this special power; their parents share in this honor too.[26] This attitude to twins is to be applauded. It makes it extremely urgent to hold a cultural palaver among Africans in which various ethnic groups can enrich one another with the positive elements in their own understanding of life. Only such an exchange of experiences, which ought initially to be restricted to Africans, can help to exorcise these negative elements and make life (in the broadest sense) possible for all Africans.

This principle of life which we have emphasized is also very important in view of the modern sins in Africa. A typical example can be seen in the abuses of power of many heads of state. In the name of the Western understanding of private property, they enrich themselves at the expense of the people; at the same time, they also appeal falsely to the African tradition, which grants a chief greater possessions. The reason for this practice in traditional Africa is, however, that the chief must be able to share his possessions with the people, so that they can have life in fullness. A chief who takes these for his own private use incurs guilt, and it would be the people's duty to depose him. This is the modern sin of many heads of state today, who avoid their traditional obligations in the name of a Western understanding of their rights. There are also male and female politicians who fill their own pockets, but instead of thinking of the people as a whole, they share only with the members of their clan fellowship. Here the clan fellowship plunders the country. This offends against the traditional principle of life whereby even a foreigner has a right to life, since (as we have said) he too is *Muntu-wa-Bende-wa-Mulopo,* "human person from Bende from God." Egotistic self-enrichment, corruption, and nepotism withhold life from the people as a whole, and this is precisely the opposite of the tradition of the ancestors.

The same applies to a parasitic existence that falsely appeals to the urban lifestyle to justify sponging off one's relatives, acquaintances, or friends. Such persons must be reminded of the traditional value of work. The community, in all its three dimensions, can grow in life only when all people—even the guests—endeavor to bear their share of the family work. This fundamental African principle, derived from the tradition, is also a challenge to the modern state to ensure that all its citizens can find work. Thus, one of the main concerns of the state must be the fight against unemployment, so that all have enough to live on. This will remove the temptation to live as parasites.

The last modern sin we must mention is today's ethnic conflicts, which lead to all-out war or even to genocide. This contradicts the African tradition, which attached great value to the rites of reconciliation even in the case of a war. These rites ensured that today's genocide could not take place. Thanks to colonialism and Christianity, the feeling grew that these rites were primitive or even magical, and people in Africa were urged to abandon them. The result was a collapse of the African universe of meaning. Instead of resolving their problems through the palaver and the rites of reconciliation, which often led to alliances with the groups that had been their enemies, people today resort at once to immensely powerful weapons which do not bestow life, but make possible mass annihilation. This makes it all the more urgent to reflect once more on the good tradition and to recall the rites of reconciliation which the ancestors institutionalized on the basis of solid reflection and of their own experience. Even where these rites cannot be taken over literally, it ought to be possible to find inspiration in their spirit. Christianity encounters a treasure here that is a precious aid in the inculturation of its own message of reconciliation.

These brief remarks, which have drawn particular attention to the negative element of the African concept of community, do not intend to play down the preponderantly good traits. Many elements of the ancestral tradition represent a genuine challenge to today's society, and especially to the church, to question elements of its own practice. The process by which norms are established in the palaver is important here, since this leads to a new understanding of authority in laying down norms.

THE MAGISTERIUM AND THE AUTHORITY OF THE PALAVER

A comparison between the procedure of the magisterium and that of the palaver in ethical questions does not mean a confrontation between these two models; rather, we shall argue in this section that the understanding of authority on the part of the magisterium must let itself be critically enriched and inculturated with the help of the African model. Only when this work has been carried out, can we hope for a moral theology, inspired by Christianity, which will succeed in bringing the gospel to people in Africa. We begin with the claim that the magisterium makes with regard to the clarification of ethical questions for Catholic believers, and then we take up the palaver model.

The Magisterium in Ethical Questions

Naturally, we cannot offer here even a rough discussion of a problem of such complexity as the competence of the magisterium in moral questions; this has been the object of many relevant studies, and I refer the reader to these authors.[27] We shall discuss here only a few aspects of the claim made by the magisterium, namely, those that are potentially relevant to a comparison with the African understanding in the palaver process.

The doctrine of the competence of the magisterium in moral questions found an extreme formulation in the First Vatican Council:

> When the Roman bishop speaks *ex cathedra,* i.e. when he exercises his office as pastor and teacher of all Christians and decides on the basis of his supreme apostolic authority that a doctrine of faith or morals must be held fast by the whole church, then he possesses—thanks to the divine assistance which was promised to him in blessed Peter—that infallibility which the divine Redeemer wished to bestow on his church in the definition of the doctrine of faith or morals; for this reason, such definitions of the Roman bishop are of themselves immutable, not thanks to assent on the part of the church. (*DH* 3074)

A. Auer suggested in 1971 that the word pair *fides et mores* is very ancient, going back to the New Testament, and he said that a historical investigation of the development of this term was urgently necessary.[28] This study has since been carried out, and two dissertations deserve special mention.[29] The result of Josef Schuster's research is interesting here: he holds that ethical norms for behavior in relation to noninfallible doctrine are not "the *mystērion* of the faith," nor can they "be deduced from propositions of the faith." If one considers their logical structure, they are "synthetic a posteriori judgments." Schuster writes: "They may contain as implicit elements an ethical evaluation and non-ethical judgments about values and facts. For a judgment about facts, professional competence is required, and the genuine authority of the church and its magisterium in communicating the faith does not bestow such a competence upon the church."[30] This means that the specific task of "drawing up a list of preferential values" does not belong exclusively to the church, or to the magisterium, or to scholarship, nor does it belong to any one group within society. This is because it involves a variety of anthropological, cultural, and economic presuppositions. If there is indeed anything in the field of *mores* that is immediately derived from the Christian faith (*fides*), then it is the *et* in the word pair *fides et mores*—not in the sense of a mere addition ("faith and also morals") but consequentially ("faith and therefore morals").[31] We must, however, face the fact that current teaching is not content with distinguishing between "addition" and "consequence," but seems to extend the competence of the magisterium to cover the entire sphere of ethics.

Some Statements of the Magisterium about Doctrinal Competence

We should note that Vatican II gave greater precision to the teaching of Vatican I, and that it considers infallibility in questions of ethics as coterminous with "the deposit of divine revelation" (*LG* 25).[32] The Pastoral Constitution *Gaudium et spes* draws clear inferences from this: "The Church is guardian of the heritage of the divine Word and draws religious and moral principles from it, but she does not always have the answer to every question. Still, she is eager to associate the light of revelation with the experience of mankind in trying to clarify the course upon which mankind has just entered" (*GS* 33). This statement bids farewell to the monologue and opens the way to a dialogue in which each partner listens to the other, and professional knowledge provides the orientation.[33]

Joseph Ratzinger pointed out in 1970 that while the three colleges of "community, presbyterate, and episcopate" cannot "be reduced to parliamentary models, there nevertheless exist *relationships.*"[34] He draws attention to the teaching of Cyprian in the patristic period, where the three-dimensional character of dialogue in the church is clearly emphasized. On the one hand, he admonishes that nothing should be done without the bishop (*nihil sine episcopo*); on the other hand, he tells his presbyterate very directly that he too can do nothing without their counsel (*nihil sine consilio vestro*); but it is just as important that one do nothing without the consent of the people (*nihil sine consensu plebis*).[35] Ratzinger remarks: "The classical model of ecclesial democracy lies in this threefold form of collaboration in building up the community. This is derived not from a meaningless transposition of models that are in fact alien to the church, but from the inner structure of the ecclesial *order* itself. This is why it is appropriate to the specific demands made by the church's essence."[36]

It is a pity that many postconciliar statements by the magisterium have not maintained the principle of dialogue; a particularly glaring example of this was the publication of the encyclical *Humanae vitae,* where the majority opinion in the ad hoc commission was ignored. Other documents too seem to invoke the authority of the magisterium rather than emphasizing listening to and struggling with one another to find what is right within the fellowship of the church as a whole. Thus, the Congregation for the Doctrine of the Faith underlines the infallibility of the magisterium "in matters of faith and morals" (*fides et mores*) and follows *Humanae vitae* in affirming that "the competence of the magisterium also extends to that which concerns the natural law."[37] "Revelation also contains moral teachings" which the natural reason can discover; but "access to them is made difficult by man's sinful condition." This instruction emphasizes, in accord with the teaching of the First Vatican Council,[38] that: "It is a doctrine of the faith that these moral norms can be infallibly taught by the magisterium" (*DV* 16). Further, when the bishops in fellowship with the successor of Peter affirm in the exercise of their authentic teaching office a doctrine which is not declared to be either infallible or binding, consent in "religious obedience" is required.[39] This category of truths involves neither the *doctrina de fide credenda* nor the doctrine *de fide tenenda,* but the teaching that is proposed by the pope or the college of bishops as *true,* or at least as *certain,* so that "one may not safely teach" the opposite.[40] The instruction *Donum veritatis* adds: "The documents issued by this Congregation expressly approved by the Pope participate in the ordinary magisterium of the successor of Peter" (*DV* 18). This means that one is obliged to receive such documents with "religious obedience."

It is striking that *Donum veritatis* has so much to say about the fellowship of the bishops and the pope, but says nothing about the rest of the faithful—although they too are involved in the process of discovering the truth, as the words of *Lumen gentium* imply: "The whole body of the faithful who have an anointing that comes from the holy one (cf. 1 John 2:20, 27) cannot err in matters of belief. This is shown in the supernatural appreciation of the faith [*sensus fidei*] of the whole people, when, 'from the bishops to the last of the faithful,' they manifest a universal consent in matters of faith and morals" (*LG* 12). For when the people "spread abroad a living witness to Christ, especially by a life of faith and love," they share in the *prophetic* ministry of Jesus Christ (see ibid.). Although the Congregation for the Doctrine of the Faith does not attach any emphasis to this dimension of the people of God in the instruction *Donum veritatis,* it does at least mention the possibility in some cases of a dialogue between the magisterium and theologians (see *DV* 25, 40). The Congregation speaks with reserve on this point, perhaps envisaging it only in cases of emergency; but it is precisely such a dialogue—not least in view of the African palaver—that must be developed. All the partners must act in the spirit of the gospel and make the one truth in Jesus Christ their goal.

This must involve above all the third category of truths, which are neither infallible nor definitive, and which can be extremely important *in rebus moralibus.*[41] Such a dialogue would introduce some nuances into the affirmation of the encyclical *Fides et ratio* about inculturation: "In engaging great cultures for the first time, the church cannot abandon what she has gained from her inculturation in the world of Greco-Latin thought. To reject this heritage would be to deny the providential plan of God who guides his church down the paths of time and history" (*FR* 72). Although this refers primarily to India, and Africa is only mentioned *en passant* (see ibid.), the palaver model could offer a significant contribution by showing that the one revelation in Jesus Christ cannot be reduced to one particular philosophical system. The encyclical itself notes: "In preaching the gospel, Christianity first encountered Greek philosophy, but this does not mean that all other approaches are precluded" (ibid.). If it is indeed true that no culture is excluded by revelation, this path should be pursued without wavering (see *FR* 71), bearing in mind that one must emphasize not only the negative and sinful aspects of the various cultures but also their positive aspects, which invite a genuine inculturation of the gospel (see ibid.). But before we discuss these questions, let us consider briefly what some theologians have to say about the teaching competence of the magisterium.

The Positions of Some Theologians on the Competence of the Magisterium

If a fruitful dialogue is to take place between theology and the magisterium, it must be assumed that both belong, each in its own way, to the pilgrim church, the people of God on its wanderings, which is not yet in possession of the promised land. The kingdom of God has not yet been fully realized.[42]

This means that both theologians and the magisterium must be aware of their limitations and their imperfection, as M. Löhrer rightly affirms: "The magisterium and theologians must remember above all that *listening* has priority over *teaching*. Listening is understood here to mean fundamentally a listening to the Word of God in the contemporary situation."[43] Although the magisterium has the task of explaining the Word of God in a binding manner, the Second Vatican Council says with unmistakable clarity that it is not "over the Word of God"; this is a service, and the magisterium may not teach anything other than "that which is handed down" (*see DV* 10). It must be equally clear that the theologian likewise is under the Word of God, although he does not expound it in the same binding manner as the magisterium; and the fact that both are bound to the Word necessarily implies that they *listen to one another.* Löhrer continues: "This kind of 'listening to one another' includes an element of mutual criticism, in a positive sense. This 'critical element' will be more readily understood if one remembers the inherent unity between listening to the *Word* and reflection on the concrete *situation* which the Word addresses."[44] Each partner needs the other, and neither can refuse to take part in the dialogue, since each must learn from the other. Doubtless theology, as the science of faith, can be carried out only as an ecclesial service; to detach itself from the church would result in the opposite of what theology genuinely intends to do, viz., to strengthen or renew the community of faith. On the other hand, the magisterium too must take seriously the endeavors and the results of theological research.

In this context, Max Seckler has drawn attention to the function of theology "in state, church, and society" in the Middle Ages.[45] Seckler offers an interpretation of a picture by an unknown master (ca. 1520) depicting Thomas Aquinas's authority as theological master and concludes that the painting's inclusion of the emperor and the pope among those who listen to Thomas "intends to say something about the task of theology and its role in society." The state and church learn from the theologian here in such a way that one can say: "The teaching office belongs to theology."[46] Thomas exemplifies the understanding of theology in the Middle Ages, which ought to be valid today too. "It is not a question of 'freeing' theology from the church and the magisterium. But it is difficult for those with authority for the official and public proclamation of the faith to continue to consider themselves 'free' vis-à-vis the results of theological research and teaching. Theology and church must be capable of dialogue in the framework of universal rationality."[47]

However, the greatest obstacles to a fruitful dialogue come from the church's magisterium itself, which appeals a priori to lapidary formulations which justify and defend its own authority, giving the impression that the magisterium perhaps speaks too much and listens too little. In the eschatological tension between "already" and "not yet," people wish to experience not only the "already" but also the "not yet." In other words, they wish to experience the church—even in its magisterium —as a body that genuinely *seeks,* though ultimately this body can trust to the sure guidance of the Holy Spirit.[48] There can be no question of employing parliamentary procedures to define the faith; even so, the texts from Cyprian quoted above show clearly that the magisterium is no autocracy.[49] If the church commits itself actively in favor of human dignity, solidarity, subsidiarity, human rights, and so on, it cannot lag behind the ideal that it itself proclaims. At the very least, it must be clear that the church is endeavoring to attain this ideal.[50]

The problem of dialogue today concerns in a particular manner the relationship between the magisterium and moral theology. The problem was posed most clearly and acutely in the discussion of *Humanae vitae.* The theologians ask whether, in view of the responsibility of "the personal human being" and of "the mutability of earthly realities" the magisterium can make authoritative and binding moral claims.[51] One must also inquire whether the moral solutions offered by the magisterium pay sufficient heed to today's multicultural world, especially with regard to the non-Western peoples. Josef Fuchs has pointed out here that the pastors of the church must ensure that "all arbitrariness" is excluded "from the way Christians structure their lives": the life of a Christian must be in harmony with the gospel. This does not, however, mean that the pastors have a definitive (or universal) solution to all moral questions.[52]

Fuchs notes that even Jesus in his moral teaching did not venture to lay down universal norms that would be applicable to all times and cultures. Jesus did indeed criticize contemporary deviations and errors, in accordance with existing moral prescriptions, and he drew attention to the significance of interior attitudes; "but he was far from teaching a moral code for correct inner-worldly behavior, different from the code accepted at that time, or even a perpetual code laying down all correct human conduct in this world for all times and in all cultures. He—the Son from

Nazareth—could not do so." Nor did Paul behave differently from Jesus. The proclamation of the gospel of Jesus Christ did not prevent him from respecting existing ethical norms and insisting on them anew in the light of the Good News; but in responding to practical questions in the life of the community he did not intend to provide definitive answers that would apply to the whole future course of history. We may sum up by saying that Jesus and Paul were interested in the problems of their own period, but "they do not elaborate a 'Christian' moral theology on particular issues which would be valid for all history. This is how ethical leadership (the 'ministry') in the Christian community, in the church, began."[53]

These acute observations by J. Fuchs suggest that the church's magisterium ought to bear in mind the distinction that the Pastoral Letters make between *parathēkē* ("deposit") and *didaskalia* ("teaching"). We find the first concept in 1 Timothy 6:20 and 2 Timothy 1:14.[54] In his very convincing analysis of these passages, Gerhard Lohfink concludes: "The *parathēkē* is substantially identical with the gospel," and this is the "decisive" element that "constitutes the church." "It is the gospel—in the specific sense that the gospel was entrusted by God to the church, and must be preserved inviolate until the return of Christ." The concept of *didaskalia* is found at 1 Timothy 1:10, 2 Timothy 4:3, and Titus 1:9; 2:1. According to Lohfink, the exegesis of this concept in the Pastoral Letters shows that it refers to the totality of that which is guaranteed by the authority of Paul *qua* apostle: this totality is now to be found as the apostle's bequest in the three Pastoral Letters. Although the *didaskalia* must be connected with the *parathēkē,* it is not simply to be equated with the gospel. "Apart from the gospel, it is the totality of the teaching that Paul has bequeathed to the church."[55] If this is correct, then the same distinction must apply to the magisterium of the church today; while it is absolutely necessary to preserve the "deposit" (*parathēkē*), the way in which it is proclaimed can change.[56] It ought therefore to be possible to discuss the *didaskalia* of the magisterium with all respect. As a minimum requirement, the magisterium ought to enter into a dialogue with other believers before the *didaskalia* is declared to be truly a "bequest."

We have spoken up to this point primarily of the magisterium and theologians, but the dialogue should not be limited to those with "professional competence." The entire people of God should participate in the discussion, as the magisterium's dialogue partner. This problem also affects academic theology, which risks speaking in the place of the people and reducing nontheologians to silence. Dietrich Wiederkehr is right to say that the acceptance of other voices and the recognition of their theological relevance would be healthy for theology and the magisterium: "The *sensus fidei* of the entire people of God calls into question every monopoly on the truth, both that of the magisterium and that of the scholars."[57] If the church is the community of believers, one must avoid the impression that faith is discussed and lived only by an elite. Many members of the people of God have not yet been given any possibility of participating in the process whereby ethical norms are established; it seems that, despite *Lumen gentium* 12, the *sensus fidei* of the people is not taken seriously. Only when the various *sensus fidei* (in the plural) are taken seriously and are allowed to encounter one another "in the palaver" will it be possible to arrive at a *con-sensus.*[58]

Something similar can be said about the various cultures and the local churches. Where we hear of a "consensus," this often denotes only very limited, "regional" agreements, mostly affecting Europe, which are then extended without any dialogue to the entire church in every culture.[59] This leads to conflicts in non-Western churches and to tensions between the magisterium and the local churches. In the case of Africa, the theology of marriage or the matter of the eucharistic sacrament is an example. From an African perspective, the palaver model tries to tackle the problems in a different manner from the West, aiming at the elaboration of an ecclesiology that is rooted in the local culture and prefers a different procedure in questions of *fides et mores.* This implies not an antithesis but a complement—and this can already be sensed in a number of new approaches by Western theologians. It is only here that the entire project can be carried out consistently in the framework of the world of African thought.

The Palaver as a Complementary Practice

Before suggesting a complementary model to the magisterium, it is important to return briefly to what we have said above.[60] Particular importance attaches here to awareness of the function of the word, for otherwise one cannot understand completely the African palaver praxis.

The Role of the Word in the Palaver

All the palaver genres listed in part 1 give clear expression to the dependence of individual and communal life on dealings with the word. On this point, people in Africa feel very close to the biblical message: the word is understood in the Bible as genuinely accomplishing what it was sent to do. The creation narrative is ultimately based on the power of the word: "And God said: 'Let there be light'; and there was light" (Genesis 1:3; see also Psalm 33:6–9). The prophet Isaiah emphasizes this power even more clearly, when God says: "As the rain and the snow come down from heaven, and return not thither but water the earth, making it bring forth and sprout, giving seed to the sower and bread to the eater, so shall my word be that goes forth from my mouth; it shall not return to me empty, but it shall accomplish that which I purpose, and prosper in the thing for which I send it" (Isaiah 55:10–11). The New Testament also shows us the power of God's word. Jesus often performs miracles by speaking, so that the centurion in Capernaum can say: "Lord, I am not worthy to have you come under my roof; but only say the word, and my servant will be healed" (Matthew 8:8; cf. John 4:46b–53). The Letter to the Hebrews calls the word of God "living and active, sharper than any two-edged sword, piercing to the division of soul and spirit, of joints and marrow, and discerning the thoughts and intentions of the heart" (Hebrew 4:12).

People in Africa feel a deep affinity to all these texts. The word in Black Africa is seen in close connection with chewing, eating, ruminating, and digesting. *Hearing* too is extremely important, since it is only the one who hears the word that can also chew it, eat it, ruminate and digest it. Louis-Vincent Thomas has pointed out that the Dogon in Mali compare the ear with the mouth and the eardrum with the teeth, indicating the necessity of eating and chewing the word.[61] Special emphasis is laid on the resemblance between the ear and the sexual organs, above all those of women: as the woman's sexual organ receives the male seed, so that this may be transformed into life, so the ear receives the word which is equipped with seed, in order to transform it into life.[62]

Recall our remarks about the significance of the chief's ears among the Manja in the Central African Republic. Because of its big ears, the hare is the totem of the Manja chief, who ought to have large ears like a hare, to bring him closer to God, the ancestors, and the people. This, however, means that the chief must pay attention to everything that happens in the community. Above all, he is obliged to receive everything by patient *listening* and then to try to digest it well. Being a good *listener* and digesting the word are linked in general in Black Africa to the chief, since he is the link between God or the ancestors and the people; and this function is to be exercised not in a solitary manner but in close collaboration with the council of elders. He is the last to speak, after having carefully examined all the aspects of a problem and digested the word well. But first he must propose his own word for debate, at least in the palaver of the elders.

In other words, the word must be made available for rumination.[63] In this connection, we have also mentioned the Bambara in Mali, who speak of the immensity of the word, which is not only something sacred but embraces the whole of humanity. When it is spoken, it is healthy and *healing.* The Bambara raise an important point here, which we shall take up later in connection with the magisterium, namely, that the word cannot be monopolized by a single individual; it is too much for one mouth. The word is not a private possession, but belongs to all humankind.

It follows that any one person can possess only a small part of the word. Accordingly, each individual must be willing to share with others, for only so can he come closer to the depth of a word. Precisely this is the meaning of the palaver in Black Africa.[64] Although we have already spoken of the African palaver procedure, it is important to mention some of its practical aspects here.

In addition, the word must prove its innocence before being put at the service of humanity. The aim of the palaver is not to dazzle or lead the participants astray by rhetoric. Rather, the community seeks a good and correct word, testing its capacity to heal and to build up the community. People in the palaver are like ruminants: they must again chew a word that was received, eaten, or drunk long ago, before it can be transformed into flesh and blood. This means that the word of the individual is tested, so that the entire community can either confirm or reject it based on whether it is good or life-giving. In short, the African palaver is the place where various words are compared, to see whether they have been well received, chewed, and digested, so that they may not bring harm to the community.[65] This in turn presupposes that not only the chief but all the other participants in the palaver have large, broad ears and that they distinguish themselves as listeners before they speak. When they speak, they must be willing to share the word with other members of the palaver, since it is too large and wide for the mouth of one individual.

The whole procedure implies that each member is aware that there is a reciprocal begetting and giving birth in the palaver: for if the word has seed, and the ear can be compared to the sexual organs, this means that the acts of speaking and hearing can be compared to the acts of begetting and conceiving and giving birth. A good and correct word to which one listens well, a word correctly chewed and digested, is constitutive of the human person. In the African context, this means that each human being has "two genders": one is both man and woman. Thanks to the analogy of mouth, ear, and sexual organs, the man who speaks or listens and digests the word is simultaneously a begetter and conceiver who gives birth to life, just like the woman, who is likewise a begetter and conceiver who gives birth. This has nothing to do with homosexuality. It is of course possible to assert that a sexual relationship between two men or two women has a basis in African anthropology, since each human person has two genders to a large degree, so that sexuality need not necessarily be expressed through the encounter between a man and a woman; but such an interpretation would not do justice to African anthropology. The word through which a mutual begetting and giving birth takes place is not limited to two persons or only some members of the community, but embraces the community in its totality. As I have shown, this totality concerns the three-dimensional nature of the community, in regard to the living, the dead, and those not yet born. Only in this three-dimensional reality does the word exercise its communitarian function fully, for here too the word is much too large and wide for the community of the living and the dead alone—it must be shared with an even more comprehensive community, viz., with that of those as yet unborn. Only when the word extends to *this* community does it disclose its extraordinary life-giving dynamic and power to the full.

On the other hand, it is also clear that this community of the unborn can be reached only by a loving exchange of words between man and woman. This confirms that it is ultimately the word that constitutes the humanity of the human being in all three dimensions, once this word loses its poisonous character and allows its healing and beneficent dimension to appear. According to the African understanding, this is possible only where the word is not monopolized, but is chewed and shared in the community.

All this leads to the question whether the ecclesial community could learn from the way Black Africans handle the word. At any rate, the Christian communities in Africa expect that their tried and tested palaver tradition will be allowed to make its own contribution to the church's reflections on all the questions of *fides et mores.* They do not wish to articulate their *sensus fidei* otherwise than in the African context.

The Church's Magisterium and the African Palaver Model

One of the fruits of the Roman Synod on Africa in 1994 was the wish of the synodal fathers and mothers that the church in Africa be looked on as a family.[66] This word must not be understood in the Western sense of a nuclear family. In Kiswahili, one would speak of *jamaa,* a much more comprehensive expression covering all the relatives of the extended family,[67] which itself includes the living, the dead, and those not yet born. To these we must add all who belong to this three-dimensional community by means of a covenant in blood. It must be borne in mind that the family in the African sense, the *jamaa,* lives from the word of one common ancestor: the word he bequeathed is central to the community. This is not, however, followed blindly, without holding a palaver; it is subject to a constant process of interpretation. In order that it may be faithfully observed, the interpretation of the individual members is examined with care in the palaver, to determine whether the inherited word has been understood aright, that is, whether it has been properly heard, chewed, and digested. I believe it to be indubitable that this model could benefit the church too, which ought to accept inspiration from this source.

A genuinely African model of the church must necessarily have recourse to the idea of the ancestors. The concept of a founding ancestor who keeps together the community of the living, the dead, and those not yet born, resembles the Old Testament idea that the assembly of the Lord (*qahal Yahweh*) is ultimately derived from the tribal organization. The "twelve tribes of Israel" (Genesis 49:1–28; Deuteronomy 33) who form the people of Yahweh have only one founding father, namely, Abraham, the model of obedience and of faith in the God whose promises he receives. It is the covenant between God and Abraham that has made Israel God's people.[68] The New Testament develops the idea of "God's people": Jesus called an inner circle, "the Twelve," and had intense contact with them (Mark 3:14; Luke 6:12f.). The Twelve stand symbolically for the twelve tribes of Israel. By reestablishing the people of twelve tribes in the new covenant, Jesus shows that he is the founding father of the eschatological Israel, which one day is to include all peoples (see Luke 10:1–20). Siegfried Wiedenhofer comments:

> By choosing the "twelve" for fellowship with the messianic messenger and for participating in his activity of gathering people together, Jesus posits a highly symbolic sign. "Twelve" was the number of the tribes of Israel, but de facto only two and a half tribes still existed (Judah, Benjamin, and half of Levi); the reestablishment of the people with all twelve tribes was expected only in the era of salvation. Thus, by means of this symbolic action, Jesus reveals himself to be the founding father of the eschatological Israel.[69]

When the movement of gathering people together which Jesus had initiated takes place in specific, multicultural communities, this includes "the totality of Israel and of the human race"[70] in such a way that the human race becomes the new Israel in the community founded by Jesus. All this means that Jesus takes the place of Abraham: he is the new Abraham. Just as Abraham founded the people of Israel, so Jesus founds a new people, that is, a new community consisting of those who believe in him.

From a Black African perspective, this means that Jesus founds a new clan fellowship and is himself its founding ancestor, who thus combines in himself the roles of ancestor and father of the tribe. Through his death and resurrection, however, he infinitely transcends both Abraham's role as ancestor and father of the tribe, and the African concept of ancestors. Jesus is not simply the primal or founding ancestor, but the proto-ancestor, and this means that he alone initiates the eschatological dimension of the living, the dead (i.e., the living dead), and those not yet born.

As far as African ecclesiology is concerned, I believe that we find in the New Testament not only the model of Christ as "brother" but also another trajectory that points to Christ (the new Abraham) as "father," and would make possible a new model of the church. If Christ can be called "father of the tribe" and "proto-ancestor," then the pope and bishops must give up their claims to the title "father." As representatives of the "twelve tribes" of a new Israel, they are all brothers.

This is not intended to call into question the legitimacy of the doctrine of the Second Vatican Council, when *Lumen gentium,* the Dogmatic Constitution on the Church, describes the relationship between priests and their bishop as that of *sons* (and friends) to their *father* (see *LG* 28). Nevertheless, the model of "brothers" at which the New Testament hints seems to correspond better to Black African realities. This will also lead to a new understanding of church and hierarchy, for if the African sense of family is taken as the basis of ecclesial life, with Christ as the father of the tribe and proto-ancestor and the bishops (including the pope) as brothers, then the palaver is an essential instrument for keeping all the members together: all decisions must be made in common. Here the pope is the oldest son who has received from the father of the tribe the commission to administer the common inheritance, that is, the church, together with his other brothers. The "older brother" and "older sister" do not possess any emphatically hierarchical authority in Black Africa; rather, they bear responsibility for younger brothers and sisters. This responsibility means that they are always available to their siblings. The wisdom of the oldest brother or sister will be acknowledged only when they consistently respect and listen to the wisdom of their siblings, and this is precisely the model on which an ecclesiology inculturated in Africa draws in its reflections on the pope. It is indeed his task to strengthen his brothers and sisters in the faith, but he may never take a solitary decision without a "palaver" with other local churches and cultures.

The pope, as oldest brother, may never intervene in the affairs of the local churches without a fraternal dialogue, since this would contradict the African palaver procedure, in which the function of the word must be examined by the community. A one-sided decision would mean putting one's confidence in a word digested by only one individual, without requiring it to prove its innocence and capacity to serve the community. The wisdom of the Manja is helpful here: the chief must have large and broad ears, and he must listen well before he speaks. When he speaks, his word in turn must be confirmed in the community. What applies to the chief applies naturally also to the oldest brother and indeed to all the siblings, where these share in the inheritance and in the wisdom of the father of the tribe: they too must develop large, broad ears. Likewise, everyone should remember the wisdom of the Bambara, who see the word as too large and broad for one single mouth. Precisely in the church, whose business is the word of God, only a common endeavor can penetrate more deeply into the immensity of this mystery.

This palaver model has interesting implications for the interpretation of scripture and tradition in the church. On this view the entire church is the interpreter, that is, the fellowship of those who believe in Christ, and not only the magisterium. While all the members (including the oldest brother) read and hear the same sacred scripture and tradition, the word that is heard is first chewed and digested on the individual level, before rumination takes place on the public level of the community. In order that the word from scripture and tradition which the individual has heard and digested may not be falsely monopolized in some kind of "situation ethics," leading to the destruction of the community of the church, it is necessary that all the members should present their understanding of scripture and tradition in an ecclesial palaver where they are exposed to questioning. Only so can God's word unfold its healing and saving effect to the full. If the magisterium were to seek to impose its own interpretation (itself the fruit of a historical process) in an exclusive manner and without any palaver with other cultures, this would fail to do justice to the fact that the word is much greater and more comprehensive than the mouth of the individual—in this case, the mouth of the magisterium itself. The word of God is inexhaustible, and permits a much wider spectrum of interpretation!

The Indian theologian Felix Wilfred is right to observe that the understanding of revelation that we find in holy scripture and tradition "embraces much more" than just "the doctrinal aspects" that have occupied the central position since the Council of Trent.[71] In the New Testament, for example, there are various christological interpretations which all attempt to understand *one and the same* Christ; none of these can fully grasp the mystery of Jesus Christ, since this is too great for one "single mouth." The task of the magisterium is to permit all cultures and peoples to hold a palaver, in order to discern their own understanding of Christ and his message, without, however, reducing the basis of the faith that is common to all. This presupposes that the magisterium first *listens* and develops large, broad ears.

This makes words of the encyclical *Fides et ratio,* quoted above, appear questionable: "In engaging great cultures for the first time, the church cannot abandon what she has gained from her inculturation in the world of Greco-Latin thought. To reject this heritage would be to deny the providential plan of God who guides his church down the paths of time and history" (*FR* 72). But do we not in fact see an alien system of thought imposed on other cultures, a system that most assuredly cannot be equated with the Christian faith? In terms of the African palaver procedure, the Greco-Latin influence on the interpretation of the faith must certainly be taken seriously; but the interpretation generated by this Western thinking may not present itself as more than one of many possible models. It cannot become the norm for all cultures. It is true "that no one culture can ever become the criterion of judgment, much less the ultimate criterion of truth with regard to God's revelation" (*FR* 71); but fidelity to this fundamental principle would make it impossible to accept without correction the passages about Greco-Latin thinking which we have quoted from *Fides et ratio* 72,[72] since it must be possible to bid farewell to even the most cherished intellectual system, if this becomes an unjust yoke on the shoulders of other cultural worlds. Such a farewell would not necessarily contradict the plan of divine providence.

In the process of inculturation, the kingdom of God does not require replacing one set of cultural "clothes" with a new one. I would prefer to compare the kingdom of God, in the perspective of inculturation, with good soil which allows the seed or grains to grow up at once, provided that these are healthy. God's field, which contains only good soil, accepts all the positive elements of every culture and allows them to grow up and bear fruit. Thus it is always the same field, but with a variety of plants which reflect the richness of the soil. Similarly with the various cultures: in their inculturation of the revelation, they reflect the multiple riches of God in his inexhaustible mystery. This is yet another confirmation of the principle that guides African ecclesiology, viz., that the word—here, the revelation and the kingdom of God—is far too large and broad for any single mouth or any one culture.

We have used the model of brotherhood in speaking of the magisterium, but it would be wrong to think that this is restricted only to the pope, bishops, and professional theologians. All believers are siblings, since baptism makes them equal members of the ecclesial palaver. Furthermore, it is not only the pope who is the oldest brother: at every phase and in every context, each member of the church community can be an *older brother or sister.* For example, on the diocesan level, the bishop is the oldest brother; in the parish, this role belongs to the priest. This model can be transposed to the *basic Christian communities:* those in charge of these communities are older brothers and sisters.

We may sum up as follows: the sibling model attaches great weight to the *Christian palaver,* which begins with the Gospel, the word of God. Here everything that concerns community life is discussed (*fides et mores*), and the attempt is made to take consensual decisions for the common future. If the African church itself took this model seriously, it could lead to a genuine renewal and a radical departure from a rigidly hierarchical pattern of thought. According to this model, the results of the Christian palaver in the remote villages would have to be proposed for debate in the parishes; the parishes would then have to come together on the diocesan level, to join the bishop (as oldest brother) in "ruminating" again on the word that has been digested. All the dioceses can then meet on the national level, before seeking the last phase of the palaver with the pope, the oldest brother of the universal church. It is not unimaginable that the oldest brother would accept the opinion of the local church in this palaver, even if absolutely definitive clarity had not yet been attained. The *immensity* of the word of God, which remains inexhaustible even *in rebus moralibus,* may lead one to be content with a "partial truth" for the time being; it is also possible that the oldest brother has complete confidence in his brothers and sisters, who are better acquainted with the local and cultural aspects of the question under discussion. Only so does the pope act as an older brother who has big ears to listen with, who knows that the word is too broad for one single mouth and therefore respects and listens to the wisdom of his younger siblings. A church understood in this way deserves to be called a family in the broad sense, encompassing the living, the dead, and those not yet born.

If the magisterium were to behave in accordance with the understanding of the church proposed here, it would deal differently with the African church in many questions that concern not only the *fides* but also the ethical life of the faithful. The principles deduced from natural law would not be imposed indiscriminately as something universal on another, non-Western culture that solves its problems differently—viz., not in accordance with a rationality conditioned by the natural law—but without thereby contradicting the intention of divine revelation.[73] This leads us to the ethics of marriage as a whole. Ought one not to encourage the African church to find its own solutions, for example in the question of the stages by which a marriage is contracted? Provided that such solutions do not clash with the gospel, they need not in the final analysis be absolutely identical to the guidelines laid down by canon law or Western theology. Here we should recall the plea that remains the testament of the late Cardinal Joseph-Albert Malula of Kinshasa. He demanded urgently that the customary doctrine of the *matrimonium ratum et consummatum* (marriage which is contracted and consummated) be studied thoroughly and if necessary be revised in the African context, since it seems to be based on a Western way of looking at things.[74] The problem of levirate marriage ought not to be too quickly condemned on the basis of Western categories: rather, it must be seen in the context of African marriage. In Africa, the marriage bond lasts beyond death, and marriage includes the extended family in all its three dimensions (the living, the dead, and those not yet born).

We must also mention canon law, which determines church order as a whole—including ethical directives. A genuinely African ecclesiology must endeavor to develop its own canon law, which would permit the palaver model to exercise its influence to the full.

Another example concerns the matter of the Eucharist. This is not a liturgical or dogmatic question, but ultimately concerns ethics. The Eucharist has an essential connection with the hospitality that is so significant in Africa. Meals play an extremely important role here, and the kind of food which is eaten is not a neutral issue. Here we should reflect whether the eucharistic matter under the forms of bread and wine—non-African products—is an appropriate expression of hospitality shared with Christ and with all believers. Africans are left with the unpleasant feeling that God ultimately does not accept them completely, since he is not willing to identify himself with the fruits of their own soil and fields. What then does "incarnation" mean? Does not the rejection of the African fruits amount to discrimination? Besides this, one cannot resist the impression that bread and wine imported from abroad also serve commercial interests, that is, that this is an economic exploitation of black people. In view of all these questions, we need a palaver, and the magisterium ought not to intervene *ab extra,* but rather charge the local churches with the task of examining this issue in depth, involving all the members of the church—including the laity.

I hope that these few examples have shown how urgent it is to proclaim the Christian faith in the context of a moral theology rooted in the specific culture. This should not be considered as destructive of the faith. The exact opposite is true: as the African Synod in 1994 made perfectly clear, all efforts to achieve inculturation aim at giving the Christian faith a chance of success. This faith must be always aware that there is not *one* Christianity, but many *Christianities.* All of these appeal to the same revelation, but express it in different ways.

It is important, precisely in the age of globalization, that the church is not led astray into a kind of cultural cloning. It must overcome this temptation in the name of the supreme mystery of the Trinity of God, the mystery that the church can never abandon. It is impossible to reduce the Christian God in his oneness to one single Person: it is only in three distinct Persons that he is the one God. Only in these three Persons is the inexhaustible and unfathomable mystery of the one God fully expressed. None of the three Persons is leveled down: each retains his full identity. The life of Father, Son, and Holy Spirit is a mutual exchange, and they work in the world in different ways in order to bestow on this world the one life in differentiation, that is, life "in the plural." In the same way, the church must respect the identity of every culture, since the cultures in all their variety are derived from the one God, but each reflects the richness of the triune God in its own manner. It follows that evangelization must decisively renounce the monoculture, for such a leveling down would utterly destroy the fullness of the triune God.

Concluding Remarks

MY AIM IN THIS INVESTIGATION HAS BEEN TO ENGAGE IN DIALOGUE with various Western ethical models, while at the same time demonstrating the autonomy and potential of the Black African model, as well as its limitations (especially in part 2, chapter 3). I conclude by presenting by way of examples those points where the African community and palaver ethics most clearly criticize and challenge the Western models that have been discussed in this book. I shall then look ahead, to make a special plea for a genuinely African ethics and theology.

LOOKING BACK

Unlike many of the principles of the natural law, but also unlike discourse ethics, the Black African palaver model does not begin with abstractions. It takes up contextual questions and proceeds by way of discourse, without, however, narrowing down participation in this discourse to an exclusively intellectual performance. The comparison with the *intrinsece malum* of Catholic moral theology, with its orientation to the natural law, has shown that African ethics is not content with abstract principles or intellectual performance alone. The example of the prohibition of incest has made this clear: we have seen that even something that is the object of an absolute negative or positive commandment must first be discussed in the community. This discussion takes place anamnetically; it is a fundamental principle that it takes into account the experience of the ancestors. This experience is not, however, something inviolable: in the encounter with new contexts, it can be questioned critically and even radically attacked. The main criterion for evaluating and establishing ethical norms is the life of the individual and of the entire community; the aim is not the realization of isolated individuals—perhaps even against the community, as is possible on the natural-law model—but rather a mutual relationship of all persons, which alone can make the human person truly human. This means refusing both the natural-law model and discourse ethics with its emphasis on the community, since both are ultimately based on the *cogito*-pattern, which plays a central role in the definition of the person; we see this, for example, in the discussion of the definition of the embryo as a person.[1]

If we take our starting point, as the African concept suggests, in a network of relationships that includes the community of the ancestors in the process whereby one becomes a person, we are entitled to pose a number of questions to the Western ethical models. These are too much interested in trying to define the precise possibility of a development in the direction of reason in the unborn child (e.g., the cerebrum), or to define precisely when one can speak of the individual *qua* individual. I should like to suggest that a dialogue with African ethics could contribute new aspects to the whole debate about abortion, and to questions such as euthanasia.

Another question in need of further reflection and clarification is without doubt the holistic dimension of African ethics, which does not operate with a separation of sacred and profane in the Western sense. We must ask here to what extent religious freedom or pluralistic thinking is acceptable. This is also the context in which we must reflect on the complex problem of human rights.

When we reflect on religious freedom or pluralistic thinking, we must bear in mind that "sacred" and "secular" are not to be understood in the Western sense, which seems to view these concepts as alternatives. We certainly may not try to grasp the African model from the perspective of *theocracy* or of Augustine's *City of God.* In my opinion, it is more correct to say that Africans *mostly behave in concreto* "as if God did not exist," even if everything is ultimately traced back to God and the ancestors. The entire procedure in palaver ethics is oriented to the good of the community: the problems debated concern people in their daily social living, without an over-hasty appeal to a religious or theocratic justification. The ancestors play an important role only because they are the forefathers of the earthly community and have bequeathed specific experiences to it, to make possible and enrich life in the present and in the future. This observation is confirmed by the fact that the majority of ethnic groups in Africa have never conducted a religious war in the name of their god or their religious conviction; nor do they do so today. It is striking how most of the ethnic groups in Black Africa have either adopted other religions such as

Christianity and Islam without any notable resistance, or else have allowed these religions to practice their faith in freedom. There has been no persecution of the members of these "new" religions in the name of traditional African religiosity. The only decisive factor is their positive contribution to the common good or their potential to destroy the common good. This too is a reason for the existence of the palaver, which makes it possible to discern whether a different religion, or an individual who thinks differently, genuinely destroys the common good—for it is possible that in the last analysis, the same ideal is being maintained, viz., the bestowal and strengthening of life in fullness. This is why Black African religion is not sacralizing and fundamentalist. It seeks to make the world a more humane place and criticizes and enriches itself through contact with other modes of thought and religious convictions.

African community ethics goes much further than this in its respect for religious freedom. Not only are the various peoples with their worldviews and religious convictions fully accepted; even within one and the same community and family, individual members are given the freedom to articulate their own religious convictions and worldviews. It is not rare to encounter siblings or relatives in today's Africa who are members of the same family but belong to different confessions, religions, or sects; this does not lead to conflicts or mutual excommunication. This raises at least implicitly the question of human rights, as these are understood in the West. If the individual is essentially dependent on the community in the process by which he becomes himself, and it is not possible to make an unambiguous separation between sacred and profane, or to detach morality from rights, then we must ask whether this means that the human rights that are conceived in terms of the individual are "absorbed" by the community and hence sacralized.

In view of what has been said above, we can answer this question briefly. Let us first emphasize that rights do not exist in isolation: an ethical justification is required, if they are to be established and applied. The aim here is the common good, which entails the strengthening of everyone's life. This also means that the individual and the community depend on one another in the field of human rights: one must define and preserve the rights of the individual vis-à-vis the community and clarify the rights of the community vis-à-vis the individual. By respecting the rights of the individual, the community preserves its own identity, and the same is true of the individual himself. It follows that freedom of the press is understood somewhat differently in Black African than in the West. An African is not satisfied with the justification of this right on the basis of the inalienable dignity of the human being *qua* individual, as is conceivable in terms of natural law or discourse ethics; the decisive factor is the context, where one must ask whether freedom of the press, understood and justified as a "naked," abstract freedom, gives a life more in accord with human dignity to children, the illiterate, and so on. In African ethics (unlike communitarianism), "context" means not only that one must take into account the relevance to the community, but also (and primarily) that the individual must find help in the community to understand his rights correctly and to put them into practice.

It is precisely here that the palaver plays a central role, by giving the individual a guideline for ethically responsible conduct, but without depriving him of the personal decision that only he can take. I have already indicated clearly that this procedure has its limitations, and that there is a potential risk (but only a *risk*) that the community may assume an absolutist position vis-à-vis the individual.[2] Nevertheless, the ideal of community and palaver ethics remains valid and productive in Black Africa, especially when compared to the procedure of natural-law ethics and discourse ethics, which emphasize the individual's right to action to such a degree that the opposite risk results, viz., that the individual seeks to realize and enjoy his freedom without the community. Even communitarianism, as we have described this, lags behind the African ideal and intention, since, although it understands the individual right as rooted in the community, it offers the individual member no *active* help in the community that would allow the application of this right to be visibly realized in the community context. It might be a good idea for all these ethical models to conduct a palaver dialogue among themselves, in order to correct their methodological (and other) deficits and to enrich one another, without abandoning their own identity.

Another point of difficulty—at least for Westerners, or those who have received a Western education—is the complex problem of the individual conscience as ultimate authority. I have already answered this question, which is connected with the individual freedom that we have just discussed; I return to it briefly here. In view of all that I have said,[3] and of the African proverbs that have often been quoted in the course of this book, it is certainly incorrect to assert that the individual conscience is absorbed into the community. In the chapter on the conscience, I indicated that the palaver permits the individual to retain his own experiences, if no agreement between the individual and the palaver community can be reached. But the positive and negative experiences are followed by a new palaver process in which the entire community is to learn from the individual, thus being enriched by new experiences, both positive and negative. If it is the individual who is right, rather than the community, this entails the abolition once and for all of what was hitherto normative;

this is replaced by something new. If one compares this procedure with the Western models, especially that of natural-law ethics, and bears in mind the problem of *prophecy* on the theological level, one will find that the Western mode of thought, in the models presented here, sees the prophetic element primarily in individual actions, where the individual can go on his own way even without paying heed to the community. According to the African model, the community will always provide the context in which the individual reflects on his actions—not in the sense that he may not make any personal decisions, but rather in the sense that the community participates in his actions and profits from them. In other words, even where the individual makes a decision that runs contrary to the opinion of the community, he wants his private insight to be shared by the community. If the action of the individual is prophetic, this does not remain a private prophecy, but tends to form a prophetic community which breaks through the unjust structures and abolishes them *as a community.* Since an African ecclesiology takes its starting point in the family (in the sense of an extended family), this is important. The endeavors of a prophetic community will ultimately lead to an "alternative community" which in its entirety assumes the charism of its individual members, in order truly to be the salt of the earth through its critique of other unjust communities or societies.

Here too, of course, a dialogue with the Western models is useful, so that the individual may be protected from the risk of simply running along with the crowd in the community; but African ethics in turn can also show clearly the limitations of the traditional Western doctrine of the conscience. The individual conscience certainly plays a central role. We must, however, inquire whether an excessive emphasis on the final authority of one's own conscience leads to an impasse. The example of decisions of the magisterium in the Catholic Church illustrates this well, since it frequently happens, where a conflict with the directives of the magisterium occurs, that individuals emphasize the primacy of the individual conscience as the ultimate authority, which in certain circumstances may act autonomously, against the guidelines issued by the ecclesial magisterium. This can make a fruitful dialogue with the magisterium difficult or even impossible, for example, if the one who has authority in the church likewise appeals to his own conscience, which insists that he propose the teaching in question. This is precisely where the palaver model appears suggestive and significant, since it urges all the members of the community to listen to one another and analyze the word or digest it in common, before individuals start asserting that they alone are right. This emphasizes the *ecclesial* dimension of conscience more strongly than traditional Western moral theology.

When social ethics points out the danger of a globalization that simply absorbs the individual, this too shows the limitations of an overemphasis on the solitary subject, since one cannot completely exclude a certain arbitrariness here. It also seems to me clear that an "unfettered ego" that is too much interested in its own rights could easily develop into a despotic authority that must inevitably destroy the common good.[4]

In this context, I should also like to recall what was written above in part 2 about the identification of ethical responsibility with certain external things:[5] according to the African understanding of ethics, the internal conviction or ethical corruption can also manifest itself externally, in a purely biological manner. No doubt, we can no longer defend such a view, for that could do grave injustice to many innocent persons—and that is intolerable. Nevertheless, we must take seriously the deepest concern of this affirmation, viz., that ethical behavior is not a private matter, but has social consequences, either establishing or destroying the community. There is an interaction between internal and external actions. The important thing is to check the internal evil, so that the community may become a place of life in fullness.

This raises the final question: the positive elements presented in this book have the potential to contribute to the elaboration of a genuinely African palaver morality bearing the imprint of Christianity. How can these be developed?

Looking Ahead

I hope that this book has made it clear that the proper character of African ethics must be taken seriously in the Christian kerygma. This means that one cannot simply accept the following observation by Cardinal Joseph Ratzinger: "It is clear where the problems lie. But one must say that the longed-for *théologie africaine* or *African theology* is more a program than a reality at present."[6] One must of course reach agreement about the concept "theology" and ask whether this can be applied only in keeping with the traditional, but very Western, definition that has been dominant until now; this is not the place to debate and answer this question. I would like to remark only that the path that has been taken by men and women theologians in Africa until now deserves to be called "theology," not merely a "program," even if it does not correspond to the expectations of the Western way of thought: these are reflections on the Christian faith in one specific cultural context, as numerous publications attest. It is true that not everything here is new, and that recourse is often had to the results of Western theologians' researches. Nevertheless, one should not be too sure "that much of what is considered 'African' is in reality an import from Europe. The classical Christian tradition has much more to say to the genuine African traditions than do such imports."[7] One could adduce many examples that contradict this thesis. At any rate, as I wrote in the preface to this book, one cannot simply categorize the elements presented here as European imports, even if the book as a whole also reflects on the European dimension—something that I do to indicate clearly not only the similarities but also the differences.

The understanding of family and community, the palaver procedure, and the attitude to freedom surely allow the reader to see an anthropology that is not identical with that of the West. These elements pose questions to the European models (including those with a Christian character), and demand the acknowledgment of their own identity in the ethical sphere. This brings us to the problem of pluralism in ethics, which must not be silenced, even or especially by Christianity: Robert Schreiter's attempt at a typology of regional theologies applies to moral theology too.[8] On the basis of Noam Chomsky's theory about the acquisition of language, Schreiter posits an analogy between the Christian tradition and the entire system of language. According to Chomsky, this system includes both "competence" (e.g., in one's native language) and "performance" (in relation to expressions which are de facto produced in language). While correctness is inherent in competence (one speaks one's native language perfectly, even if one has not learned its rules), a performance can be either good or bad. Grammar can do no more than describe the language, not generate it; thus grammar must change when the language develops. Nor is grammar capable of justifying exceptions and idiomatic expressions.[9]

Schreiter argues that, if one applies all this to the Christian tradition, faith is analogous to linguistic competence. Theology and tradition as forms of praxis (e.g., liturgy) have a similar relationship to linguistic performance, while orthodoxy (sacred scripture, convictions about the faith, councils, magisterium, creeds) is comparable to the grammar "which links competence and performance."[10] This means that the faith which baptism bestows as linguistic competence can be expressed in a variety of performances, none of which is capable of giving exhaustive expression to the faith. The consequence for our own topic is that one can speak only in the plural of theology as performance, and that every theology which seeks to interpret the faith in its own context cannot be other than *fragmentary.* The task of orthodoxy as grammar is to inquire into the rules that must be followed. Schreiter writes:

> The *loci* of orthodoxy do not create any theology for a community. Theology is not generated by these *loci,* any more than performances are gener-

> ated by grammar. . . . To deduce the theology of a community exclusively from a theological or biblical doctrinal system would be like deducing idioms from rules of grammar.[11]

This does not mean that orthodoxy has nothing to do with theology; it means that orthodoxy is not the source of texts, but "the guarantee of the correct elaboration of texts for performance."[12] When the correctness or incorrectness of a theology is to be evaluated, orthodoxy understands "faith" as linguistic competence.

What has been said about orthodoxy must also apply to orthopraxis, which endeavors to make it possible to put orthodoxy into practice. The consequence, however, is that the moral theology for one particular community cannot be prescribed by orthopraxis—which ultimately belongs to the sphere of the "grammar" of faith, since the magisterium lays claim to orthopraxis too, in view of the word-pair *fides et mores.* If ethics in a Christian context is a theological reflection on the praxis of the faith, this means that it is an aspect of that performance which seeks to express the faith (as "competence") anew and in a specific manner in the various contexts and cultural spheres, without ever doing so exhaustively. To employ concepts that we have met above: only the *parathēkē,* as *depositum,* is that which must always be preserved. The *didaskalia* is ultimately more concerned with the context, so that it can be understood as "grammar." This is decisively important for the local churches, since this makes it possible for them to interpret the *depositum* even *in rebus moralibus* in a "performance" in the context of their own cultures and to elaborate their own moral theologies as new idioms which do not in the least contradict the *depositum* as *parathēkē.* In order that these moral theologies may not remain restricted to scholars alone, but may determine the praxis of the communities, it is necessary to urge the bishops, who are the first preachers of the gospel, not to appeal to an alien and incomprehensible idiom (i.e., Western theology) to forbid those new attempts at an interpretation of the faith that are rooted in the culture of the faithful, but rather to allow these to be realized in the specific pastoral reality.

It is certainly not superfluous to emphasize this precisely in Africa, where there is a risk that the difference between theological reflections and the substance of the faith may be leveled down. Only when bishops, theologians, and other believers are truly convinced that African culture[13] is a providential instrument for one legitimate reading (among many others) in the question of *fides et mores,* will it also be possible to demand a Christianity incarnated in Africa. This will mean growth, and hence enrichment, for the entire church of Jesus Christ.

Notes

Preface

1. P. Schmitz, *Fortschritt ohne Grenzen? Christliche Ethik und technische Allmacht* (Freiburg i. Br., 1997), 14.

2. See the judgment by G. W. F. Hegel, *Vorlesungen über die Philosophie der Geschichte,* Theorie-Werkausgabe 12 (Frankfurt a. M., 1970), 120ff.

3. See *Collectaneae Sacrae Congregationis de Propaganda Fide* (Rome, 1907), I, no. 134.

4. See *Sylloge praecipuorum documentorum Summorum Pontificum et Sacrae Congregationis Romanorum ad usum Missionariorum* (Rome, 1939), no. 206.

5. See the collection of texts in V. Mulago, "Evangélisation et authenticité dans l'enseignement du Magistère," in *Aspects du Catholicisme au Zaïre,* ed. V. Mulago (Kinshasa, 1981), 7–45.

6. S. Brechter, "Kommentar," *LThK-E,* III, 83.

7. See the *Lineamenta* for the Synod on Africa (Vatican City, 1990/1993), nos. 61–72, and the *Instrumentum Laboris,* nos. 101–7; cf. also John Paul II, *Ecclesia in Africa* (14 September 1995), no. 67.

8. See B. Bujo, *Die ethische Dimension der Gemeinschaft: Das afrikanische Modell im Nord-Süd-Dialog* (Freiburg i. Ue./Freiburg i. Br., 1993).

9. F. Furger, "Zur theologischen Ethik," *SKZ* 163 (1995): 447–54, at 451.

10. Bujo, *Die ethische Dimension,* 8.

11. See *Ad Gentes* 22, which speaks of "paths to a profounder adaptation."

Part 1
Fundamental Questions of African Ethics

1. See, e.g., R. Friedli, *Le Christ dans les cultures: Carnets de routes et de déroutes. Un essai de théologie des religions* (Freiburg i. Ue./Paris, 1989), 114–66; K.-H. Ohlig, *Ein Gott in drei Personen? Vom Vater Jesu zum "Mysterium" der Trinität* (Mainz/Lucerne, 1999), 16–18.

2. See E. N. Mujynya, "Le mal et le fondement dernier de la morale chez les bantu interlacustres," *Cahiers des Religions Africaines* 3 (1969): 55–78, esp. 68f.; B. Bujo, *African Christian Morality at the Age of Inculturation* (reprint, Nairobi, 1998), 77.

Chapter 1
Starting Point and Anthropology

1. Cf. *inter alia* P. Tempels, *Bantu-Philosophie: Ontologie und Ethik* (Heidelberg, 1956); idem, *Notre rencontre* (Léopoldville, 1962); V. Mulago et al., *Des prêtres noirs s'interrogent* (Brussels, 1956); A. Kagame, *La philosophie bantu-rwandaise* (Brussels, 1956); V. Mulago, *Un visage africain du Christianisme: L'union vitale bantu face à l'unité vitale ecclésiale* (Paris, 1965); J. S. Mbiti, *Afrikanische Religion und Weltanschauung* (Berlin, 1974); J. S. Pobee, *Grundlinien einer afrikanischen Theologie* (Göttingen, 1981); B. Bujo, *African Christian Morality at the Age of Inculturation* (reprint, Nairobi, 1998).

2. See W. Reese-Schäfer, *Was ist Kommunitarianismus?* (Frankfurt a.M./New York, 1994).

3. See the summary of Ben Barber's arguments against liberalism in Reese-Schäfer, *Was ist Kommunitarianismus?* 90: "The epistemological framework of liberalism is Cartesian, i.e., based on the supposition that there exists an independent starting-point from which the concepts, values, goals and standards of political life can be inferred deductively. According to the liberal contract theory, one is a citizen because one has at some time or other assented to some abstract truths. According to Berber's communitarian position, on the other hand, one is a citizen of a common history, and this is why one shares some common ideas about value with other persons."

4. J. Ratzinger, *Einführung in das Christentum: Vorlesungen über das Apostolische Glaubensbekenntnis* (Munich, 1968), 176.

5. Ibid., 178.

6. Ibid., 177.

7. See ibid., 178.

8. Ibid., 176f.

9. See ibid., 177.

10. Ibid.

11. See ibid., 126ff.

12. See here the position of P. Singer, *Praktische Ethik,* 2nd ed. (Stuttgart, 1994). See also the discussion by K. Arntz, "Der umstrittene Personbegriff in der Bioethik: Anmerkungen zu den Thesen Peter Singers," *ThG* 41 (1998): 196–206; H. Hoping, "Göttliche und menschliche Personen: Die Diskussion um den Menschen als Herausforderung für die Dogmatik," *ThG* 41 (1998): 126–74.

13. I return to this question in greater detail when examining the question of "being a person" in part 2.

14. This is a translation of the fundamental principle of the Sotho in South Africa: *Motho ke motho ka batho ka bang.* There is a striking parallel in Martin Luther King's unforgettable speech in 1961, "I Have a Dream," where he says: "Strangely enough, I can never be what I ought to be until you are what you ought to be. You can never be what you ought to be until I am what I ought to be"; quoted by J. H. Cone, *Martin–Malcolm–America* (Maryknoll, N.Y., 1993), 80. Cf. the reference and commentary by E. E. Uzukwu, *A Listening Church: Autonomy and Communion in African Churches* (Maryknoll, N.Y., 1996), 37.

15. This is discussed in greater detail below.

16. See Bujo, *African Christian Morality,* 96f.

17. See, above all, D. Nothomb, *Un humanisme africain: Valeurs et pierres d'attente* (preface by A. Kagame) (Brussels, 1969), 240ff.

18. For more on this, see Bujo, *African Christian Morality,* 100f.; Nothomb, *Un humanisme africain,* 21–39. We shall return to this question in greater detail in part 2.

19. See Kagame's preface to Nothomb, *Un humanisme africain,* 9.

20. This is well set out by B. K. Vahwere, "Le problème moral de l'éducation sexuelle en Afrique noire: L'éthique sexuelle Nande à la lumière de la morale chrétienne selon Xavier Thévenot" (Licentiate dissertation, Kinshasa, 1994), 31, 33.

21. See ibid., 28–30.

22. See, e.g., Ambrose of Milan, *De Nabute Iezraelita* 1.1.2: "For we are not born with clothing, nor are we begotten with gold and silver. We first saw the light of day naked, lacking food, covering, vessels" (*PL* 14:767).

23. M. Walzer, *Sphären der Gerechtigkeit: Ein Plädoyer für Pluralität und Gleichheit* (Frankfurt a.M./New York, 1992), xiv; quoted in Reese-Schäfer, *Was ist Kommunitarianismus?* 132.

24. R. Forst, *Kontexte der Gerechtigkeit: Politische Philosophie jenseits von Liberalismus und Kommunitarismus* (Frankfurt a.M., 1994), 259.

25. See ibid., 258f.

26. Ibid., 261.

27. See ibid.

28. See M. Walzer, *Interpretation and Social Criticism* (Cambridge, Mass./London, 1987); see also Reese-Schäfer, *Was ist Kommunitarianismus?* 119–45.

29. See L. Lévy-Bruhl, *Les fonctions mentales dans les sociétés inférieures* (Paris, 1910); idem, *La mentalité primitive* (Paris, 1922); idem, *L'âme primitive* (Paris, 1927); idem, *Le surnaturel et la nature dans la mentalité primitive* (Paris, 1931); idem, *L'expérience mystique et les symboles chez les primitifs* (Paris, 1938); R. Allien, *La psychologie de la conversion chez les peuples non-civilisés* (Paris, 1925). We also recall the remarks by G. W. F. Hegel, *Vorlesungen über die Philosophie der Geschichte,* Theorie Werkausgabe 12 (Frankfurt a.M., 1970), 120ff.

30. The debate about rationality is summarized briefly by S. Streiff and H. Ruh, *Zum Interesse theologischer Ethik an der Rationalität* (Zurich, 1995), 7–29. The most important study is K.-O. Apel and M. Kettner, eds., *Die eine Vernunft und die vielen Rationalitäten* (Frankfurt a.M., 1996).

31. Reese-Schäfer, *Was ist Kommunitarianismus?* 129–30; cf. Walzer, *Interpretation and Social Criticism,* 48.

32. See Reese-Schäfer, *Was ist Kommunitarianismus?* 130.

33. See E. Schockenhoff, *Naturrecht und Menschenwürde: Universale Ethik in einer geschichtlichen Welt* (Mainz, 1996), 55–142 (Eng. trans. by Brian McNeil in preparation).

34. See the essays by K. Demmer, *Christliche Existenz unter dem Anspruch des Rechts: Ethische Bausteine der Rechtstheologie* (Freiburg i.Ue./Freiburg i.Br., 1995); Schockenhoff, *Naturrecht und Menschenwürde.*

35. See O. H. Pesch, "Kommentar," in *DThA* 13:633–739; Schockenhoff, *Naturrecht und Menschenwürde,* 200–209, although the author does not refer to this outstanding study by Pesch.

36. *SCG* III c. 122 n. 2950 (Marietti edition).

37. Ibid.

38. Ibid., n. 2955.

39. L. Oening-Hanhoff, "Der Mensch: Natur oder Geschichte? Die Grundlagen und Kriterien sittlicher Normen im Licht der philosophischen Tradition," in *Naturgesetz und christliche Ethik: Zur wissenschaftlichen Diskussion nach Humanae vitae,* ed. F. Henrich (Munich, 1970), 13–47, at 34. The "conservation of the species" is indeed ultimately understood in connection with nature, but this is a nature understood from the perspective of the community, not a nature expounded in the narrow sense.

40. See Augustine, *De bono coniugali,* chs. 17–18, nos. 19–22 (*PL* 40:386ff.). On this, see also J. Ratzinger, "Zur Theologie der Ehe," in *Theologie der Ehe,* ed. G. Krems and R. Mumm, 2nd ed. (Regensburg/Göttingen, 1972), 88–90.

41. See B. Bujo, *Moralautonomie und Normenfindung bei Thomas von Aquin unter Einbeziehung der neutestamentlichen Kommentare* (Paderborn/Munich et al., 1979), 291.

42. *STh* I q. 1 a. 1c; see also *STh* II-II q. 2 a. 4; *SCG* Ic. 4; *3 Sent.* d. 24 q. 1 a 3. P. Synave offers a good commentary on these texts: "La révélation des vérités divines naturelles d'après saint Thomas d'Aquin," in *Mélanges Mandonnet: Etudes d'histoire littéraire et doctrinale du Moyen-Age,* I (Paris, 1930), 227–30.

43. On this, see Bujo, *Moralautonomie und Normenfindung,* 163–72, with references to the relevant texts in Thomas. A useful study here is also O. H. Pesch, *Thomas von Aquin: Grenze und Größe mittelalterlicher Theologie,* 3rd ed. (Mainz, 1995), 208–27.

44. Among the numerous studies by L. Kohlberg, see especially *Essays on Moral Development,* I, *The Philosophy of Moral Development: Moral Stages and the Idea of Justice* (San Francisco, 1981); II, *The Psychology of Moral Development: The Nature and Validity of Moral Stages* (San Francisco, 1984); for further bibliography on Kohlberg, see F. Osen and W. Althof, *Moralische Selbstbestimmung: Modelle der Entwicklung und Erziehung im Wertebereich: Ein Lehrbuch—mit einem Beitrag von Detlef Garz* (Stuttgart, 1992); the reflections in this book develop these themes. L. Kohlberg's concept is also important for J. Habermas, *Moralbewußtsein und kommunikatives Handeln* (Frankfurt a.M., 1983); see also Schockenhoff, *Naturrecht und Menschenwürde,* 90–92.

45. See G. Nummer-Winkler, "Moralischer Universalismus—kultureller

Relativismus: Zum Problem der Menschenrechte," in *Universale Menschenrechte im Widerspruch der Kulturen,* ed. J. Hoffmann, Symposium 2 (Frankfurt a.M., 1994), 79–103, at 82f.; eadem, "Gibt es eine weibliche Moral?" in *Weibliche Moral: Die Kontroverse um eine geschlechtsspezifische Ethik,* ed. G. Nummer-Winkler (Frankfurt a.M./New York, 1991), 145–61, esp. 153ff.; eadem, "Der Mythos von den Zwei Moralen," in *Und drinnen waltet die züchtige Hausfrau: Zur Ethik der Geschlechterdifferenz,* ed. H. Kuhlmann (Gütersloh, 1995), 49–68, esp. 61: "Children everywhere already have an appropriate cognitive understanding of morality at a relatively early age: they know simple moral rules and know that these possess intrinsic validity."

46. Schockenhoff, *Naturrecht und Menschenwürde,* 84.

47. See L.-V. Thomas and R. Luneau, *La terre africaine et ses religions: Traditions et changements* (Paris, 1975), 94f. Thomas and Luneau write about a dimension of marriage that is almost mystical, since this is not a question of a wife or husband who genuinely exists; nevertheless, they point out that true marriage transcends the visible, earthly sphere. It derives its binding force from the invisible, heavenly partnership, which cannot be regulated by a contract. Other forms of marriage in Africa, such as that between in-laws, likewise point to this non-contractual, heavenly dimension.

48. See B. Bujo, *Die ethische Dimension der Gemeinschaft: Das afrikanische Modell im Nord-Süd-Dialog* (Freiburg i. Ue./Freiburg i. Br., 1993), 102f.

49. The remarks about heterologous artificial insemination do in fact point to the community dimension, but more should be said about this.

50. On the very cautious discussion of *Humanae vitae* and *Familiaris consortio* in the African context, see J. Andavo, *La responsabilité négro-africaine dans l'acceuil et le don de la vie: Perspective d'inculturation pour les époux chrétiens* (Fribourg/Paris, 1996), 116–29.

51. *Catechism of the Catholic Church* (*CCC*), 2357f.

52. See, e.g., *STh* I-II q. 94 a. 3 ad 2.

53. On this, see Bujo, *Moralautonomie und Normenfindung,* 233–42, where the relevant texts are presented.

54. See, *inter alia, STh* I-II q. 94 a. 3 ad 2.

55. See, *inter alia, SCG* II c. 55 n. 1209; *SCG* III c. 44 n. 2213; c. 48 n. 2257; c. 51 n. 2284; c. 57 n. 2334; *In Eth. Nic.* I c. 11 lect. 16 n. 202; *CTh* I c. 104 n. 208.

56. See B. Bujo, *Die Begründung des Sittlichen: Zur Frage des Eudämonismus bei Thomas von Aquin* (Paderborn/Munich, 1984), esp. 94ff.

57. See ibid., 137–82.

58. See Bujo, *Moralautonomie und Normenfindung,* 265–73; W. Korff, "Der Rückgriff auf die Natur: Eine Rekonstruktion der thomanischen Lehre vom natürlichen Gesetz," *PhJ* 94 (1987): 285–96.

59. See *CCC* 2381, which speaks of marriage both as a covenant and as a contract. For a critique, see B. Bujo, "Ehe als Bund und Prozeß in Afrika," *StdZ* 213 (1995): 507–20.

60. See Bujo, *Moralautonomie und Normenfindung,* 289–97.

61. See ibid., 290f., with reference to *4 Sent.* d. 33 q. 1 a. 1 ad 8 and q. 1 a. 2 sol. 2.

62. Bujo, *Moralautonomie und Normenfindung,* 293–96.

63. On this, see B. Bujo, "Die Bedeutung des Spirituellen im Leben des Afrikaners als Ansatzpunkt für eine gesunde Ökologie," in *Ökologisches Weltethos im Dialog der Kulturen und Religionen,* ed. H. Kessler (Darmstadt, 1996), 88–101.

64. See Schockenhoff, *Naturrecht und Menschenwürde,* 233.

65. Compare some other sexual practices among the Masai in East Africa; but see also the critical observations on polygamy in part2, chapter 3.

66. Schockenhoff, *Naturrecht und Menschenwürde,* 299.

67. Ibid.

68. Ibid.

69. Ibid., 233.

70. See the observations in ibid., 118.

71. See ibid., 197–232.

72. Ibid., 228f.

73. See, for example, the condemnation of polygamy in the Apostolic Exhortation *Familiaris consortio* of John Paul II (1981), no. 19. Although this passage argues in personalistic terms, it is well known that natural law also plays a part in the background of the thinking of the magisterium. On this, see the analysis by F. Böckle, "Was bedeutet 'Natur' in der Moraltheologie?" in *Der umstrittene Naturbegriff: Person–Natur–Sexualität in der kirchlichen Morallehre* (Düsseldorf, 1987), 45–68.

74. See John Paul II, encyclical *Veritatis splendor* (VS) (1993), no. 82.

75. See, e.g., F. Böckle, *Fundamentalmoral,* 5th ed. (Munich, 1985), 307–19.

76. See *STh* I-II q. 94 a. 5 ad 2; II-II q. 64 a. 6 ad 1; O. H. Pesch, "Kommentar," in *DThA* 13:583f. and 639; Schockenhoff, *Naturrecht und Menschenwürde,* 202 n. 94 and 203 n. 96f. (with no mention of Pesch's interesting commentary).

77. See P. Grelot, "Notes," in *Thomas d'Aquin, Somme théologique,* vol. 2 (Paris, 1984), 685 n. 38. However, I believe that P. Grelot is wrong to say that Thomas does not take seriously the literal meaning of scripture here. He does not wish to take refuge in the spiritual interpretation of the Bible, and this is why he takes it literally, in order to interpret the ethically offensive passages on the basis of God as a lawgiver who can command such things as murder, theft, or adultery. Thomas rejects here the Augustinian principle which says that whatever in the divine Word cannot be taken to refer either to uprightness of conduct or the truth of the faith must be understood as uttered metaphorically (see Augustine, *De doctrina christana* 3.10.14; *PL* 34:71).

78. Habermas, *Moralbewußtsein,* 92; cf. Bujo, *Die ethische Dimension,* 43ff.

79. See Forst, *Kontexte der Gerechtigkeit,* 304.

80. Ibid.

81. See ibid., 302f.

82. Ibid., 302.

83. In the Kilendu language: *Nza nga dani rero tsu nanga dani vi nzî.*

84. In the original Kilendu: *Nza nga bini rero tsu nanga bini vi nzî.*

85. Taabu Sabiti, *Proverbes et dictons en Swahili et en Kingwana* (n.p.: Editions Saint Paul-Afrique, 1976), 31, no. 4. In the original: *Kobe haumi mguu wa chui.*

86. Ibid., no. 2: *Mtumbwi uheshimi maji na maji yaheshimu mtumbwi.*

87. Ibid., 33, no. 12: *Sikio halipitii kichwa.*

88. Ibid., 34, no. 22: *Mtoni ukavuma; chini mna mawe,* or: *Mto ukavuma, chini mna mawe.*

89. See Bujo, *Die ethische Dimension,* 63–66, 185–96.

90. See J. C. Katongole, "Ethos Transmission through African-Bantu Proverbs: Proverbs as a Means for Transmitting Values and Beliefs among Africans with the Example of Bantu-Baganda" (dissertation, Würzburg, 1997), 27–38.

91. A. T. Sanon, *Das Evangelium verwurzeln: Glaubenserschließung im Raum afrikanischer Stammesinitiationen* (Freiburg/Basel/Vienna, 1985), 33.

92. See ibid., 34.

93. See ibid., 37.

94. Ibid., 38.

95. A. MacIntyre, *After Virtue: A Study in Moral Theory,* 2nd ed. (Notre Dame, Ind., 1981), 121.

96. Ibid., 130.

97. See ibid., 205–6.

98. See ibid., 192–93.

99. Ibid.

100. See ibid., 209. The example of a recipe from a cookbook makes this very clear: the book may, for example, direct: "'Take six eggs. Then break them into a bowl. Add flour, salt, sugar, etc.' But the point about such sequences is that each element in them is intelligible as an action only as a-possible-element-in-a-sequence. Moreover even such a sequence requires context to be intelligible. If in the middle of my lecture on Kant's ethics I suddenly broke six eggs into a bowl and added flour and sugar, proceeding all the while with my Kantian exegesis, I have *not,* simply in virtue of the fact that I was following a sequence prescribed by Fanny Farmer, performed an intelligible action."

101. The same is true of a male or female murderer. In the case of women, this applies mostly to those who kill with poison.

102. As I have mentioned above, it goes without saying that the term adultery applies equally in the context of a polygamous marriage, since all the wives are regarded as legitimate spouses. One should also emphasize that the dowry is not a purchase price; it has a merely symbolic significance. On this, see Bujo, *Die ethische Dimension,* 85–111.

103. O. F. Bollnow, *Wesen und Wandel der Tugenden* (reprint, Frankfurt a.M./Berlin/Vienna, 1975), 13f.

104. See ibid., 14.

105. *Katholischer Erwachsenen-Katechismus,* II, *Leben aus dem Glauben,* ed. German Episcopal Conference (Freiburg i.Br., 1995), 75.

106. See J. Fuchs, "Weltethos oder säkularer Humanismus?" in *Für eine menschliche Moral: Grundfragen der theologischen Ethik,* IV, *Auf der Suche nach der sittlichen Wahrheit* (Freiburg i.Ue./Freiburg i.Br., 1997), 44, 45, 47.

107. J. Fuchs, "Sünde—Bemerkungen zu einem unzeitgemäßen Begriff," in ibid., 102f.

108. M. Vidal, "Die Enzyklika 'Veritatis splendor' und der Weltkatechismus: Die Restauration des Neuthomismus in der katholischen Morallehre," in *Moraltheologie in Abseits? Antwort auf die Enzyklika "Veritatis splendor,"* ed. D. Mieth, 2nd ed. (Freiburg i.Br., 1994), 244–70, at 248–57 (on virtue, see p. 255).

109. See E. Arens, "Glaube und Handeln aus handlungstheoretischer Sicht," in *Theologische Ethik im Diskurs: Eine Einführung,* ed. W. Lesch and A. Bondolfi (Tübingen/Basel, 1995), 37. On the whole cluster of problems associated with narrating, testifying, and confessing, see ibid., pp. 25–41; idem, *Christopraxis: Grundzüge theologischer Handlungstheorie* (Freiburg i.Br., 1992).

110. P. Schmitz, "Tugend—der alte und neue Weg zur inhaltlichen Bestimmung des sittlich richtigen Verhaltens," *ThPh* 54 (1979): 161–82, at 181. On the classical doctrine of virtue, see the representative studies by D. Mieth, *Die neuen Tugenden: Ein ethischer Entwurf* (Düsseldorf, 1984); O. H. Pesch, "Die Theologie der Tugend und die theologischen Tugenden," *Concilium* 23 (1987): 233–45. On Thomas Aquinas, see E. Schockenhoff, *Bonum hominis: Die anthropologischen und theologischen Grundlagen der Tugendethik des Thomas von Aquin* (Mainz, 1987).

111. See the comments by Reese-Schäfer, *Was ist Kommunitarianismus?* 128.

Chapter 2
Ethics and Anamnesis

1. On this, see B. Bujo, "Anamnetische Solidarität und afrikanisches Ahnendenken," in *Anerkennung der Anderen: Eine theologische Grunddimension interkultureller Kommunikation,* ed. E. Arens (Freiburg i.Br., 1995), 31–63.

2. See John S. Mbiti, *African Religions and Philosophy* (reprint, London/Ibadan/Nairobi, 1983), 133 and 126.

3. See E. Mveng, *L'Afrique dans l'Eglise: Paroles d'un croyant* (Paris, 1985), 35ff.

4. On this and the following ideas, see B. Bujo, "Universalité des normes et agir particulier des cultures: L'éthique négro-africaine face au christianisme," in *The Kairos of a Synod: Sedos Symposium on Africa,* ed. W. von Holzen and S. Fagan (Rome, 1994), 86–104; idem, "Sexualverhalten in Afrika," *ThG* 36 (1993): 203–19.

5. On the distinction between biography and autobiography, see B. Bujo, *Afrikanische Theologie in ihrem gesellschaftlichen Kontext* (Düsseldorf, 1986), 83 n. 7.

6. On this and on what follows, see Bujo, "Sexualverhalten," 212ff.

7. See B. Kisembo, L. Magesa, and A. Shorter, *African Christian Marriage,* 2nd ed. (Nairobi, 1998), 93–95.

8. Ibid. I discuss this in greater detail below in part 2, chapter 1.

9. See Yoka Lye Mudaba, "Bobongo: La danse sacrée et la libération," *Cahiers des Religions Africaines* 16 (1982): 277–91.

10. On this, see Bujo, "Anamnetische Solidarität," 57f.

11. See Mulamba-Mutatayi, "Regard sur la statuaire Kuba," *Cahiers des Religions Africaines* 16 (1982): 113–33. The following observations about masks are based on this study.

12. See ibid., 118f.

13. See ibid., 125ff.

14. See, *inter alia,* M. K. Mikanza Mobyem, "Mort éternelle pour une profusion de vie: La force dramatique du masque," *Cahiers des Religions Africaines* 16 (1982): 258f.; Lema Gwete, "Essai sur la dimension religieuse de l'art négro-africain," *Cahiers des Religions Africaines* 16 (1982): 71–111.

15. See Mulamba-Mutatayi, "Regard," 125–28.

16. A. A. MacIntyre, *After Virtue: A Study in Moral Theory,* 2nd ed. (Notre Dame, Ind., 1981), 220.

17. Ibid., 220–21.

18. See O. Höffe, *Vernunft und Recht: Bausteine zu einem interkulturellen Rechtsdiskurs* (Frankfurt a.M., 1996), 59–60, 64.

19. There is an immense secondary literature on discourse ethics and communitarianism. See, *inter alia, Habermas und die Theologie: Beiträge zur theologischen Rezeption, Diskussion und Kritik der Theorie kommunikativen Handelns,* ed. E. Arens (Düsseldorf, 1989); idem, *Kommunikatives Handeln und christlicher Glaube: Ein theologischer Diskurs mit Jürgen Habermas* (Paderborn et al., 1997); H.-J. Höhn, *Vernunft—Glaube—Politik: Reflexionsstufen einer christlichen Sozialethik* (Paderborn et al., 1990); C. Kissling, *Gemeinwohl und Gerechtigkeit: Ein Vergleich von traditioneller Naturrechtsethik und Gerechtigkeit* (Freiburg i.Ue/Freiburg i.Br., 1993)*;* A. Honneth, ed., *Kommunitarismus: Eine Debatte über die moralischen Grundlagen moderner Gesellschaften,* 2nd ed. (Frankfurt a.M., 1994). There is also a good introduction to communitarianism in W. W. Reese-Schäfer, *Was ist Kommunitarianismus?* (Frankfurt a.M./New York, 1994); C. Zahlmann, ed., *Kommunitarismus in der Diskussion: Eine streitbare Einführung,* 2nd ed. (Berlin, 1994). One should, however, concentrate on the representatives of the respective theories mentioned throughout this study: K.-O. Apel, J. Habermas, C. Taylor, M. Walzer, and others.

20. On this, see J.-G. Bidima, *La palabre: Une juridiction de la parole* (Paris, 1997).

21. For further details, see B. Bujo, *Die ethische Dimension der Gemeinschaft: Das afrikanische Modell im Nord-Süd-Dialog* (Freiburg i. Ue./Freiburg i. Br., 1993); idem, *Dieu devient homme en Afrique noire: Méditation sur l'Incarnation* (Kinshasa, 1996), esp. 23–36.

22. On this, see Bujo, *Dieu devient homme,* 75–82; idem, "Auf der Suche nach einer afrikanischen Christologie," in *Der andere Christus: Christologie in Zeugnissen aus aller Welt,* ed. H. Dembowski and W. Greive (Erlangen, 1991), 87–99, esp. 94–97 (also published under the title "Jesus afrikanisch gesehen," in

Jesus: Auf der Suche nach einem neuen Gottesbild, ed. J. Tille [Düsseldorf/Vienna, 1993], 333–50). See also R. Dzaringa-Jisa, "Towards the Theology of the Cross in the Light of the Ficus-tree among the Bahema of Zaire" (Licentiate dissertation, Nairobi, 1997).

23. If a patient is no longer able to take part in a conversation, the relatives are invited to the verbal palaver. This, however, is not to be equated with the argumentation of a law-court, since the relatives are not required to assume a vicarious function. They are invited to relate the genesis of the illness, and if necessary, to describe the entire family atmosphere in which the patient has lived or still lives.

24. See E. J. Lartey, "Two Healing Communities in Africa," in *The Church and Healing: Echoes from Africa,* ed. E. J. Lartey, D. Nwachuku, and Kasonga wa Kasonga (Frankfurt a.M., 1994), 33–48, at 43.

25. See Okot p'Bitek, *Africa's Cultural Revolution* (Nairobi: Macmillan, 1973), 88; cf. the quotations in J. G. Donders, *Afrikanische Befreiungstheologie: Eine alte Kultur erwacht* (Olten/Freiburg i.Br., 1986), 141–42; also B. Bujo, "Krankheit und Gemeinschaft aus negro-afrikanischer Sicht," in *Heilende Gemeinschaft? Von der sozialen Dimension der Gesundheit,* ed. G. Koch and J. Pretscher (Würzburg, 1996), 9–25.

26. On this, see the details in Bujo, *Afrikanische Theologie,* 34f.; idem, "Anamnetische Solidarität," 31–63.

27. See Kasonga wa Kasonga, "African Christian Palaver: A Contemporary Way of Healing Communal Conflicts and Crises," in *The Church and Healing,* ed. Lartey, Nwachuku, and Kasonga wa Kasonga, 48–65, at 56.

28. Even on this level some palaver procedures are not judicial, but take up other problems concerning the common good. The goal may be to advise the king or chief so that he takes a correct decision, or to prepare a great ceremony for the people as a whole; sometimes it may be the fixing of prices on the market, or obligations incumbent on the people or the king or chief. The members of this kind of palaver tend to be the wise persons of the community, or else the king/chief with his council of elders, who are delegated by the people. We must therefore explicitly underline the fact that even the extra-familial or administrative palaver need not be conflictual; it not infrequently has an irenic character. On this, cf. J.-G. Bidima, *La palabre,* 10.

29 On this whole topic, see O. Ndjimbi-Tshiende, *Réciprocité—coopération et le système palabrique africain: Tradition et herméneutique dans les théories du développement de la conscience morale chez Piaget, Kohlberg et Habermas* (St. Ottilien, 1992), 222ff.

30. See J. C. Katongole, "Ethos Transmission through African-Bantu Proverbs: Proverbs as a Means for Transmitting Values and Beliefs among Africans with the Example of Bantu-Baganda" (dissertation, Würzburg, 1997).

31. H. Scholler, "Das afrikanische Rechtssprichwort als hermeneutisches Problem," in *Dimensionen der Hermeneutik: Arthur Kaufmann zum 60. Geburtstag,* ed. W. Hassemer (offprint, no date or place of publication), 135–55, at 134; quoted by Ndjimbi-Tshiende, *Réciprocité—coopération,* 224 n. 368.

32. See Ndjimbi-Tshiende, *Réciprocité—coopération,* 224.

33. H. Scholler, "Anknüpfungspunkte für eine Rezeption der abendländischen Menschenrechte in der afrikanischen Tradition," in *Menschenrechte und kulturelle Identität,* ed. W. Kerber (Munich, 1991), 117–42, at 141.

34. Scholler thinks along similar lines ("Anknüpfungspunkte").

35. See Ndjimbi-Tshiende, *Réciprocité—coopération,* 212–14.

36. See the example in Ndjimbi-Tshiende, *Réciprocité—coopération,* 189–92, with further comments on pp. 240–43.

37. J. Gründel explains the so-called convergence argumentation in a similar way: "Die Bedeutung einer Konvergenzargumentation für die Gewißheitsbildung und für die Zustimmung zur absoluten Geltung einzelner sittlicher Normen," in *Wahrheit und Verkündigung: Festschrift zum 70. Geburtstag von Michael Schmaus,* II, ed. L. Scheffczyk, W. Dettloff, and R. Heinzmann (Munich et al., 1967), 1607–30.

38. See Ndjimbi-Tshiende, *Réciprocité—coopération,* 242.

39. See the palavers documented by Ndjimbi-Tshiende, *Réciprocité—coopération,* 195–202, 389–403.

40. See the secondary literature indicated in n. 19 above.

41. See R. Alexy, "Eine Theorie des praktischen Diskurses," in *Normbegründung, Normdurchsetzung,* ed. W. Oelmüller (Paderborn, 1978); (reference in J. J. Habermas, *Moralbewußtsein und kommunikatives Handeln* [Frankfurt a.M., 1983], 123n. 66); Habermas, *Moralbewußtsein,* 97-100.

42. Habermas, *Moralbewußtsein,* 99.

43. See Bujo, *Die ethische Dimension,* 21–82; Ndjimbi-Tshiende, *Réciprocité —coopération,* 195ff.

44. Habermas, *Moralbewußtsein,* 99.

45. See Ndjimbi-Tshiende, *Réciprocité—coopération,* 247.

46. See E. A. Hoebel, *The Law of Primitive Man: A Study in Comparative Legal Dynamics* (Cambridge, 1967), 252–54; quoted by Ndjimbi-Tshiende, *Réciprocité—coopération,* 246f.

47. Bundesversammlung der Schweizerischen Eidgenossenschaft, *Bundesbeschluss über eine nachgeführte Bundesverfassung* (Bern, 1998), preamble.

48. See Ndjimbi-Tshiende, *Réciprocité—coopération,* 246f.

49. See P. Tempels, *Bantu-Philosophie: Ontologie und Ethik* (Heidelberg, 1956), 33.

50. E. Mveng, "Essai d'anthropologie négro-africaine," *Bulletin de Théologie Africaine* 1 (1979): 229–39, at 234. On this topic as a whole, see Bujo, *Die ethische Dimension,* 179ff.

51. See E. Mveng, *L'Afrique dans l'Eglise,* 11.

52. More on this in Bujo, *Die ethische Dimension,* 200.

53. See Ndjimbi-Tshiende, *Réciprocité—coopération,* 247.

54. J. Habermas, *Erläuterungen zur Diskursethik* (Frankfurt a.M., 1991), 184.

55. Ibid.

56. See ibid., 184–85.

57. Ibid., 185.

58. See ibid., 146ff.
59. Ibid., 147.
60. Ibid., 148.
61. Ibid.
62. Ibid., 148f.
63. Ibid., 150–51.
64. Ibid., 151.
65. See ibid., 151–52.
66. Ibid., 152.
67. On this topic, see Tshiamalenga-Ntumba, "Afrikanische Philosophie: Zum originären Vertrauen des afrikanischen Menschen," in *Eglise et droits de la société africaine,* ed. A. Mutombo-Mwana and E.-R. Mbaya (Mbujimayi, 1995), 109–20, at 112.
68. See ibid., 113.
69. Ibid., 116f.
70. See ibid., 117ff.
71. Ibid., 118.
72. Ibid., 118f.
73. Ibid., 119.
74. Ibid.
75. See ibid.
76. On discourse ethics, see K.-O. Apel, *Diskurs und Verantwortung: Das Problem des Übergangs zur postkonventionellen Moral* (Frankfurt a.M., 1988), esp. 103–78; idem, "Normative Begründung der 'Kritischen Theorie' durch Rekurs auf lebensweltliche Sittlichkeit? Ein transzendentalpragmatisch orientierter Versuch, mit Habermas gegen Habemas zu denken," in *Im Prozeß der Aufklärung: Jürgen Habermas zum 60. Geburtstag,* ed. A. Honneth, T. McCarthy, C. Offer, and A. Wellmer (Frankfurt a.M., 1989), 15–65; Habermas, *Moralbewußtsein;* idem, *Erläuterungen.*
77. See D. K. Musonda, *The Meaning and Value of Life Among the Bisa and Christian Morality* (Rome, 1996).
78. See Apel, *Diskurs und Verantwortung,* 116f. and n. 17/2.
79. See F. Tönnies, *Gemeinschaft und Gesellschaft: Grundbegriffe der reinen Soziologie* (Berlin, 1887), quoted from 8th ed., 1935; reference in Höffe, *Vernunft und Recht,* 168.
80. Tönnies, *Gemeinschaft und Gesellschaft,* 178; see O. Höffe, *Vernunft und Recht,* 169.
81. See F. Tönnies, *Gemeinschaft und Gesellschaft,* 176–78; cf. the commentary by Höffe, *Vernunft und Recht,* 169.
82. Tönnies, *Gemeinschaft und Gesellschaft,* 3f.; quoted by Höffe, *Vernunft und Recht,* 169.
83. See Tönnies, *Gemeinschaft und Gesellschaft,* 251.
84. See Höffe, *Vernunft und Recht,* 169f., 180.
85. See ibid., 179.
86. Ibid.

87. Ibid.

88. See ibid., 180.

89. Höffe criticizes Tönnies's definition of community, in view of modern law and the reality of the modern state: "Even where one religion is dominant, such as Christianity or Islam or Judaism, it disintegrates in various directions (denominations, etc.); in addition to this, there are practicing members and members who have long stopped practicing, as well as persons who have taken the formal step of leaving the religious community, so that a large measure of homogeneity can be established only by (public or concealed) coercion. This is why at least one characteristic, viz. harmony, is lacking" (*Vernunft und Recht,* 180). Here, however, it must be borne in mind that ecumenism essentially occurs by means of dialogue. This is completely in accord with the African understanding of community, where conflicts are not excluded, but there is always the endeavor to reestablish unity and harmony.

90. Höffe, *Vernunft und Recht,* 180.

91. African ethics too would have to criticize Tönnies's definition of community, which sees its characteristics *inter alia* as "birth," language, customs, and faith; see Tönnies, *Gemeinschaft und Gesellschaft,* 3f.

92. C. Taylor, "Die Motive einer Verfahrensethik," in *Das Problem Hegels und die Diskursethik,* ed. W. Kuhlmann (Frankfurt a.M., 1986), 101–35, at 130.

93. See ibid., 133 and 119.

94. See MacIntyre, *After Virtue,* passim.

95. We recall here what Habermas writes in *Erläuterungen,* 184f.

96. See, e.g., his *Moralbewußtsein.*

97. Habermas, *Erläuterungen,* 139.

98. Ibid., 139f.

99. See ibid., 114–40.

100. Ibid., 114.

101. See ibid., 140.

102. Ibid., 114; cf. 141f.

103. See ibid., 114.

104. See ibid.; see also p. 196 (against Apel).

105. See Apel, *Diskurs und Verantwortung,* 145f.

106. See ibid.

107. Ibid., 146–47.

108. Ibid., 147, 150.

109. See Habermas, *Erläuterungen,* 197; see also the criticism by C. Kissling, *Gemeinwohl und Gerechtigkeit,* 436–51. (Kissling also criticizes Habermas here.)

110. See O. Höffe, ed., *Aristoteles, Nikomachische Ethik* (Berlin, 1995); idem, *Aristoteles* (Munich, 1996); idem, *Vernunft und Recht,* 172–85.

111. See Aristotle, *Rhetoric* 1.5, 1360b 19-24; quoted by Höffe, *Aristoteles,* 213.

112. See ibid.

113. See Aristotle, *Nicomachean Ethics* 2.2, 1104b 3ff.; 3.12, 1117a 17; reference in Höffe, *Vernunft und Recht,* 175.

114. See Höffe's commentary and the texts he adduces in evidence.

115. Höffe, ed., *Aristoteles, Nikomachische Ethik,* 183; idem, *Aristoteles,* 230f.

116. See Habermas, *Erläuterungen,* 199–208.

117. See ibid., 178, 184.

118. See Habermas's discussion of the theses of C. Taylor in *Erläuterungen,* 176–85.

119. Höffe, *Vernunft und Recht,* 183.

120. This is precisely the process by which proverbs—at least in Africa—are generated. They give apposite expression in one sentence to something confirmed by many experiences, so that the outcome of these experiences can now be universalized.

121. See *STh* I-II q. 56 a. 3c; q. 57 a. 4-6; II-II q. 47 a. 1-3. For more on this, see Bujo, *Die ethische Dimension,* 47f.

Part 2
Identity and the Understanding of Freedom

1. On this, see B. Bujo, *The Ethical Dimension of Community: The African Model and the Dialogue between North and South* (Nairobi, 1998), 165.

2. S. T. Pinckaers has assembled a good international bibliography: *Pour une lecture de "Veritatis splendor"* (Paris, 1995), 69–76.

Chapter 1
Western Christian Ethics and African Anthropology

1. [Translator's note: all texts of the Council and the magisterium are quoted in the officially approved English translations. This explains the occasional employment of non-inclusive language.]

2. See A. Auer, *Autonome Moral und christlicher Glaube: Zweite um einen Nachtrag erweiterte Auflage* (Düsseldorf, 1984), 147.

3. See ibid., 15.

4. J. Pieper, *Die Wirklichkeit und das Gute,* 5th ed. (Munich, 1949), 11; cf. Auer, *Autonome Moral,* 16.

5. See Auer, *Autonome Moral,* 17.

6. Ibid., 18.

7. See ibid.

8. On this, see H. Hirschi, *Moralbegründung und christlicher Sinnhorizont: Eine Auseinandersetzung mit Alfons Auers moraltheologischem Konzept* (Freiburg i.Ue. et al., 1992).

9. See Auer, *Autonome Moral,* 39–43; also Hirschi, *Moralbegründung,* 25f.

10. See A. Auer, "Was heißt 'Dialog der Kirche mit der Welt'? Überlegungen zur Enzyklika 'Ecclesiam suam' Pauls VI.," in A. Auer, *Zur Theologie der Ethik: Das Weltethos im theologischen Diskurs* (Freiburg i.Ue./Freiburg i.Br., 1995), 11–36.

11. Auer, *Autonome Moral,* 39.
12. See ibid., 12.
13. See A. Auer, "Interiorisierung der Transzendenz: Zum Problem Identität oder Reziprozität von Heilsethos und Weltethos," in Auer, *Zur Theologie,* 131ff.
14. See Auer, *Autonome Moral,* 55ff.
15. See Auer, "Interiorisierung," 131–50.
16. Ibid., 142.
17. See Josef Fuchs, "Gibt es eine unterscheidend christliche Moral?" in J. Fuchs, *Für eine menschliche Moral: Grundfragen der theologischen Ethik,* I, *Normative Grundlegung* (Freiburg i.Ue./Freiburg i.Br., 1988), 101–16.
18. See ibid., 106f.
19. Ibid., 113.
20. Ibid., 121.
21. See Auer, *Autonome Moral,* 189–97.
22. On this concept, see D. Mieth, "Autonome Moral im christlichen Kontext: Zu einem Grundlagenstreit der theologischen Ethik," *Orientierung* 40 (1976): 31–34.
23. For Pius XII, see the texts quoted in Auer, *Autonome Moral,* 138; Paul VI, *Humanae vitae,* no. 4.
24. See Vatican II: *OT* 16; *GE* 10; and most recently John Paul II, encyclical *Fides et ratio* (1998), no. 43f., where the abiding significance of Thomas's teaching is especially emphasized.
25. This law is to be understood as an analogy, since not only the human person but other beings too can participate in the *lex aeterna,* each in its own way.
26. *STh* I-II q. 91 a. 2c: "Besides this, the rational creature is subject in a more excellent way to the divine providence, since it itself becomes a sharer in providence, providing for itself and for others."
27. See *DThA* 13:480 n. 4.
28. O. H. Pesch, "Kommentar," in *DThA* 13:554.
29. See Pesch, "Kommentar," in *DThA* 13; W. Kluxen, *Philosophische Ethik bei Thomas von Aquin,* 2nd ed. (Hamburg, 1980); K.-W. Merks, *Theologische Grundlegung der sittlichen Autonomie: Strukturmomente eines "autonomen" Normbegründungsverständnisses im lex-Traktat der Summa theologiae des Thomas von Aquin* (Düsseldorf, 1978); B. Bujo, *Moralautonomie und Normenfindung bei Thomas von Aquin unter Einbeziehung der neutestamentlichen Kommentare* (Paderborn/Munich et al., 1979).
30. See especially Auer, *Autonome Moral,* 127–31; idem, "Die Autonomie des Sittlichen nach Thomas von Aquin," in *Christlich glauben und handeln: Fragen einer fundamentalen Moraltheologie in der Diskussion,* ed. K. Demmer and B. Schüller (Düsseldorf, 1977), 31–54.
31. For bibliography, see B. Bujo, *Die Begründung des Sittlichen: Zur Frage des Eudämonismus bei Thomas von Aquin* (Paderborn/Munich, 1984), 75 n. 199.
32. See M.-D. Chenu, "Le plan de la Somme théologique de saint Thomas," *RThom* 47 (1939): 93–107; M. Seckler, *Das Heil in der Geschichte: Geschichtstheologisches Denken bei Thomas von Aquin* (Munich, 1964); O. H. Pesch, "Um

den Plan der Summa Theologiae des hl. Thomas von Aquin: Zu Max Secklers Deutungsversuch," *MThZ* 16 (1965): 128–37; idem, *Theologie der Rechtfertigung bei Martin Luther und Thomas von Aquin: Versuch eines systematisch-theologischen Dialogs,* 2nd ed. (Mainz, 1985), 918–35.

33. See F. Böckle, "Theonome Autonomie: Zur Aufgabenstellung einer fundamentalen Moraltheologie," in *Humanum: Moraltheologie im Dienst des Menschen (Festschrift Egenter),* ed. J. Gründel, F. Rauh, and V. Eid (Düsseldorf, 1972), 17–46; see idem, "Theonomie der Vernunft," in *Fortschritt wohin? Zum Problem der Normenfindung in der pluralen Gesellschaft,* ed. W. Oelmüller (Düsseldorf, 1972), 63–86.

34. Böckle, "Theonomie der Vernunft," 76.

35. See Hirschi, *Moralbegründung,* 141ff.

36. A typical example is B. Stoeckle, *Grenzen der autonomen Moral* (Munich, 1974).

37. See the studies by A. Auer, J. Fuchs, and F. Böckle cited above.

38. A. Auer, "Ist die Kirche heute noch 'ethisch bewohnbar'?" in *Moraltheologie im Abseits? Antwort auf die Enzyklika "Veritatis splendor,"* ed. D. Mieth, 2nd ed. (Freiburg i.Br., 1994), 296–315, at 296.

39. See ibid., 297.

40. See D. Mieth, "Die Moralenzyklika, die Fundamentalmoral und die Kommunikation in der Kirche," in *Moraltheologie im Abseits?* ed. Mieth, 9–24, at 17.

41. Auer, "Ist die Kirche," 302.

42. See B. Bujo, "Erste allgemeine Eindrücke zur Enzyklika 'Veritatis splendor': Wahrheit und Freiheit in der modernen Welt," *Freiburger Nachrichten,* 6 October 1993, p. 5.

43. J. Fuchs, "Die sittliche Handlung: das intrinsece malum," in *Moraltheologie im Abseits?* ed. Mieth, 177–93, at 181.

44. See the periodical *Concilium* 20 (1984), fascicle 2.

45. See M. Vidal, "Läßt sich die Autonomie als Moralgrundlage mit der Befreiungsethik vereinbaren? Der notwendige Dialog zwischen 'Autonomie' und 'Befreiung,'" *Concilium* 20 (1984): 154–59, at 155.

46. Ibid., 154f.

47. Ibid., 155. In addition to M. Vidal, see also F. M. Rejón, "Auf der Suche nach dem Reich und seiner Gerechtigkeit: Die Entwicklung oder Ethik der Befreiung," *Concilium* 20 (1984): 115–20, esp. 118f.

48. See Vidal, "Läßt sich die Autonomie," 156ff.

49. P. Tempels, *Bantu-Philosophie: Ontologie und Ethik* (Heidelberg, 1956), 67; cf. V. Mulago, *Un visage africain du Christianisme: L'union vitale bantu face à l'unité vitale ecclésiale* (Paris, 1965), 121.

50. See A. Kagame, *La Philosophie Bantu comparée* (Paris, 1976), 289, no. 275.

51. See Tempels, *Bantu-Philosophie,* 67.

52. Ibid., 69.

53. Ibid.

54. Ibid., 70.

55. See part 1 of the present book.

56. A. Halder, article "Person," *LThK,* 2nd ed. 8:288.

57. K. Demmer, "Optionalismus—Entscheidung und Grundentscheidung," in *Moraltheologie im Abseits?* ed. Mieth, 69–87, at 71.

58. Charles Nyamiti has attempted to define the person on the basis of a similar context; cf. "The Incarnation Viewed from the African Understanding of Person," *African Christian Studies* 6 (1990): 3–27. After mentioning various conceptions linked to sciences such as cultural anthropology, sociology, and so on (p. 3), he decides in favor of a methodology that sees the person in the light of Black African anthropology: "We shall try to find out the elements which, according to the African, are indicative of an individual's true worth, honour and importance" (p. 4). He continues: "We have preferred to limit ourselves to the above-mentioned conception not only owing to the impossibility of dealing adequately with all the aspects of the topic within the scope of our essay, but especially because we believe that, when used for theological purposes, the African conception we have chosen will lead to more fruitful and original results" (ibid.). Nyamiti emphasizes the significance of the community for the individual. It seems that the individual belongs to the community, rather than vice versa: "The individual's relationship to the community is so intimate that he belongs to it more than the community belongs to him. His individuality, personal responsibilities and rights are acknowledged but they are dominated by the community idea. That is why the acquisition of his personality depends upon his official acknowledgment or acceptance as an adult (person) by the community (e.g., through initiation rituals)" (p. 9). One who is not embedded in a community lacks all personality: he or she is in effect extinguished. Even the deceased receive their personal Being through their relationship to the community of those they leave behind on earth (cf. ibid.). I shall return below to the significance of individuals for the community. D. K. Musonda emphasizes other aspects than Nyamiti and myself, but his definition includes our position; see Musonda, *The Meaning and Value of Life Among the Bisa and Christian Morality* (Rome, 1996), 122–31.

59. *Kudha radi ngü dhedho dzdjo.*

60. *Nru si tsu naro nza.*

61. *Umuryâmbwá aba umwé agatukisha umuryango.*

62. See the original in Kagaragu Ntabaza, *Emigani Bali Bantu: Proverbs et maximes des Bashi* (Bukavu, 1984), 141, no. 1095: *Isu likalaka n'izulu linalake.*

63. See the original in J. C. Katongole, "Ethos Transmission through African-Bantu Proverbs: Proverbs as a Means for Transmitting Values and Beliefs among Africans with the Example of Bantu-Baganda" (dissertation, Würzburg, 1997), 248: *Ekitta obusenze buba bunaanya.*

64. See the original in Kagaragu Ntabaza, *Emigani,* 340, no. 2729: *Orhunyegere rhubiri rhurhayabirwa n'ihanzi.* See also the Swahili proverbs in Taabu Sabiti, *Proverbes et dictons en Swahili et en Kingwana* (n.p.: Editions Saint Paul-Afrique, 1976), 63, no. 8: *Kidole kimoja hakivunji chawa* ("One finger cannot kill

a louse"); no. 15: *Wa kuume haukati wa kushoto* ("The right hand does not cut the left hand off"); no. 16: *Meno ya mbwa hayaumani* ("The teeth of a dog do not bite one another").

65. See Kagaragu Ntabaza, *Emigani,* 63, no. 490: *Ebibwa bibiri birhayabirwa n'ivuha.*

66. See ibid., 1, no. 8: *Abaganda barhankabire benge, ci baba banga.*

67. See Katongole, "Ethos Transmission," 339: *Eyawukana ku mugendo: y'e-fuuka kaasa.*

68. See part 1 of this book.

69. See Bujo, *Die ethische Dimension der Gemeinschaft: Das afrikanische Mod-ell im Nord-Süd-Dialog* (Freiburg i. Ue./Freiburg i. Br., 1993), 138f.; idem, *African Christian Morality at the Age of Inculturation* (reprint, Nairobi, 1998), 96f.

70. See Bujo, *Die ethische Dimension,* pp. 138f.

71. See Kagaragu Ntabaza, *Emigani,* 7, no. 55: *Aga nyandumà mishi gagayun-juliza.*

72. See Taabu Sabiti, *Proverbes,* 138, no. 30: *Mali ya mjomba si ya mwipwa.*

73. See ibid., 134, no. 3: *Ukipenda karanga ("kalanga"), upakatie gae.*

74. See Katongole, "Ethos Transmission," 303: *Ke werimidde: kakira "mbegeraako."*

75. See ibid., 306: *Mazzi masabe: tegamala nnyonta.*

76. See ibid., 307: *Omuggo oguli ewa munnó: tegugoba ngo.*

77. *Ndjale adhuri nikotso.*

78. See Katongole, "Ethos Transmission," 307: *Olwoya lwo mu nnyindo, olweggya wekka.*

79. See ibid., 308: *Kateyanira: kafa omutego.*

80. See ibid.: *"Kambuukire baaba (munnange) w'abuukidde": kwe kuywa mu ntubiro.*

81. See Kagaragu Ntabaza, *Emigani,* 119, no. 924: *Erhi omuntu anywerha, omurhume.*

82. Auer, *Autonome Moral,* p. 185.

83. See ibid., 186.

84. See J. Fuchs, "Gibt es eine unterscheidend christliche Moral?" 101–16.

85. See Auer, *Autonome Moral,* 186.

86. See B. Bujo, *The Ethical Dimension of Community: The African Model and the Dialogue between North and South* (Nairobi, 1998), 157–80.

87. See ibid.

88. See Tempels, *Bantu-Philosophie,* 63.

89. See Bujo, *Ethical Dimension,* 93–98; J. S. Mbiti, *African Religions and Philosophy* (reprint, London/Ibadan/Nairobi, 1983), 133–48; V. Mulago, *Mariage traditionnel africain et mariage chrétien* (Kinshasa, 1981). Cf. also the unpublished dissertation by H. Mitendo Nkelenge, "Mariage contrat ou mariage alliance. Pour une éthique matrimoniale africaine."

90. See B. Bujo, "Krankheit und Gemeinschaft aus negro-afrikanischer

Sicht," in *Heilende Gemeinschaft? Von der sozialen Dimension der Gesundheit,* ed. G. Koch and J. Pretscher (Würzburg, 1996), 9–25.

91. See H. de Lubac, *Surnaturel: Etudes historiques* (Paris 1946; new ed., 1991 with a preface by M. Sales). On de Lubac, see also A. Vanneste, "Saint Thomas et le problème du surnaturel," in Vanneste, *Nature et grâce dans la théologie occidentale: Dialogue avec H. de Lubac* (Louvain, 1996), 161–83.

92. See O.H. Pesch, *Theologie der Rechtfertigung,* 924.

93. See Seckler, *Das Heil in der Geschichte,* 37ff.

94. Pesch, *Theologie der Rechtfertigung,* 929 n. 51.

95. See ibid.

96. *SCG* II c. 55 n. 1309: *Impossibile est naturale desiderium esse inane: natura enim nihil facit frustra.*

97. Enumeration of the Marietti edition.

98. On this whole topic, see Bujo, *Die Begründung des Sittlichen,* 108–22.

99. *Aptitudo ad gratiae susceptionem.* Cf. *De Malo* q. 2 a. 11c and 14.

100. *Iustificatio impii non est miraculosa.*

101. This is set out in greater detail in Bujo, *Die Begründung des Sittlichen;* and Deman, "Kommentar," in *DThA* 14:416.

102. Deman, "Kommentar," in *DThA* 14:416.

103. See the commentary by Vanneste, "Saint Thomas," 142.

104. See ibid., n. 34.

105. *Duplex hominis beatitudo seu felicitas.* Cf. *STh* I-II q. 5 a. 5.

106. *Duplex veritatis modus.*

107. *Novum lumen superadditum.*

108. See E. E. Schockenhoff, *Bonum hominis: Die anthropologischen und theologischen Grundlagen der Tugendethik des Thomas von Aquin* (Mainz, 1987), 286ff.

109. See Vanneste, "Saint Thomas," 174.

110. See ibid., 181. Vanneste refers, *inter alia,* to *In Boet. de Trin.* q. 67 a. 1.

111. Schockenhoff, *Bonum hominis,* 290f.

112. See Bujo, *Die Begründung des Sittlichen,* 93–136. On this whole question of the unity or split in the human person according to Thomas, see O. H. Pesch, "Sünde und Menschsein bei Thomas von Aquin: Eine theologiegeschichtliche Meditation," in *Die Einheit der Person: Beiträge zur Anthropologie des Mittelalters. Richard Heinzmann zum 65. Geburtstag,* ed. M. Thurner (Stuttgart, 1998), 85–98, esp. 93ff.

113. See O. Schilling, *Die Staats- und Soziallehre des hl. Thomas von Aquin* (Paderborn, 1923), 59. See also Bujo, *Moralautonomie und Normenfindung,* 298.

114. Pesch, "Kommentar," in *DThA* 13:740.

115. On this whole question, see Bujo, *Moralautonomie und Normenfindung,* 299ff.

116. See also Schilling, *Die Staats- und Soziallehre,* 93f.

117. See B. Bujo, "Die Frage nach der Entstehung von Moral und Recht aus nichtokzidentaler Sicht," in *Kirche–Kultur–Kommunikation: Peter Henrici zum 70. Geburtstag,* ed. U. Fink and R. Zihlmann (Zurich, 1998), 67–73.

118. See B. Bujo, *Afrikanische Theologie in ihrem gesellschaftlichen Kontext* (Düsseldorf, 1986).

119. See B. Bujo, "Auf der Suche nach einer afrikanischen Christologie," in *Der andere Christus: Christologie in Zeugnissen aus aller Welt,* ed. H. Dembowski and W. Greive (Erlangen, 1991), 87–99, at 98.

120. See above, part 1, chapter 2.

121. Bujo, *Afrikanische Theologie,* 97.

122. See John Paul II, encyclical *Redemptor hominis* (1979), no. 10.

123. On the forms of the Petrine and Pauline privileges, see K.-H. Peschke, *Christliche Ethik: Spezielle Moraltheologie* (Trier, 1995), 536.

124. The doctrine of the two natures, as defined by the Council of Chalcedon, must be interpreted differently in the African context. The fact that Christ has two natures means that God confirms the one vocation of the human person through the same Christ; Christ as God-man is the proof that the humanity of the human person finds fulfillment in God.

Chapter 2
Sin and Freedom of Conscience

1. See H. Küng, *Projekt Weltethos* (Munich/Zurich, 1990); idem, *Weltethos für Weltpolitik und Weltwirtschaft* (Munich/Zurich, 1997); *Erklärung zum Weltethos: Die Deklaration des Parlamentes der Weltreligionen,* ed. H. Küng and K.-J. Kuschel (Munich/Zurich, 1993); *Wissenschaft und Weltethos,* ed. H. Küng and K.-J. Kuschel (Munich/Zurich, 1998).

2. On the discussion from a Black African perspective, see B. Bujo, "Welches Weltethos begründet die Menschenrechte?" *Jahrbuch für christliche Sozialwissenschaften* 39 (1998): 36–53, with bibliographical references to the wider debate on this topic.

3. See B. Bujo, *Die ethische Dimension der Gemeinschaft: Das afrikanische Modell im Nord-Süd-Dialog* (Freiburg i. Ue./Freiburg i. Br., 1993), 53–82.

4. See B. Bujo, *Moralautonomie und Normenfindung bei Thomas von Aquin unter Einbeziehung der neutestamentlichen Kommentare* (Paderborn/Munich et al., 1979), 196.

5. *Instigare ad bonum et remurmurare malo.*

6. *Tota vis conscientiae examinantis vel consiliantis ex iudicio synteresis pendet, sicut tota veritas rationis speculativae pendet ex principiis primis.* See also *STh* I q. 79 a. 13 ad 3.

7. See R. Heinzmann, "Der Mensch als Person: Zum Verständnis des Gewissens bei Thomas von Aquin," in *Das Gewissen: Subjektive Willkür oder oberste Norm?* ed. J. Gründel (Düsseldorf, 1990), 34–52, at 44ff.

8. *Propter se et in specie et in individuo.*

9. See Bujo, *Die ethische Dimension,* 76, where I point out that each one,

including the one who exercises the magisterium, can appeal to his own personal conscience, and that this leads the discussion into an impasse.

10. See T. G. Belmans, "Le paradoxe de la conscience erronée d'Abélard à Karl Rahner," *RThom* 90 (1990): 570–86, at 574. In n. 20, he quotes Bonaventure, II *Sent.* d. 39 a. 1 q. 3 (*Opera omnia,* II, Quaracchi ed., 1985, p. 905B): *Conscientia est sicut praeco Dei et nuntius, et quod dicit non mandat ex se, sed mandat quasi ex Deo, sicut praeco cum divulgat edictum regis, et hinc est quod conscientia habet virtutem ligandi.* See also *VS* 58.

11. See J. Ratzinger, "Wenn Du den Frieden willst, achte das Gewissen jedes Menschen," in Ratzinger, *Vom Wiederauffinden der Mitte: Grundorientierungen. Texte aus vier Jahrzehnten,* ed. S. O. Horn, V. Pfnür, V. Twomey, S. Wiedenhofer and J. Zöhrer (Freiburg i.Br. et al., 1997), 279ff.

12. Ibid., 280.

13. See ibid., 280–81.

14. Ibid., 281.

15. See ibid., 282, 283.

16. See Ratzinger, "Wenn Du den Frieden willst," 278.

17. On this, see C. Maurer, article "Synoida/Syneidesis," *TWNT* 7:905.

18. Bujo, *Die ethische Dimension,* 69.

19. H. Rotter, "Das personale Denken in der Moraltheologie," *StdZ* 206 (1988): 518–28, at 526.

20. A. K. Ruf, *Sünde—Was ist das?* (Munich, 1972), 34f.

21. See the interpretation by H. Krings, article "Existentialismus," in *LThK,* 2nd ed. 3:1305, with references to Sartre's writings.

22. J.-P. Sartre, *Les Mouches* (Paris, 1943), 135.

23. L. Monden, *Sünde, Freiheit und Gewissen* (Salzburg, 1968), 85.

24. J.-P. Sartre, *L'Etre et le néant* (Paris, 1943), 414.

25. See J. M. Aubert, *Abrégé de la morale catholique: La foi vécue* (Paris, 1987), 134.

26. T. Steinbüchel, *Die philosophische Grundlegung der katholischen Sittenlehre,* I (Düsseldorf, 1938), 238.

27. See ibid., 238, 242, 243.

28. S. Kierkegaard, *Fear and Trembling,* Kierkegaard's Writings 6 (Princeton, 1983), 55.

29. Ibid., 55, 56.

30. Ibid., 60–62.

31. See Monden, *Sünde, Freiheit,* 88f., esp. 89.

32. R. Egenter, article "Situationsethik," *LThK,* 2nd ed., 9:805.

33. John A. T. Robinson, *Honest to God* (London, 1963), 106.

34. Ibid., 107, 109–13.

35. Ibid., 114.

36. Ibid., 114, 115.

37. Ibid., 118.

38. John A. T. Tobinson, *Christian Morals Today* (London, 1964), 12 (italics original).

39. Ibid., 18, 20.

40. See Robinson, *Honest to God,* 119, 115.

41. J. Fletcher, *Situation Ethics: The New Morality* (Philadelphia/London 1966), 60.

42. Ibid., 131, 120, 121, 123.

43. Ibid., 142–43. Fletcher discusses the Catholic seal of confession on p. 132: the substance of the confession must be divulged, if love requires it: "when a priest learns 'under the seal' that an innocent man is about to die for the penitent's crime. Canon law forbids him to reveal what he knows. . . . Why is the priest's seal more sacrosanct than the life of the luckless victim of circumstances, waiting in death row? . . . Therefore, in the relativities of this world where conscience labors to do the right thing, we may always do what would be evil in some contexts if in *this* circumstance love gains the balance." In his *Moral Responsibility: Situation Ethics at Work* (Philadelphia, 1967), Fletcher applies his basic principle to specific cases.

44. See Rotter, "Das personale Denken," 518–28.

45. See *AAS* 44 (1952): 413–19.

46. See Ruf, *Sünde,* 40.

47. See ibid., 46.

48. See ibid., 48f.

49. See the excellent remarks by Rotter, "Das personale Denken," 522f.

50. See ibid.

51. See the detailed observations in Bujo, *Die ethische Dimension,* 73–77.

52. Ibid., 63–73, 77–82.

53. On the interpretation of this question, see B. Bujo, *African Christian Morality at the Age of Inculturation* (reprint, Nairobi, 1998), 95ff.

54. See, e.g., D. Nothomb, *Un humanisme africain: Valeurs et pierres d'attente* (preface by A. Kagame) (Brussels, 1969), 240ff.; E. N. Mujynya, "Le mal et le fondement dernier de la morale chez les bantu interlacustres," *Cahiers des Religions Africaines* 3 (1969): 77; V. Mulago, *La religion traditionnelle des Bantu et leur vision du monde,* 2nd ed. (Kinshasa, 1980), 175.

55. See part 1, chapter 1.

56. Kilendu is the language of the Walendu and Bahema in northeastern Congo-Kinshasa.

57. These examples show how questionable is the thesis of Eloi Messi Metogo, who maintains that no proper philosophy can be derived from language. His criticism is directed above all at A. Kagame's book *La Philosophie Bantu comparée* (Paris, 1976). In *Dieu peut-il mourir en Afrique? Essai sur l'indifférence religieuse et l'incroyance en Afrique Noire* (Paris, 1997), 197, E. Messi Metogo writes: "How can one fail to see—to take one example—that no language, whether African or other, contains a vision of the world or a defined philosophy?" In support of his thesis, he quotes at length the radical criticism by Marcien Towa

an Kagama (ibid., n. 3): "In order to make it clear what I mean here, let us imagine that someone wished to infer French philosophy from the French language. You give him a French grammar, the small or large edition of Larousse or the 'Littré.' Now, there is no one in the world who can infer Descartes from French grammar and Larousse. One cannot infer any defined philosophical system from the linguistic structure of a language or from the dictionary of this language, because language is not in fact a theory or a vision of the world. . . . The French language can express all kinds of conceptions of the world . . . which belong to Chinese or Hindu philosophy. . . . And what I say here about French applies to all languages, without any distinctions." This thesis by M. Towa, which Messi Metogo adopts uncritically, cries out for a thorough examination; since this is not possible within the framework of the present book, a few points must suffice. Naturally, no philosophical theory exists in a particular language, nor does it contain any already existing system. But every language reflects a particular rationality which is based on a particular worldview—and this in turn is indispensable for the elaboration of a philosophical theory. Even if one cannot discern an individual system such as Aristotelianism, Thomism, Cartesianism, and so on, it is nevertheless possible, by means of the linguistic concepts employed, to trace every system back to its *Sitz im Leben* and the cultural coordinates in which it was born. It is strange that Messi Metogo has not noticed that a European and an African have different ideas of what is signified by such words as "older brother" or "ancestor." Is it not possible to use this as the starting point for the development of different philosophical or theological theories, each with its own rationality? Besides this, the quotation from Vanneste (see Messi Metogo, *Dieu peut-il mourir en Afrique?* 176) completely ignores the numerous discussions on this point, which considerably relativize the ideas of this author. See the references in B. Bujo, *Afrikanische Theologie in ihrem gesellschaftlichen Kontext* (Düsseldorf, 1986), 64–71.

58. On this whole subject, see Bujo, *African Christian Morality,* 100.

59. *Gûtiri mûici na mûcûûthîrîrîa,* quoted in G. J. Wanjohi, *The Wisdom and Philosophy of the Gikuyu Proverbs: The Kihooto World-View* (Nairobi, 1997), 137.

60. See ibid.

61. *Mundu utari mburi ndendaga nyama,* quoted in Wanjohi, *Wisdom,* 137.

62. On the commentary, see ibid.

63. See ibid., 138.

64. See Bujo, *Die ethische Dimension,* 63–66.

65. See L. Magesa, *African Religion: The Moral Traditions of Abundant Life* (Nairobi, 1998), 156ff.

66. See J. Bradshaw, *Bradshaw on the Family—A Revolutionary Way of Self-Discovery* (Florida, 1988), 2; quoted from Magesa, *African Religion,* 156f.

67. On this, see Bujo, *Die ethische Dimension,* 69–79, 84–89.

68. See ibid., 208ff.

69. See J. S. Mbiti, *Introduction to African Religion,* 2nd ed. (Nairobi/Kampala, 1996), 178.

70. Ibid., 179.

71. See ibid.

72. See E. E. Uzukwu, *A Listening Church: Autonomy and Communion in African Churches* (Maryknoll, N.Y., 1996), 18f., 127ff.

73. See Bujo, *African Christian Morality,* 98ff.

74. See ibid. for a more detailed discussion.

75. See Mbiti, *Introduction,* 177.

76. See Magesa, *African Religion,* 140.

77. See Mbiti, *Introduction,* 172: "It may be possible for some individuals to do some of these things, but precisely what powers and knowledge they use I do not know. The fact that most of us do not understand them does not mean they cannot be done."

78. See ibid., 170, 168.

79. Magesa, *African Religion,* 170–73.

80. See Mbiti, *Introduction,* 210, proverb 57.

81. See ibid., 209, proverb 38.

82. See Bujo, *Die ethische Dimension,* 66–73; idem, "Gibt es Demokratie im Singular? Eine Anfrage aus schwarzafrikanischer Perspektive," in *Ethik und Demokratie, 28: Internationaler Fachkongreß für Moraltheologie und Sozialethik (Sept. 1997/Münster),* ed. A. Autiero (Münster, 1998), 47–62.

83. See Bujo, "Gibt es Demokratie," 57f.

84. Many western philosophers and theologians think on similar lines: see, e.g., H. Krings, article "Freiheit," in *Handbuch philosophischer Grundbegriffe,* 2:507: "The concept of freedom is from the very outset a concept involving communication. Freedom is not primarily the attribute of an individual subject which could exist and be understood on its own; rather, the concept of an individual subject can be understood only by means of that communicative concept. In empirical terms, this means that a human being on his own cannot be free. Freedom is possible only where freedom opens itself up to others." This means that individual freedom is freedom only where it loses itself in the freedom of others, in order that these too may experience genuine human existence. See also B. Hidber, "Freiheit und Sünde: Zur theologischen Verhältnisbestimmung," in *In Christus zum Leben befreit: Für Bernhard Häring,* ed. J. Römelt and B. Hidber (Freiburg i.Br. et al., 1992), 84–111, at 98: "Freedom is realized in and through ties. . . . Freedom makes the human person a subject precisely by opening him and orienting him towards other subjects."

85. See Mbiti, *Introduction,* 177: "Even though the individual exists for his society and not vice versa, the community respects his property and life. . . . The community must show justice towards the individual, for this is a moral duty of society." I believe that it would be better to keep the concepts of "society" and "community" separate. In the African context, the latter is to be preferred. Besides this, one cannot simply assert that "society" in Africa does not exist for the individual. The palaver procedure, as described above, suggests a rather different relationship between community (or society) and individual.

Chapter 3
Critical Observation:
The Challenge of Inculturation

1. See B. Bujo, "Das Lustprinzip in der Sexualmoral," *StdZ* 215 (1997): 627–35, at 630.

2. For a representative collection of testimonies, see Awa Thiem, *Die Stimme der schwarzen Frau: Vom Leid der Afrikanerinnen* (Reinbek bei Hamburg, 1986).

3. See J. Kenyatta, *Facing Mount Kenya: The Traditional Life of the Gikuyu* (Nairobi, 1991).

4. See ibid., 135: "For years there has been much criticism and agitation against *irua* of girls by certain misinformed missionary societies in East Africa, who see only the surgical side of the *irua,* and, without investigating the psychological importance attached to the custom by the Gikuyu. These missionaries draw their conclusion that the *irua* of girls is nothing but a barbarous practice and, as such, should be abolished by law. On the other hand, the Gikuyu look on these religious fanatics with great suspicion. The overwhelming majority of them believe that it is the secret aim of those who attack this centuries-old custom to disintegrate their social order and thereby hasten their Europeanisation. The abolition of *irua* will destroy the tribal symbol which identifies the age-groups, and prevent the Gikuyu from perpetuating that spirit of collectivism and national solidarity which they have been able to maintain from time immemorial."

5. See ibid., 130–54.

6. See ibid., 130–33.

7. See B. Kisembo et al., *African Christian Marriage,* 2nd ed. (Nairobi, 1998), 94; Kenyatta, *Facing Mount Kenya,* 174.

8. See Kisembo et al., *African Christian Marriage,* 174: "Polygamy creates larger and more complex affinal networks which have a stabilizing effect on the institution of marriage. It is frequently remarked by anthropologists that marriage is noticeably more stable where polygamy flourishes."

9. See Kenyatta, *Facing Mount Kenya,* 176. He quotes the first wife, who is urging her husband to marry a second wife: "My husband, don't you think it is wise for you to get me a companion (*moiru*)? Look at our position now. I am sure you will realise how God has been good to us to give us a nice and healthy baby. For the first few days I must devote all my attention to nursing our baby. I am weak. . . . I can't go to the river to bring water nor to the field to bring some food, nor to weed our gardens. You have no one to entertain them. I have no doubt that you realise the seriousness of the matter. What do you think of the daughter of so-and-so? She is beautiful and industrious and people speak highly about her and her family. Do not fail me, my husband. Try and win her love. I have spoken to her and found that she is very interested in our homestead. In anything I can do to help you I am at your sevice, my husband. Even if we have not enough sheep and goats for the dowry our relatives and friends will help you so that you can get her into our family. You are young and healthy and this is the best time for us to have healthy children and so enlarge our family group, and thereby

perpetuate our family name after you and I have gone. My husband, please act quickly as you know the Gikuyu saying: *Mae megotherera matietagerera mondo onyotie* ('The flowing water of the river does not wait for a thirsty man')."

10. On this question, see C. Haule, *Bantu "Witchcraft" and Christian Morality: The Encounter of Bantu Uchawi with Christian Morality. An Anthropological and Theological Study* (Immensee, 1969); T. M. Buakasa, *L'Impensé du discours: "Kindoki" et "nkisi" en pays kongo du Zaïre,* 2nd ed. (Kinshasa, 1980); M. P. Hebga, *Sorcellerie et prière de délivrance* (Paris/Abidjan, 1982). See also Lufuluabo Mizeka, *L'Anti-sorcier face à la science,* with a preface by Cardinal Malula (Mbujimayi, 1977).

11. See Buakasa, *L'Impensé du discours;* L. Magesa, *African Religion: The Moral Traditions of Abundant Life* (Nairobi, 1998), 165–74. Magesa correctly notes: "In addition to malevolent witches, sorcerers, medicine-doctors and herbalists may possess the same powers as witches, but they are not necessarily malevolent. On the contrary, sometimes they use their power in benevolent ways. Because of the mystical power that they share with a 'witch proper', they too are referred to as witches (using the vernacular)" (p. 165). The Kiswahili language in Congo-Kinshasa makes the distinction between *mchawi* and *mlozi.* While a *mchawi* always harms other people, a *mlozi* is one who knows exactly the same techniques and secret practices as the *mchawi,* but does not share his desire to hurt; however, his deep knowledge of the techniques of a *mchawi* means that he could in fact inflict harm. The Kilendu language in Eastern Congo-Kinshasa distinguishes between *djaiba* and *nruba.* The latter, who possesses all the knowledge of the former, can help people to discover who is the true *djaiba* (sorcerer) with evil intent. The Chagga in Tanzania speak of *msawi* (sorcerer) and *muwanga* (healer). Every *muwanga* is, however, a potential *msawi,* since he could also misuse the weapons which are meant to be employed against sorcerers. On this, see S. N. A. Mosha, "Sin in the African Practices of Medicine, Healing and 'Divination'" (M.A. dissertation, manuscript, Nairobi, 1987), 15–16; B. Bujo, "Krankheit und Gemeinschaft aus negro-afrikanischer Sicht," in *Heilende Gemeinschaft? Von der sozialen Dimension der Gesundheit,* ed. G. Koch and J. Pretscher (Würzburg, 1996), 10–11.

12. See Buakasa, *L'Impensé du discours,* 283ff.

13. See ibid., 304ff.

14. For a commentary, see Magesa, *African Religion,* 168ff.

15. See the case of Kimputu, presented by Buakasa, *L'Impensé du discours,* 36ff. On p. 51, he gives the following interpretation: since Kimputu works with the whites, he loses respect for old persons—and it is precisely these who are the elders of the community.

16. See Buakasa, *L'Impensé du discours,* 38, 51. On p. 38, Kimputu relates what the *nganga* (healer) has said to him: "I feel sorry for you and Wumba. Lord Mbwanga has had you tied to the fetish Mpungu in the land of the Ntandu, because if you start to work, you will have no more respect for the elders."

17. See Magesa, *African Religion,* 137–39; J. S. Mbiti, *Introduction to African Religion,* 2nd ed. (Nairobi/Kampala, 1996), 95f.

18. See Magesa, *African Religion,* 137.

19. See J. Nyerere, "Ujamaa—Grundlage des afrikanischen Sozialismus," in *Afrikanischer Sozialismus: Aus den Reden und Schriften von Julius K. Nyerere,* with an introduction by Gerhard Grohs (Stuttgart, 1972), 10–18, at 13.

20. Ibid.

21. On this whole subject, see B. Bujo, *Die ethische Dimension der Gemeinschaft: Das afrikanische Modell im Nord-Süd-Dialog* (Freiburg i. Ue./Freiburg i. Br., 1993), 122f.

22. See part 2, chapter 2.

23. See Bujo, *Die ethische Dimension,* 99–111.

24. See ibid., 99ff.

25. G. Odi Assamoi, "Die Begegnung der christlichen Moral mit der afrikanischen Familientradition," *Concilium* 17 (1981): 794–800, at 798; see also Mariama Bâ, *Ein so langer Brief: Ein afrikanisches Frauenschicksal* (Wuppertal, 1980).

26. See Magesa, *African Religion,* 138f. He mentions here *inter alia* the Yoruba, Ganda, Nyoro, Kpelle, Dogon, and Lango. As we have seen, the negative attitude toward twins also applies in many ethnic groups to older persons, who are suspected of being a threat to life. It is alleged that they begrudge other people life.

27. See, *inter alia,* A. Ridl, *Die kirchliche Lehrautorität in Fragen der Moral nach den Aussagen des Ersten Vatikanischen Konzils* (Freiburg i.Br./Basel/Vienna, 1979); J. Schuster, *Ethos und kirchliches Lehramt: Zur Kompetenz des kirchlichen Lehramtes in Fragen der natürlichen Sittlichkeit* (Frankfurt a.M., 1984); *Der Glaubenssinn des Gottesvolkes—Konkurrent oder Partner des Lehramts?* ed. D. Wiederkehr (Freiburg i.Br./Basel/Vienna, 1994).

28. See A. Auer, *Autonome Moral und christlicher Glaube: Zweite um einen Nachtrag erweiterte Auflage* (Düsseldorf, 1984), 139.

29. See Ridl, *Die kirchliche Lehrautorität*; and Schuster, *Ethos und kirchliches Lehramt.*

30. Schuster, *Ethos und kirchliches Lehramt,* 381.

31. See ibid.

32. See *DH* 4149: "This infallibility, with which the divine Redeemer wished his church to be equipped in defining doctrine about faith or morals, is coextensive with the deposit of divine revelation which must be preserved religiously and expounded faithfully."

33. See the commentary by A. Auer on *GS* 33 in *LThK-E,* 3:380f.

34. J. Ratzinger, "Demokratisierung der Kirche," in Ratzinger and H. Maier, *Demokratie in der Kirche: Möglichkeiten, Grenzen, Gefahren* (Limburg, 1970), 43.

35. See ibid., 43f. J. Ratzinger refers (p. 44 n. 30) to Cyprian, *Ep.* 14.4 (CSEL III 2, p. 512, 16–20): "As for what our fellow-presbyters Donatus, Fortunatus, Novatus and Gordius wrote to me, I could not reply on my own, since I had resolved from the very beginning of my episcopal ministry to do nothing on the basis of my own private opinion, without your [plural] counsel and without the consent of the people." Ratzinger also quotes *Ep.* 66.8 (ibid., p. 733,

4–6): "It follows that you must realize that the bishop is in the church, and the church is in the bishop. If anyone is not with the bishop, he is not in the church."

36. Ratzinger, "Demokratisierung," 44.

37. Congregation for the Doctrine of the Faith, "Instruction on the ecclesial vocation of the theologian" (*Donum veritatis*), 1990, nos. 15–16; see also *Humanae vitae* 4.

38. See *DH* 3005; *Donum veritatis* 16 n. 17.

39. See the profession of faith in the motu proprio *Ad tuendam fidem* of Pope John Paul II (1998); see also nos. 10–11 in the "Doctrinal Notification" about this motu proprio by the Congregation for the Doctrine of the Faith, and *Donum veritatis* 17 and 23. On *Ad tuendam fidem* and the commentary by the Congregation, see the very important essay by P. Hünermann, "Schutz des Glaubens? Kritische Rückfragen eines Dogmatikers," *HK* 52 (1998): 455–60; idem, "'Den Glauben gegen Irrtümer verteidigen': Kritische Reflexionen eines Dogmatikers zu den jüngsten römischen Verlautbarungen," in *Bindung an die Kirche oder Autonomie? Theologie im gesellschaftlichen Diskurs,* ed. A. Franz (Freiburg i.Br., 1999), 291–303.

40. Congregation for the Doctrine of the Faith, Doctrinal Notification, no. 10 (*tuto doceri non potest*); see also CIC canons 752 and 1371.

41. This third category is the object of the profession of faith: see *Ad tuendam fidem* 22. See the fundamental criticism by Hünermann, "Schutz des Glaubens?" 459f.

42. See M. Löhrer, "Dogmatische Erwägungen zur unterschiedlichen Funktion und zum gegenseitigen Verhältnis von Lehramt und Theologie in der katholischen Kirche," in *Theologe und Hierarch,* ed. J. Pfammatter and E. Christen, Theologische Berichte 17 (Zurich, 1988), 11–53, at 45.

43. Ibid.

44. Löhrer, "Dogmatische Erwägungen," 46.

45. See M. Seckler, "Vom Geist und von der Funktion der Theologie im Mittelalter," in Sekler, *Im Spannungsfeld von Wissenschaft und Kirche: Theologie als schöpferische Auslegung der Wirklichkeit* (Freiburg i.Br., 1980), 149–60.

46. Ibid., 150.

47. M. Seckler, "Die Theologie als kirchliche Wissenschaft—ein römisches Modell," in Sekler, *Im Spannungsfeld,* 62–84, at 83.

48. On this, see also Löhrer, "Dogmatische Erwägungen," 48f.

49. See Ratzinger, "Demokratisierung," 43.

50. See S. Wiedenhofer, "Ekklesiologische Implikationen eines demokratischen Stils in der Ethik," in *Ethik und Demokratie 28: Internationaler Fachkongreß für Moraltheologie und Sozialethik,* ed. A. Autiero (Münster, 1998), 141–56, at 151f.

51. See J. Fuchs, "Magisterium und Moraltheologie," in Fuchs, *Für eine menschliche Moral: Grundfragen der theologischen Ethik,* III, *Die Spannung zwischen objektiver und subjektiver Moral* (Freiburg i.Ue./Freiburg i.Br., 1991), 127–38, at 130.

52. See ibid., 127.

53. Ibid., 128.

54. See G. Lohfink, "Die Normativität der Amtsvorstellungen in den Pastoralbriefen," *ThQ* 157 (1977): 93–106, at 96.

55. See ibid., 98, 99.

56. See Schuster, *Ethos und kirchliches Lehramt,* 305, with reference to *GS* 62: "The deposit and the truths of faith are one thing, the manner of expressing them is quite another—provided the meaning and understanding of them is safeguarded."

57. D. Wiederkehr, "Sensus vor Consensus: Auf dem Weg zu einem partizipativen Glauben—Reflexionen einer Wahrheitspolitik," in *Der Glaubenssinn des Gottesvolkes,* ed. D. Wiederkehr (Freiburg i.Br./Basel/Vienna, 1994), 182–206, at 186.

58. See ibid., 191.

59. See ibid., 190.

60. See part 1, chapter 2.

61. See L.-V. Thomas, "Corps et société: Le cas négro-africain," in *L'Afrique et ses formes de vie spirituelle* (Kinshasa, 1981), 193–214, at 202f.

62. See ibid., 203–5; B. Bujo, "Sexualverhalten in Afrika," *ThG* 36 (1993): 209–18.

63. See E. E. Uzukwu, *A Listening Church: Autonomy and Communion in African Churches* (Maryknoll, N.Y., 1996), 127ff.

64. This is stated at greater depth in Uzukwu, *A Listening Church,* 129f.

65. See B. Bujo, *Dieu devient homme en Afrique noire: Méditation sur l'Incarnation* (Kinshasa, 1996), 26–28.

66. See also John Paul II, *Ecclesia in Africa,* no. 63.

67. The Kiswahili spoken in Tanzania distinguishes between *familia* and *jamaa.* The former word is completely Western, and does not reflect the African reality.

68. See B. Bujo, "Auf dem Weg zu einer afrikanischen Ekklesiologie," *StdZ* 212 (1994): 254–66, at 255.

69. S. Wiedenhofer, *Das katholische Kirchenverständnis: Ein Lehrbuch der Ekklesiologie* (Graz, 1992), 79.

70. Ibid.

71. See F. Wilfred, "Vom Schattenboxen zum Dialog. Grundlegende Probleme einer asiatischen Theologie," *HK* 53 (1999): 26–33, at 27.

72. The encyclical runs a kind of slalom. It emphasizes on the one hand that it does not intend to declare any one system to be compulsory, but this is in fact what it ultimately does. See, e.g., *FR* 49, 64, 71, 72, 78.

73. For an example of this, see what we have written above about homosexuality.

74. See J.-A. Malula, "Mariage et famille en Afrique," in *Œuvres complètes du Cardinal Malula,* VII, ed. L. de Saint Moulin (Kinshasa, 1997), 135–45: "Certainly, it is *de fide divina* that Christ affirmed and taught the indissolubility of

marriage. We in Africa know this, and we teach it too. But we also believe that Christ did not say how persons were to marry among different peoples, nor when a validly contracted marriage becomes or is absolutely indissoluble. This is why only the affirmation of indissolubility should be held as being *de fide divina* and an absolute imperative. But has God revealed the manner of constituting the marriage bond (e.g., the canonical form) and the conditions for its indissolubility (consummation by one single sexual act)? Are these not cultural phenomena in time and space?" (p. 143). See also Luc Auguste Sangare (Archbishop of Bamako in Mali), "Mariage et famille: Propositions," and Raphael S. Mwana'a Nzeki Ndingi (Bishop of Nakuru in Kenya), "Reconnaître le mariage traditionnel," both in *Le Synode africain: Histoires et textes,* ed. M. Cheza, with a preface by Jean-Marc Ela (Paris, 1996), 124f., 126–28. We should also note the statement by Alberto Setele (Bishop of Inhambane in Mozambique), "Mariage et famille: Défis pastoraux," ibid., 123f.

Concluding Remarks

1. See part 2, chapter 1.
2. See, e.g., part 2, chapter 3.
3. See part 2, chapter 2.
4. I have discussed this question in detail in B. Bujo, *Die ethische Dimension der Gemeinschaft: Das afrikanische Modell im Nord-Süd-Dialog* (Freiburg i. Ue./Freiburg i. Br., 1993), 63–82.
5. See part 2, chapter 2.
6. J. Ratzinger, *Zur Lage des Glaubens: Ein Gespräch mit Vittorio Messori* (Munich, 1985), 207.
7. Ibid.
8. See R. Schreiter, *Abschied vom Gott der Europäer: Zur Entwicklung regionaler Theologien,* with a preface by Edward Schillebeeckx (Salzburg, 1992).
9. See ibid., 177–79.
10. Ibid., 179.
11. Ibid., 180f.
12. Ibid., 181.
13. Many people, especially Western scholars and thinkers, hold that one must speak of Black Africa in the plural, since there is no one native African culture. For example, Cardinal Ratzinger says in the conversation quoted above: "The 'pure' African tradition as such does not exist. It has many layers, some of them mutually contradictory, depending on the provenance of the strata" (*Zur Lage,* 208). On the following page, he repeats that Africa "is a continent with so many strata that it cannot be reduced to one general structure." This thesis can no longer be maintained today, thanks to the work of African scholars who—despite variations in detail—agree that the fundamental orientations and concepts are the same among most of the peoples of Black Africa, for example, the

attitude to God, the ancestors, the community, illness and healing; the differences arise when it is a question of the specific prayers, rites, and so on, through which the common goal is to be attained. The project of an African theology or an African Christianity is concerned with the fundamental reality, not with the details. On the common elements and the unity of religion and ethics in Africa, see most recently L. Magesa, *African Religion: The Moral Traditions of Abundant Life* (Nairobi, 1998).

Bibliography

1. Documents of the Church

Vatican Council I

Dogmatic Constitution on the Catholic Faith (*Dei Filius*). April 24, 1870.

Dogmatic Constitution on the Church of Christ (*Pastor aeternus*). July 18, 1870.

Vatican Council II

Dogmatic Constitution on the Church (*Lumen gentium*). November 21, 1964.

Decree on Priestly Training (*Optatam totius*). October 28, 1965.

Declaration on Christian Education (*Gravissimum educationis*). October 28, 1965.

Dogmatic Constitution on Divine Revelation (*Dei verbum*). November 18, 1965.

Pastoral Constitution on the Church in the Modern World (*Gaudium et spes*). December 7, 1965.

Decree on the Mission Activity of the Church (*Ad gentes*). December 7, 1965.

Declaration on Religious Freedom (*Dignitatis humanae*). December 7, 1965.

Paul VI

Encyclical *Humanae vitae*. July 25, 1968.

John Paul II

Encyclical *Redemptor hominis.* March 4, 1979.

Apostolic exhortation *Familiaris consortio.* November 22, 1981.

Congregation for the Doctrine of the Faith

Instruction *Donum vitae.* February 22, 1987.

Instruction on the Ecclesial Vocation of the Theologian (*Donum veritatis*). May 24, 1990.

Catechism of the Catholic Church. 1993.

John Paul II

Encyclical *Veritatis splendor.* August 6, 1993.

Post-Synodal apostolic exhortation *Ecclesia in Africa* (On the Church in Africa and Its Evangelizing Mission towards the Year 2000). September 14, 1995.

Apostolic letter motu proprio *Ad tuendam fidem.* May 18, 1998.

Encyclical *Fides et ratio.* September 14, 1998.

2. Selected Bibliography

Adeolu-Adegbola, E. A. "The Theological Basis of Ethics." In *Biblical Revelation and African Beliefs,* ed. K. A. Dickson and E. Ellingworth, 116–36. London, 1969.

Andavo, J. *La responsabilité négro-africaine dans l'accueil et le don de la vie: Perspective d'inculturation pour les époux chrétiens.* Fribourg/Paris, 1996.

Apel, K.-O. *Diskurs und Verantwortung: Das Problem des Übergangs zur postkonventionellen Moral.* Frankfurt a.M., 1988.

———, and M. Kettner, eds. *Die eine Vernunft und die vielen Rationalitäten.* Frankfurt a.M., 1996.

Auer, A. *Autonome Moral und christlicher Glaube: Zweite um einen Nachtrag erweiterte Auflage.* Düsseldorf, 1984.

———. *Zur Theologie der Ethik: Das Weltethos im theologischen Diskurs.* Freiburg i.Ue./Freiburg i.Br., 1995.

Awa Thiem. *Black Sisters Speak Out. Black Women and Oppression in Black Africa.* 1996.

Barrett, A. J. *Sacrifice and Prophecy in Turkana Cosmology.* Nairobi, 1998.

Bidima, J.-G. *La palabre: Une juridiction de la parole.* Paris, 1997.

Böckle, F., ed. *Fundamentalmoral.* 5th ed. Munich, 1985. English, *Fundamental Moral Theology,* 1980.

Bradshaw, J. *Bradshaw on the Family: A Revolutionary Way of Self-Discovery.* Florida, 1988.

Browne, M., ed. *The African Synod. Documents, Reflections, Perspectives.* Maryknoll, N.Y., 1996. Pp. 139–51.

Buakasa, T. K. M. *L'impensé du discours. "Kindoki" et "nkisi" en pays kongo du Zaire.* 2d ed. Kinshasa, 1980.

Bujo, B., "A Christocentric Ethic for Black Africa." *Theology Digest* 30 (1982): 143–46.

———. *African Christian Morality at the Age of Inculturation.* Nairobi, 1998 (new printing).

———. *African Theology in its Social Context.* 2d ed. Nairobi, 1999.

———. "Can Morality Be Christian in Africa?" *African Christian Studies* 32 (1985): 230–34.

———. *Christmas. God Becomes Man in Black Africa.* Nairobi, 1995.

———. *Do We Still Need the Ten Commandments?* 2d ed. Nairobi, 1990.

———. "On the Road toward an African Ecclesiology. Reflections on the Synod." In *The African Synod. Documents, Reflections, Perspectives,* ed. E. Browne, 139–51. Maryknoll, N.Y., 1996.

———. "Polygamy in Africa: A Pastoral Approach." *Theology Digest* 32 (1985): 230–34.

———. "Solidarity and Freedom: Christian Ethic in Africa." *Theology Digest* 34 (1987): 48–50.

———. *The Ethical Dimension of Community. The African Model and the Dialogue between North and South.* Nairobi, 1998.

Cone, J. H. *Martin—Malcolm—America.* Maryknoll, N.Y., 1993.

———, and B. Schüller, eds. *Christlich glauben und handeln: Fragen einer fundamentalen Moraltheologie in der Diskussion.* Düsseldorf, 1977.

Dickson, K. A., and E. Ellingworth, eds. *Biblical Revelation and African Beliefs.* London, 1969.

Fabella, V. M. M., and A. M. Oduyoye, ed. *With Passion and Compassion: Third World Women Doing Theology.* Maryknoll, N.Y., 1988.

Fletcher, J. *Moral Responsibility: Situation Ethics at Work.* Philadelphia, 1967.

———. *Situation Ethics: The New Morality.* Philadelphia, 1966.

Forst, R. *Kontexte der Gerechtigkeit. Politische Philosophie jenseits von Liberalismus und Kommunitarismus.* Frankfurt a.M., 1994.

Fuchs, J. *Für eine menschliche Moral: Grundfragen der theologischen Ethik.* Vol. 1, *Normative Grundlegung.* Freiburg i.Ue./Freiburg i.Br., 1988.

———. *Für eine menschliche Moral: Grundfragen der theologischen Ethik.* Vol. 3, *Die Spannung zwischen objektiver und subjektiver Moral.* Freiburg i.Ue./Freiburg i.Br., 1991.

———. *Für eine menschliche Moral: Grundfragen der theologischen Ethik*, Vol. 4, *Auf der Suche nach der sittlichen Wahrheit.* Freiburg i.Ue./Freiburg i.Br., 1997.

Greshake, G. *Der dreieine Gott: Eine trinitarische Theologie.* 2nd ed. Freiburg i.Br., 1997.

Gründel, J., ed. *Das Gewissen: Subjektive Willkür oder oberste Norm?* Düsseldorf, 1990.

Habermas, J. *Erläuterungen zur Diskürsethik.* Frankfurt a.M., 1991. English, *Justification and Application.* Cambridge, Mass., 1993.

———. *Moralbewußtsein und kommunikatives Handeln.* Frankfurt a.M., 1983. English, *Moral Consciousness and Communicative Action.* Cambridge, Mass., 1992.

Haule, C. *Bantu "Witchcraft" and Christian Morality: The Encounter of Bantu Uchawi with Christian Morality. An Anthropological and Theological Study.* Immensee, 1969.

Healey, J., and D. Sybertz. *Towards an African Narrative Theology.* Nairobi, 1996.

Heinzmann, R. "Der Mensch als Person. Zum Verständnis des Gewissens bei Thomas von Aquin." In *Das Gewissen: Subjektive Willkür oder oberste Norm?* ed. J. Gründel, 34–52. Düsseldorf, 1990.

Hillman, E. *Polygamy Reconsidered: African Plural Marriage and the Christian Church.* Maryknoll, N.Y., 1975.

Hirschi, H. *Moralbegründung und christlicher Sinnhorizont: Eine Auseinandersetzung mit Alfons Auers moraltheologischem Konzept.* Freiburg i.Ue./ Freiburg i.Br., 1992.

Hoebel, E. A. *The Law of Primitive Man: A Study in Comparative Legal Dynamics.* Cambridge, 1967.

Höffe, O. *Aristoteles: Nikomachische Ethik.* Berlin, 1995.

———. *Aristoteles.* Munich, 1996.

———. *Vernunft und Recht: Bausteine zu einem interkulturellen Rechtsdiskurs.* Frankfurt a.M., 1996.

Holzen, W. von, and S. Fagan, eds. *Africa: The Kairos of a Synod. Sedos Symposium on Africa.* Rome, 1994.

Honneth, A., ed. *Kommunitarismus: Eine Debatte über die moralischen Grundlagen moderner Gesellschaften.* 2nd ed. Frankfurt a.M., 1994.

———, Th. McCarthy, C. Offe, and A. Wellmer, eds. *Zwischenbetrachtungen. Im Prozeß der Aufklärung. Jürgen Habermas zum 60. Geburtstag.* Frankfurt a.M., 1989. English, *Philosophical Interventions in the Unfinished Project of Enlightenment.* Cambridge, Mass., 1992.

Idowu, E. B. *African Traditional Religion: A Definition.* 12th ed. London, 1983.

Ifesieh, E. L. "Some Factors Affecting the Stability of Marriage among the Yoruba and the Igbo of Nigeria." *Cahiers des Religions Africaines* 19 (1985): 213–26.

Joas, H. *Die Entstehung der Werte.* Frankfurt a.M., 1997. English, *The Genesis of Values.* Chicago, 2001.

Kagame, A. *La Philosophie Bantu comparée.* Paris, 1976.

———. *La philosophie bantu-rwandaise.* Brussels, 1956.

Kagaragu Ntabaza. *Emigani Bali Bantu: Proverbes et maximes des Bashi.* Bukavu, 1984.

Kanyandago, P. M. *Evangelizing Polygamous Families: Canonical and African Approaches.* Eldoret, 1991.

Kasonga wa Kasonga. "African Christian Palaver. A Contemporary Way of Healing Communal Conflicts and Crises." In *The Church and Healing: Echoes from Africa,* ed. E. J. Lartey, D. Nwachuku, and Kasonga wa Kasonga, 48–65. Frankfurt a.M., 1994.

Katongole, J. C. "Ethos Transmission through African-Bantu Proverbs: Proverbs as a Means for Transmitting Values and Beliefs among Africans with the Example of Bantu-Baganda." Dissertation, Würzburg, 1997.

Kenyatta, J. *Facing Mount Kenya: The Traditional Life of the Gikuyu.* Nairobi, 1991.

Kierkegaard, S. *Fear and Trembling.* Kierkegaard's Writings 4. Princeton, N.J., 1983.

Kirwen, M. C. *African Widows: An Empirical Study of the Problems of Adapting Western Christian Teachings on Marriage to the Leviratic Custom for the Care of Widows in Four Rural African Societies.* Maryknoll, N.Y., 1979.

Kisembo, B., L. Magesa, and A. Shorter, eds. *African Christian Marriage.* 2d ed. Nairobi, 1998.

Kofon, N. E. *Polygyny in Pre-christian Bafut and New Moral Theological Perspectives.* Frankfurt a.M., 1992.

Kohlberg, L. *Essays on Moral Development.* 2 volumes. San Francisco, 1981, 1984.

Küng, H. *Projekt Weltethos.* Munich/Zurich, 1990. English, *Global Responsibility. In Search of a New World Ethic.* New York, 1991.

———. *Welthethos für Weltpolitik und Weltwirtschaft.* Munich/Zurich, 1997.

———, and K.-J. Kuschel, eds. *Erklärung zum Weltethos: Die Deklaration des Parlamentes der Weltreligionen.* Munich/Zurich, 1993. English, *A Global Ethic: The Declaration of the Parliament of the World's Religions.* 1993.

———, and K.-J. Kuschel, eds. *Wissenschaft und Weltethos.* Munich/Zurich, 1998.

Lartey, E. J. "Two Healing Communities in Africa." In *The Church and Healing: Echoes from Africa,* ed. E. J. Lartey, D. Nwachuku, and Kasonga wa Kasonga, 33–48. Frankfurt a.M., 1994.

———, D. Nwachuku, and Kasonga wa Kasonga, eds. *The Church and Healing: Echoes from Africa.* Frankfurt a.M., 1994.

Lévy-Bruhl, L. *L'âme primitive,* Paris, 1927. English, *The "Soul" of the Primitive.* London and New York, 1928.

———. *L'expérience mystique et les symboles chez les primitifs.* Paris, 1938.

———. *La mentalité primitive.* Paris, 1922. English, *Primitive Mentality.* London and New York, 1923.

———. *La mythologie primitive.* Paris, 1935. English, *Primitive Mythology.* Queensland, 1983.

———. *Le surnaturel et la nature dans la mentalité primitive.* Paris, 1931. English, *Primitives and the Supernatural.* New York, 1935.

———. *Les fonctions mentales dans les sociétés inférieures.* Paris, 1910. English, *How Natives Think.* New York, 1925.

MacIntyre, A. *After Virtue: A Study in Moral Theory.* Notre Dame, Ind., 1981; 2d ed., 1984.

Magesa, L. *African Religion: The Moral Traditions of Abundant Life.* Nairobi, 1998.

Malula, J.-A. "Mariage et famille en Afrique." In *Œuvres complètes du Cardinal Malula,* Bd. 7, ed. L. de Saint Moulin, 135–45. Kinshasa, 1997.

Mariama Bâ. *Ein so langer Brief: Ein afrikanisches Frauenschicksal.* Wuppertal, 1980. English, *So Long a Letter.* 1991.

Masolo, D. A. *African Philosophy in Search of Identity.* Nairobi, 1995.

Mbiti, J. S. *African Religions and Philosophy.* London/Ibadan/Nairobi, 1983 (new edition).

———. *Introduction to African Religion.* 2d ed. Nairobi/Kampala, 1996.

Mieth, D., ed. *Moraltheologie im Abseits? Antwort auf die Enzyklika "Veritatis splendor."* 2nd ed. Freiburg i.Br., 1994.

———. *Die neuen Tugenden: Ein ethischer Entwurf.* Düsseldorf, 1984.

Milingo, E. *The World in Between: Christian Healing and the Struggle for Spiritual Survival.* Maryknoll, N.Y., 1984.

Mosha, S. N. A. "Sin in the African Practices of Medicine, Healing and 'Divination.'" (M.A. Degree-Arbeit, MS). Nairobi, 1987.

Mugambi, J. N. K., and A. Nasimiyu-Wasike, eds. *Moral and Ethical*

Issues in African Christianity: Exploratory Essays in Moral Theology. Nairobi, 1992.

Mujynya, E. N., *L'homme dans l'univers des Bantu.* Lubumbashi, 1972.

Mulago, V., ed. *Aspects du Catholicisme au Zaire.* Kinshasa, 1981.

———, et al. *Des prêtres noirs s'interrogent.* Brussels, 1956.

———. *La religion traditionnelle des Bantu et leur vision du monde.* 2d ed. Kinshasa, 1980.

———. *Mariage traditionnel africain et mariage chrétien.* Kinshasa, 1981.

———. *Un visage africain du Christianisme: L'union vitale bantu face à l'unité vitale ecclésiale.* Paris, 1965.

Musonda, D. K. *The Meaning and Value of Life Among the Bisa and Christian Morality.* Rome, 1996.

Mveng, E. *L'Afrique dans l'Église: Paroles d'un croyant.* Paris, 1985.

Mwoleka, C. *Ujamaa and Christian Communities.* Eldoret, 1976.

Ndjimbi-Tshiende, O. *Réciprocité—coopération et le système palabrique africain: Tradition et herméneutique dans les théories du développement de la conscience morale chez Piaget, Kohlberg et Habermas.* St. Ottilien, 1992.

Nothomb, D. *Un humanisme africain: Valeurs et pierres d'attente.* Preface by M. l'Abbé A. Kagame. Brussels, 1969.

Nunner-Winkler, G., ed. *Weibliche Moral: Die Kontroverse um eine geschlechtsspezifische Ethik.* Frankfurt a.M./New York, 1991.

———. "Development of Moral Understanding and Moral Motivation." In *Individual Development from 3 to 12: Findings from the Munich Longitudinal Study,* ed. F. E. Weinert and W. Schneider, 253–90. New York, 1998.

Nyamiti, C. *African Tradition and the Christian God.* Eldoret, n.d.

———. "The Incarnation Viewed from the African Understanding of Person." *African Christian Studies* 6 (1990): 3–27.

Nyerere, J. K. "Ujamaa—Grundlage des afrikanischen Sozialismus." In *Afrikanischer Sozialismus: Aus den Reden und Schriften von Julius K. Nyerere. Mit einer Einleitung von Gerhard Grohs,* 10–18. Stuttgart, 1972. English, *Freedom and Socialism. Uhuru Na Ujamaa: A Selection from Writings and Speeches.* 1965–1967.

Ocholla-Ayayo, A. B. C. *Traditional Ideology and Ethics Among the Southern Luo.* Uppsala, 1976.

Okot p'Bitek. *Africa's Cultural Revolution.* Nairobi: Macmillan, 1973.

Omi, R. E. A., and K. C. Anyangwu. *African Philosophy: An Introduction to the Main Philosophical Trends in Contemporary Africa.* Rome, 1984.

Pesch, O. H. *Theologie der Rechtfertigung bei Martin Luther und Thomas von Aquin: Versuch eines systematisch-theologischen Dialogs.* 2d ed. Mainz, 1985.

———. *Thomas von Aquin: Grenze und Größe mittelalterlicher Theologie.* 3d ed. Mainz, 1995.

"Philosophie africaine: Rationalité et Rationalités." *Actes de la XIV*[e] *Semaine Philosophique de Kinshasa.* Kinshasa, 1996.

Pieper, J. *Die Wirklichkeit und das Gute.* 5th ed. Munich, 1949.

Ratzinger, J. *Einführung in das Christentum: Vorlesungen über das Apostolische Glaubensbekenntnis.* Munich, 1968. English, *Introduction to Christianity.* 1990.

———. *Vom Wiederauffinden der Mitte. Grundorientierungen. Texte aus vier Jahrzehnten,* ed. S. O. Horn, V. Pfnür, V. Twomey, S. Wiedenhofer, and J. Zöhrer. Freiburg i.Br. et al., 1997.

———. *Zur Lage des Glaubens: Ein Gespräch mit Vittorio Messori.* Munich, 1985. English, *Ratzinger Report: An Exclusive Interview on the State of the Church.* 1987.

———, and H. Maier. *Demokratie in der Kirche: Möglichkeiten, Grenzen, Gefahren.* Limburg, 1970.

Reese-Schäfer, W. *Was ist Kommunitarismus?* Frankfurt a.M./New York, 1994.

Robinson, J. A. T. *Christian Morals Today.* London, 1964.

———. *Honest to God.* London, 1963.

Ruf, A. K. *Sünde—Was ist das?* Munich, 1972.

Saint Moulin, L. de, ed. *Œuvres complètes du Cardinal Malula,* 7 vols. Kinshasa, 1997.

Sanon, A. T. *Das Evangelium verwurzeln: Glaubenserschließung im Raum afrikanischer Stammesinitiationen.* Freiburg i.Br./Basel/Vienna, 1985.

Sartre, J.-P. *L'être et le néant.* Paris, 1943. English, *Being and Nothingness.*

———. *Les Mouches.* Paris, 1943. English, *The Flies.*

Schockenhoff, E. *Bonum hominis: Die anthropologischen und theologischen Grundlagen der Tugendethik des Thomas von Aquin.* Mainz, 1987.

———. *Naturrecht und Menschenwürde: Universale Ethik in einer geschichtlichen Welt.* Mainz, 1996.

Schreiter, R. J. *Abschied vom Gott der Europäer: Zur Entwicklung regionaler Theologien. Mit einem Vorwort von Edward Schillebeeckx.* Salzburg, 1992. English, *Constructing Local Theologies.* 1985.

Schuster, J. *Ethos und kirchliches Lehramt: Zur Kompetenz des Lehramtes in Fragen der natürlichen Sittlichkeit.* Frankfurt a.M., 1984.

Seckler, M. *Das Heil in der Geschichte: Geschichtstheologisches Denken bei Thomas von Aquin.* Munich, 1964.

———. *Im Spannungsfeld von Wissenschaft und Kirche: Theologie als schöpferische Auslegung der Wirklichkeit.* Freiburg i.Br., 1980.

Singer, P. *Praktische Ethik.* 2d ed. Stuttgart, 1994. English, *Practical Ethics.* 2d ed. Cambridge, 1993.

Taabu Sabiti. *Proverbes et dictons en Swahili et en Kingwana.* N.p., 1976.

Taylor, C. "Die Motive einer Verfahrensethik." In *Das Problem Hegels und die Diskursethik,* ed. W. Kuhlmann, 101–35. Frankfurt a.M., 1986.

———. *Source of the Self: The Making of the Modern Identity.* Cambridge, Mass.: Harvard University Press, 1989.

Tempels, P. *Bantu-Philosophie. Ontologie und Ethik.* Heidelberg, 1956.

———. *Notre rencontre.* Léopoldville, 1962.

Tönnies, F. *Gemeinschaft und Gesellschaft: Grundbegriffe der reinen Soziologie.* 8th ed. Berlin, 1935. English, *Community and Society.* 1988.

Tshiamalenga-Ntumba. "Afrikanische Philosophie. Zum originären Vertrauen des afrikanischen Menschen." In *Église et droits de la société africaine,* ed. A. Mutombo-Mwana, and E.-R. Mbaya, 109–20. Mbujimayi, 1995.

Ukpong, J. S. "Sin and Reconciliation Among the Ibibio. A Christian Evaluation." *Cahiers des Religions Africaines* 19 (1985): 227–33.

Uzukwu, E. E. *A Listening Church: Autonomy and Communion in African Churches.* Maryknoll, N.Y., 1996.

Vanneste, A. *Nature et grâce dans la théologie occidentale: Dialogue avec H. de Lubac.* Leuven, 1996.

Walzer, M. *Interpretation and Social Criticism.* Cambridge, Mass., and London, 1987.

———. *Spheres of Justice: A Defense of Pluralism and Equality.* 1983.

Wanjohi, G. J. *The Wisdom and Philosophy of the Gikuyu Proverbs: The Kihooto World-View.* Nairobi, 1997.

Wiedenhofer, S. *Das katholische Kirchenverständnis: Ein Lehrbuch der Ekklesiologie.* Graz, 1992.

Wiederkehr, D., ed. *Der Glaubenssinn des Gottesvolkes—Konkurrent oder Partner des Lehramts?* Freiburg i.Br./Basel/Vienna, 1994.

Index